The Hutchinson Money Minder

The Hutchinson Money Minder

A LIFETIME GUIDE TO FAMILY FINANCIAL MANAGEMENT

Margaret Allen

HUTCHINSON

London · Melbourne · Auckland · Johannesburg

*For my parents, George and Agnes Sutton,
with love and thanks for everything they
did and still do for me*

Copyright © Margaret Allen 1987

First published in 1987 by
Century Hutchinson Ltd,
Brookmount House, 62–65 Chandos Place,
Covent Garden, London WC2N 4NW

Century Hutchinson Australia Pty Ltd
PO Box 496 16–22 Church Street
Hawthorn
Victoria 3122
Australia

Century Hutchinson New Zealand Limited
PO Box 40–086 Glenfield
Auckland 10
New Zealand

Century Hutchinson South Africa (Pty) Ltd
PO Box 337 Bergvlei
2012 South Africa

Set in Linotron Times by Wyvern Typesetting Ltd, Bristol

Printed and bound in Great Britain by Mackays of Chatham

British Library Cataloguing in Publication Data
Allen, Margaret, *1933–*
   The Hutchinson money minder: a lifetime
   guide to family financial management.
   1. Finance, Personal——Great Britain——
   Handbooks, manuals, etc.
   I. Title
   332.024′00941   HG179

ISBN 0–09–172724–3
ISBN 0–09–173731–1 Pbk

Contents

Introduction

Sensible financial planning can make a great deal of difference to our lives, ensuring that at each stage we are making the most of our resources. Our financial existence divides into seven phases, rather like Shakespeare's seven ages of man in *As You Like It*.

At the beginning—from birth until we begin our first job—financial decisions are made for us rather than by us, and we have few rights. Nevertheless, we do exist as people: we have the right to tax allowances, to be set against any income we may have, although generally our income is lumped together with that of our parents in assessing liability to tax. Many decisions have to be taken for us which will have an impact on the rest of our lives. Will we be sent to a state or a private school? If the latter, how will our education be financed? What tax-efficient means can our parents use to increase the money available to spend on our upbringing? What kind of savings should we have? What kind of spending allowance should they give us, if any?

Our first job moves us into the second phase of our lives. If we are under the age of majority, 18, we still do not have the full rights of an adult—for instance, we cannot normally get credit without a guarantor, because minors are not responsible for their debts. But we do become liable for tax and National Insurance contributions on our earnings; and, from our first day at work, we contribute towards the retirement pension we will eventually receive more than 40 years later.

The third major step for most of us is marriage. This is when real financial planning should start—rather earlier, if possible. Decisions taken now affect the rest of our lives; for this reason, this period is the subject of a major portion of this book. Care needs to be taken in setting up a home. Attention must be paid to the new financial obligations the marital partners have to one another. Wills should be made, or new ones, because marriage invalidates all previous wills. If at all possible, some regular saving should be embarked upon and maintained, even if periodically we have to dip into the accumulated sum. We need to look afresh at the tax system and what it implies for a married couple. Protection for the couple against illness, unemployment or even untimely death should be considered: the issue should not be shirked.

A couple can generally live quite well and easily until the onset of the fourth phase, when children arrive and family commitments increase, but the birth of the children—that of the first child in particular—can put severe strains on the family budget. Mothers cannot always continue to work, even when they want to (and many prefer a few years at home, at least when the children are small), and adaptations need to be made in the way spending is organized. We may have to dip into our savings. Life-assurance needs may change. Not all marriages run for a full lifetime, and divorce or separation, especially where there are young dependent children, can mean sharply lower standards of living for both partners.

Financial opportunities begin to open up again in the fifth stage, when the children are older. Mothers can return to work, although they may find career opportunities more limited or even blocked. This is the time to make certain that our pension arrangements are going to be adequate for our years in retirement. A will may need updating. There may be more funds available for savings schemes and life-assurance policies designed to mature at retirement, or for whole-of-life policies to minimize any inheritance tax which may eventually become payable on your estate when you die. You can probably begin to think about investing in the stock market.

Next comes stage six, the final ten years or so of your working life. This is often the most financially comfortable stage of your life. The children may have left home, or at least have become self-supporting. There may be two good incomes again. The mortgage on the home may be paid off. You may want to release some of your capital for investment and move to a smaller home. It is your last chance to look towards the years of retirement, when incomes will almost certainly fall again. It is important to check out what topping-up arrangements you can make to increase your pension, to reassess your tax position, and to go into savings schemes which offer maximum income and growth. It is probably the time when you can most afford to take a risk in the stock market, going for capital growth rather than income. You may also want to help your sons and daughters by contributing in a tax-efficient way towards the upkeep of your grandchildren; you may want to do the same for your nieces and nephews or your godchildren.

Seventh, and last, we come to the years of retirement. Now maximizing income, rather than seeking capital growth, becomes the priority. You must do your utmost to make sure that your income is not eroded by inflation, and so you must get the right sort of mix in your savings and investments for continuing good income as well as some prospect of an improvement in your capital. You must make sure that there is enough cash readily available to cope with emergencies, especially medical ones. You must make sure that you have reduced any inheritance tax on your estate to a minimum, if you have not eliminated it altogether. You must reassess your housing needs and make a final check on your will. If you are married, it is important to recognize and accept that one of you will die first and that the other will be a widow or widower: you must prepare for this situation.

Systematizing our financial planning throughout these seven 'ages' sounds a tall order, but the sooner we start the easier it is, and we find that one phase of our lives passes smoothly into the next. After a few years, you will not even realize that you are planning: it will simply be a part of life.

FROM BIRTH TO FIRST JOB

Parents have total financial control over their children until they begin their first job. This does not mean, however, that children have no rights at all. If they have an income they can be taxpayers and have tax allowances. They may get into debt, but while they are minors they cannot be held responsible for such debts. Certain decisions need to be taken very soon after a child's birth, if the parents' plans for his or her upbringing are to be achieved at a cost which is not too punitive; for instance, if private education is planned, the cost might prove prohibitive, particularly if there are more than a couple of children in the family, unless decisions are taken at the time of birth which will minimize the cost. Because children are potential taxpayers, grandparents and other relatives or friends can help fund school fees or contribute to general upkeep in a tax-efficient way. Parents, too, can use the annual exemptions on the transfer of capital to build up savings and investments for their children. Children do not need life assurance for themselves, but parents should look at the cover on their own lives to ensure that children are protected in the event of a parent's untimely death. When children begin to save on their own account, they need help in choosing the right kind of savings. A decision also needs to be taken by parents on their approach to spending allowances for children. These are all matters which come within the ambit of family financial planning, firstly by the parents and later, as the children grow, by the family as a whole.

1 | First Thoughts on Education

As soon as children are born and registered they go straight into government records. Two things, among many others, stay with them for the rest of their lives: one is their National Insurance number and the other is their right to a tax allowance against any income they may have. Children cannot pay tax themselves and, until they reach their majority or begin paid work for an employer, their income will as a general rule be lumped with that of their parents. Their tax allowance can be important, however, particularly if the time comes when their parents no longer live together. By arranging maintenance payments properly, a divorcing or separating couple can minimize tax obligations by apportioning part of the payment to the child/children. Claiming the relief against the child's income can cut a single parent's tax bill considerably, while the maintaining parent can get full tax relief on any alimony and child support.

Funding private education

However, that is not normally what one is thinking about on the birth of a child. Many parents immediately want to start saving for their children, either simply to build up a nest-egg for the child later on or to put something on one side towards eventual school fees, if the child is to be educated privately.

It is never too soon to think about funding potential school fees. When the time comes, especially at the secondary level, school fees may be prohibitively expensive. Some of the top schools are already charging fees of over £6,000 per annum, and it should not be forgotten that there are many extras on top of fees. Although £1,500 a term is about average for a private boarding school, parents of a child born in 1987 must plan to spend, over the whole school life of 13 to 14 years, a total sum for education of as much as £100,000, assuming that fees continue to rise at an average of about 5 per cent a year (some years they have risen more than that). Finding that sort of money out of taxed income is difficult, even for the very well-off, particularly if there are two or more children to be privately educated.

A lot of the sting can be taken out of school fees by making plans the moment a child is born. On the whole, the plans available involve some kind of life assurance, and may mean that parents are paying premiums for considerably longer than their children are at school. However, if the scheme is started early enough, the payments will be manageable out of income and become a paying habit that the parents almost do not notice.

In this section, we will look at the plans available to parents for their children, and then at how other interested parties, such as grandparents, aunts and uncles and godparents, might help out.

Children and life assurance

It is possible at birth to take out an endowment life-assurance policy on a child's life to contribute to school fees later. This is not, however, generally a good idea, and today insurance companies do not encourage such policies. While it is true, as we will see in Part Three, that life-assurance premiums are lower the younger and fitter we are, there is no benefit in taking out an endowment life-assurance policy on an infant (and it would have to be an endowment policy because such policies mature at a certain date and the funds can then be used for school fees) in terms of premiums simply because the child involved is a few weeks or months old. The risks of death of a baby are no lower than those of, say, a 20-year-old, so the premium levels would be about the same.

Most children, particularly when they are very young, do not need cover on their own lives, no matter what form that cover may take. Put bluntly, there will be no financial loss to a family in the event of the death of a dependent child. The financial risk is not the death of the child but the death of one or other of the parents while the child is still completely dependent on them.

The aim is to provide financial protection for an orphaned child. This involves life-assurance cover for the surviving parent and the child. We shall return to this topic in Parts Three and Four, because it is only when dependants arrive that the first real need for life assurance arises.

School-fee plans for parents

Most school-fee plans are based on life assurance. They are divided into two basic types, capital schemes and income schemes. Many schools today operate their own income schemes and, if you have definitely decided which school you want your child to go to, this may be the best plan for you—as long as you have a reasonable lump sum of money that you can put down some time in advance. This lump sum is called a 'composition fee', and can be paid to the school some years before the child will go there. The size of the lump sum involved will depend on how far ahead you put the money down and the cost of the fees at that particular school. This system benefits the school, which has the fees ahead of time and coincidentally guaranteed.

Alternatively, you can leave the payment until the child starts at the school, and pay the whole lot in advance. Although something will be built in for increases in fees, the discount you will get is likely to be in the region of 10–15 per cent. If, however, you had paid the composition fee four or five years earlier, the reduction might have been 40 per cent or more.

If you have yet to choose your child's school but still like the idea of the lump-sum payment, you can make use of one of the companies specializing in school-fee schemes. A payment now (1987) of about £11,000 for fees due to start in 1991 would, it is estimated, produce almost £20,000's worth of fees when the time came. If you could look further ahead and decide that you could cope with the school fees out of income (they are lower in junior schools) until the child reached the age of 10 or 11, then a payment of under £8,000 now would be equivalent to close on £27,000 by 1997—allowing for school fees rising on average by 5 per cent a year. Of course, that may not be the case, and it would be unwise to rely totally on the

11

single-premium policy to cover the whole of the school fees. In some years, fees have risen by as much as 14 per cent.

You may not want to tie up your money in this way, or you may not have the money available. Instead, you might choose to save regularly. But this is much more costly and requires more discipline. To get the same amount as the lump sum available through the single-premium policy you would need to save, allowing for interest, nearly £13,000.

An alternative is an endowment policy on one or both of the parents' lives. Here you pay monthly or annual premiums well before you need the school fees, perhaps starting when the child is born. You are likely to be young yourself then, so the premiums will not be onerous. Once you start needing the money for fees, the policy will provide it at the beginning of either each term or each school year, and the premiums will then rise accordingly. Your payments will probably continue for a period after the child has left school, so you could be committing yourself to 20 or 25 years of premium payments to cover the cost of fees. For many people, however, this is the simplest and most manageable system. A new policy can be added with each child. Although it can become a heavy burden, at least your financial commitment is defined. If for any reason you never activate the school-fee element of the policy, it is treated just like an ordinary endowment policy (see pages 103–5), with a sum assured when the policy eventually matures.

In recent years there has been a new development in school-fee plans. Companies and individuals have been looking at ways for people to exploit the very substantial asset many have which normally does not earn interest: their home. These plans are extremely expensive, but some people are so eager to put their children into private education that they find them attractive. What happens is that you use the difference between what you owe on the mortgage and the increased value of your home since you bought it. Say you owe £20,000 on a home you bought five years ago for £40,000, and that the value has now risen to £80,000. You would therefore have £60,000 if you sold the house. You can now borrow against part of this sum—depending on your income level and other commitments—to pay school fees. You will not be able to borrow the full amount; between 70 and 80 per cent of the current calculation of the home's value, less the first mortgage, is normal, and the interest you will have to pay on the loan is quite high—2–2.5 per cent above minimum lending rate—but it is paid only on the amount borrowed at any time, so rises as school fees are drawn on the loan facility. There will be a small arrangement fee, which may be a flat £100 or £150, or, say, 0.5 per cent of the loan facility. All the plans are based on life-assurance endowment policies or pension plans, and run for any period between 10 and 25 years. The loan is repaid through low-cost endowment in the same way as a first endowment mortgage.

Such loans may enable parents with more than one child to finance all their school fees. If you had a home valued at, say, £150,000, with an outstanding mortgage of £50,000, there would be a potential £100,000 against which you could borrow. Eighty per cent of that would be £80,000 and, if drawn gradually, could go quite a long way. But you will have to remember that, when you come to sell your house, you no longer have simply the outstanding first mortgage from a bank or building society to repay but also the new loan, so that the surplus funds from the sale of your home could be substantially lower and you might have to endure high mortgage payments on all your homes throughout your life. That is a big sacrifice, but one that many parents believe is worth making.

More and more school-fee plans using one's home will be thought up by the insurance companies; the box below shows the ones which are available at the time of writing. If you are thinking of one, check with an insurance broker to find out the full range offered. Newer ones may be rather more attractive. There is no way, however, that they can eliminate the fact that the home-owner is effectively increasing his or her mortgage quite sharply and reducing any surplus he or she may have available on the sale of the home. That said, any further increase in the home's value after the plan has been taken out does of course go to the owner on sale.

If you do not like these plans, which are in effect a second mortgage, you could instead arrange for a full remortgage. This means that the first mortgage is paid off and a new one issued, plus a loan which can be used for school fees. The legal and other costs are rather higher in these cases.

USING YOUR HOME TO PAY SCHOOL FEES

Name of scheme/ companies involved	Current rate	Arrangement fee	Percentage of house valuation	term*
Berkeley St James' Education Loan Scheme *Tel.* 01–222 8785	12.75 per cent	£100	80 per cent minus first mortgage	10 years (endow-ment only)
National Westminster Bank/ISIS/Claremont Saville *Tel.* 01–630 8795	13 per cent	£100 plus dis-bursements	70 per cent minus first mortgage	10–25 years
NEL Britannia *Tel.* 0306–887766	13 per cent	0.5 per cent of loan facility	£50,000 limit	10–20 years
Security Pacific *Tel.* 0892–44933	13.5 per cent (under review)	£80	80 per cent minus first mortgage; 75 per cent for pension mortgage	five-year rollover facility; 10–25 years
Standard Life/Bank of Scotland *Tel.* 031–225 2552	12.75 per cent	£150	80 per cent minus first mortgage	10–25 years; five-year rollover facility

*All plans endowment or pension plan unless otherwise stated

There is no reason why a grandparent or other relative should not take out one of the school-fee plans for a child, although it would be a very altruistic thing to do—even bearing in mind that grandparents are often anxious to help their grandchildren as much as possible—and a very expensive one, because life policies become increasingly costly as we get older. There are, however, other ways, which are highly tax-efficient, whereby they can provide funds at a rather more modest level. One is by executing a Deed of Covenant. A covenant is a means whereby someone (the covenantor) agrees to pay a sum of money annually to another. The attraction for children is that, although their income is lumped with that of their parents, they will, if such money is forthcoming, be allowed to reclaim tax at the standard rate as long as the gross (before tax) amount of the covenant is less than the current single person's allowance. For the tax year from 6 April 1987 to 5 April 1988, that allowance stands at £2,425. The covenantor cannot be the parent—or, at least, there is no point in covenanting a dependent child under the age of 18 because parents cannot give their children money and then reclaim tax on it. (The rules are different if the parents are separated and one is paying child support under a Court Order—see page 191.)

Let us say that a grandparent covenants a child for £2,000 a year. The parent gets the money on behalf of the child, but does not collect the full £2,000. Tax at the standard rate is deducted before the payment is made, so the grandparent or other covenantor actually hands over less—in 1987–88 terms, £1,460 (£2,000 less £540 tax at the standard rate). The parent then applies to the tax inspector for the deducted tax, again on behalf of the child, bringing the payment back up to £2,000. As long as the payment is kept within the single person's allowance, full standard-rate tax relief can be reclaimed. At higher tax rates the level of relief is gradually reduced.

Later on, when the children reach 18, and assuming that they (a) have no other income and (b) are still studying, the parent can make a similar covenant. (See pages 155–6, where the general procedure to follow is set out.)

Covenants can be drawn up by the individuals involved. There is no need to use a lawyer, but some care should be taken in the wording (see the box on page 15). You will have to satisfy the tax inspector that the covenant is genuine—the inspector will not release the tax relief if he or she thinks that it has been drawn up purely as a means of saving tax; for instance, he or she might think this if you covenanted a friend's child and the friend covenanted yours. Although tax relief is available only up to the amount of the single person's allowance, there is nothing to stop someone from covenanting more than one child. If you feel uncertain as to whether you are getting it right, you can always just buy a professionally designed Deed of Covenant form.

There are two important rules for grandparents to remember: first, they must be taxpayers themselves and, second, they must be covenanting someone who is not a taxpayer. In addition, there are some other minor rules to follow as set out on page 156. Rather than covenant a child directly, you can if you wish appoint a trustee who will make sure that the covenant is used for the child's benefit and no one else's. If you appoint a trustee, you should, after the words '. . . out of the general fund of my taxed income', insert this sentence into the Deed: 'The Trustee shall hold

WHAT THE DEED OF COVENANT SHOULD SAY

I ...., of ...., hereby covenant my grandson/daughter/
niece/nephew/godchild ...., of ...., that for seven years
from this date during the remainder of our joint lives, or until he/
she ceases to be receiving full-time education at an educational
establishment, or until he/she marries (whichever period is the
shorter), I will pay the annual sum of £..... out of the general
fund of my taxed income. Receipt of either parent shall be good
and sufficient discharge. These payments shall be made in ...
equal instalments of £..... The first payment shall be on ....,
and thereafter on .... each year (monthly or quarterly).

In witness whereof I have set my hand and seal this .... (date)

Signature ....

Signed, sealed and delivered ....

Witness's signature ....

Witness's address and occupation ....

all such annual sums upon trust for the absolute benefit of the Beneficiary
with power to pay or apply them for the benefit of the Beneficiary as the
Trustee think fit.' Naturally, if you trust the child's parents, you will not
bother with a trustee—or you can select one to be the trustee.

If you are signing a Deed of Covenant in Scotland, you do not need to
have it witnessed if it is written in your own handwriting, or if you write the
words 'adopted as holograph' above your signature. Two witnesses are
required, however, if the Deed is printed or typed. Otherwise, the rules in
Scotland are as for the rest of the country (see page 156).

Friendly-society policies

One life-assurance policy which new parents might consider taking out on
their own lives in order to benefit their children is a contract with a friendly
society. Dependent children or a spouse can be the named beneficiaries of
such policies. The government restricts the life cover (the sum assured) to
maximum premiums of £100 a year. There are other restrictions. Each
person can have only one such life or endowment policy: if a policy is
surrendered before that, no more than the gross amount of premiums paid
can be given as a surrender value—which means that, because of inflation,
you will have lost money. Such restrictions aside, however, these policies
are very good value. All the profits of friendly societies are completely
tax-free, and so is any income or growth in the fund—even tax paid on
building-society investments can be reclaimed, unlike the case for
individuals. This means that the percentage profit when the policy matures
can be much greater than with a conventional life-assurance policy,
although of course the absolute sums involved are rather small. The
maturement of the policy could, nevertheless, provide a useful contribution to funds when children reach the age of secondary education.

15

2 | Children and Their Savings

It is never too early to start a child in the savings habit. Savings of their own give children a sense of financial independence and make them appreciate the cost of things and value them accordingly. Parents can save small amounts of money for their offspring, and children can have an account in their own name as soon as they are born (although they will not normally be able to make withdrawals from the account until they are able to sign their name and understand what they are doing). Seven is a typical age for children to start using an account themselves.

In general, the income of a child from his or her savings is potentially taxable and is taxed as if it were part of the income of the parent. But if the source of the savings is anyone other than the parent, the single person's tax allowance can be set against any income. It is only in the case of children who are independently rather wealthy that there are any major tax considerations.

When choosing a saving or investment scheme it makes little difference whether one is an adult or a child. The choice should suit the individual's circumstances. Of course, infants will not understand anything very sophisticated and decisions will have to be taken for them; and, except for the very few who inherit substantial sums of money early and need to have their money professionally managed, most will choose from schemes in the banks or building societies or opt for National Savings. Building societies have long been a popular vehicle for children's savings, but it has to be said that they are a poor choice unless the child is paying tax at the standard rate; the same applies to the banks. The reason for this is that all interest from these sources is tax-paid (the box on page 17 defines the three ways in which interest can be paid): the tax paid directly to the Inland Revenue by the financial institution concerned on behalf of the saver cannot be reclaimed by that saver if he or she happens to be a non-taxpayer. As most children do not come into the tax bracket, by saving in a bank or a building society they are effectively paying tax they need not and are forgoing interest. Banks and building societies have in recent years been trying to lure children into their savings schemes by distributing porcelain piggies, pencils, magazines and the like, but it is worth explaining to older children that there is a price to be paid for these 'free gifts'— and that is lower interest on their savings.

Children are far better off using the National Savings Investment Account or, for the more affluent child, National Savings Income or Deposit Bonds, all of which pay interest gross (that is, before deduction of tax). The taxman will want to know about this interest, but it is unlikely that the average child saver's interest will be large enough to incur income tax.

Having said that, probably the easiest and simplest way for a child to make small savings is through the National Savings Ordinary Account. Children can use their National Savings Ordinary Account themselves from the age of seven, although before that the parent must deposit and withdraw on their behalf. As the account can be used at any post office throughout the country, it is very convenient for a child to use. The interest on these accounts is low, but to a child with very little money this factor is not significant, and the first £70 of interest each year is tax-free (although it should be declared to the taxman via the parent). There is a two-tier level of interest, a lower one for savings under £500 and a higher one above that, usually guaranteed by the government for a year. Explain the nature of interest earned to the child—how the money they save can be used to make more money. This concept is appealing to many children and a savings habit acquired early may never be lost. Also, parents can use the account to teach a child the beginning of money management. It is a good idea, when making a child a weekly allowance, to stipulate that part of it must be saved regularly and put towards specific projects, such as major purchases, holidays or school trips.

Parents should always make sure that the child sends his or her bank

HOW INTEREST IS PAID

Interest on savings comes in three forms:

Tax-free. This is interest on which no tax is payable. It applies to fixed-interest National Savings Certificates, index-linked Savings Certificates and the first £70 of interest on the National Savings Ordinary Account. All interest on the new Personal Equity Plan (PEP) is tax-free if the plan is held for the qualifying period. PEPs are available, however, only to those who are 18 or over.

Tax-paid. This applies to all interest outside the National Savings sector, apart from offshore funds. Tax is deducted by the financial institution on the interest paid on the deposits it holds before the interest is paid to the saver. This deducted tax cannot be reclaimed by a nontaxpayer, but anyone liable for tax at levels higher than the standard rate must eventually pay the extra. The interest must be stated on an individual's tax return. There is some benefit for standard-rate taxpayers in such tax-paid savings, because the tax paid by the financial institution is rather less than standard rate, and so the deposit-taking institution can pay a little more net interest than it could if the full standard rate had to be deducted.

Taxable but paid gross. Interest on the National Savings Investment Account, Income Bonds and Deposit Bonds and that on offshore accounts is paid gross—that is, before deduction of tax. Taxpayers benefit from the full payment, but must declare the interest on their tax return and eventually pay any tax due.

book off to the National Savings headquarters (you can get a stamped addressed envelope at any post office) after the end of each calendar year to be credited with interest. No matter how small this is, the child will quickly appreciate that simply by having money in the bank he or she has made more money.

Fixed-interest National Savings Certificates and Index-linked Certificates also make good long-term presents for children. The rise in the value of the certificates over their four-year life is not taxable and, while there may be better levels of gross interest to be had elsewhere, the certificates' rates are always competitive.

Premium Bonds, while they carry no interest, qualify for tax-free prizes in weekly and monthly draws, and therefore make good small presents for children. If the child is lucky enough to win a prize, the money can be used for the child's benefit. Money is not altogether a serious matter, and the child should learn that money management can be fun as well as profitable. Holding a few premium bonds is unlikely to make a child into a gambling addict in later years.

Details of all savings schemes and their suitability in differing circumstances are set out on pages 237–9.

Transferring money to children

One thing which parents do not consider enough is the regular transfer of some of their financial assets to their children as they grow. Since the April 1986 budget, the tax on lifetime transfers of assets, including money, has been zero as long as the transfer has been made more than seven years before death. At this early stage in their lives, parents are unlikely to want to make over large funds to their offspring, using the new Inheritance Tax rules (see pages 198–201), but many more than do could take advantage of the annual £3,000 complete exemption to build up nest-eggs for their children. When such children reach their majority, these accumulated funds can be used to pay for further-education expenses, to provide the deposit for the purchase of a home, or simply to give a young adult more financial independence than is usual.

One need not transfer the whole of the £3,000, of course, and the amount can be varied according to the financial circumstances of the family in any particular year. If there is more than one child, the funds should be equally divided and all children treated alike.

What a family does with money invested on behalf of children (and such money should be written in trust for them) depends to some extent on the family's overall wealth. It has to be remembered that, generally, the income of the child is treated for tax purposes as that of the parent (usually the father). When the parent is simply transferring money to the child there will be no tax saving, but regular saving for a child builds up funds for that child's eventual benefit. It makes sense to go for tax-free forms of saving to begin with—fixed-interest National Savings Certificates and Index-linked Certificates—and then to move on to tax-paid savings if the allowance for savings certificates has been exhausted.

If you want to go beyond that into risk-bearing investments, such as stocks and shares, the possibilities of profit over the entire period from birth to 18 are much greater, but not all companies permit minors to be shareholders, and so the process can be more complicated and bring in the

CHILDREN AND SAVINGS

Children are potential taxpayers, like any other individual. They are allowed a personal tax allowance of £2,425 for 1987–88. Income on money from their parents, however, counts as part of the parents' investment income—the father's, where the parents are living together—and not the child's. It is aggregated with the parents' income and taxed at the parents' marginal rate, once it exceeds £5 a year.

Non-taxpaying children should ideally put their money into savings which pay interest gross; e.g., a National Savings investment account, income bonds, deposit bonds, gilt-edged stock bought through the National Savings Register (see page 171). Children liable for tax at the standard rate should put their money into bank savings or building-society savings.

Children normally cannot buy stocks and shares or unit trusts, but these can be bought on behalf of the child. However, the Inland Revenue may require documentation to show that the child is really the owner.

Tax-free investments, although not tax-efficient for the non-tax-paying child, are nevertheless convenient ways to save. They are: National Savings ordinary account, National Savings certificates, and index-linked certificates.

No one under the age of 18 can take out a Personal Equity Plan (see page 51). Children under 16 cannot buy Premium Bonds, but these can be bought for them by parents, legal guardians or grandparents, although not by anyone else.

Children can use a bank account themselves, normally when they can sign their own name or have reached the age of seven.

whole question of trusts. Moving along this track is obviously worthwhile only for the more wealthy among us.

For many families, however, long-term saving for children is simply not a feasible possibility: the best we can do is to encourage our children to make small savings themselves, or to begin small savings accounts for them as soon as they are born.

3 Allowances for Children

It is a good idea to set children on the road to financial independence as soon as possible by making them an allowance the moment they are able to use money and understand its function in our lives. This can be an outright allowance (i.e., pocket money)—indeed, at least part of it should be: it is too much to expect very young children to work for all their weekly spending money. There is, however, no reason why 'extras', over and above the basic allowance, should not be earned for small jobs. It is unwise to be overgenerous with a child, but it is an excellent idea to include a little which you insist goes towards saving for holidays, treats and so on; that way the child will learn to appreciate how his or her money grows. Most children take more care of things they have bought for themselves with their own money, so there can be a general benefit all round as they learn to appreciate the value of things.

There are a few points to bear in mind when deciding the level of pocket money, which should at the beginning be given weekly or even daily, so that the child does not have either (a) too much in one go or (b) too much planning to do in order to make the allowance last more than a few days:

- As soon as a child realizes what money can buy, give a small allowance.
- Increase it on each birthday and discuss the amount with the child. Set out what it must cover and increase the level gradually to give the child more control over his or her overall spending as he or she gets older.
- Be realistic about the level. You cannot expect children to buy their own clothes out of a fiver a week.
- Try to find out what other people's children get. It is a mistake to be too generous in comparison with other parents, but at the same time it is a mistake to be too mean.
- Do not criticize the child's spending. Once you have given the allowance, it is no longer your business. Children soon learn not to spend badly once they find no more money is forthcoming until the due day.

When children reach 16, or even earlier if it is clear that they are sensible about money, allow them to open a bank account with a cheque book (assuming they want to). The bank may insist that the parent holds the account jointly with the child until he or she reaches 18, but bank managers today will usually agree to send a statement to the child alone even if the account is joint, and to contact the parent only if there are signs of trouble. If you opt for this, the (say, monthly) allowance will have to be rather more substantial than a weekly allotment, but you can by this time insist that it cover at least minor items of clothing, sports equipment, make-up, entertainment and so on, leaving yourself with only the major items. Good financial habits established early are a life-long asset.

Children at Work

4

Almost one-third of British school children earn money from jobs other than those they do at home. Although many of them are below the minimum school-leaving age of 16, there is not necessarily anything illegal about their activities. Most employed children do a paper round, or work in shops and stores at weekends, but there are also a number of budding businessmen and -women who want to set up little operations while they are still at school. There are some general points for potential employers and parents to bear in mind:

- It is illegal
  to employ anyone under the age of 13
  to employ children of school age in school hours
  to employ school children before 7am or after 7pm
  to employ school children in factories, mines or quarries, or on construction sites
  to employ school children for more than two hours on schooldays or Sundays
  to employ school children on heavy work which might cause injury.
- Anyone of school age (or under 18 and in full-time education) does not have to pay National Insurance contributions.
- All working children are potentially liable to pay income tax. There will be no tax to pay as long as their income stays below the level of the single person's allowance. Above that level there will be tax to pay, but by the parent (usually the father), as the child's income is treated as part of the general family income and taxed accordingly until the child goes into full-time employment after the age of 16. Details should be included on the paying parent's tax return.
- Self-employed children are treated like any other taxpayer, and can claim expenses to be set against their tax liability.
- Money paid by parents to their children for jobs done in the home does not count as taxable income.
- Minors are not responsible for their debts. This means that, if a child has to borrow money to help finance his or her own business, the parent will be expected to act as guarantor for the debt.

Junior entrepreneurs

If a child wants to set up a business, the cooperation of the parents can be vital; they are quite likely, apart from anything else, to provide the space needed for the business to operate. Try to ensure that the child is not simply carried away with enthusiasm and that he or she sits down and works out a plan, as anyone in business would do. This includes:

- Working out how much time is needed and how much will be available outside school hours, allowing for homework.
- Doing some market research to make sure that there actually is a demand for the thing the child wishes to make or the service he or she wants to offer.
- Working out whether any capital is needed for setting up the business. A small investment at the start may mean that the enterprise has a much greater chance of success than if the child struggles to operate without any starting capital. If you are prepared to lend a little money, do it on a businesslike basis, with clearly defined repayment terms.
- Advertising. This will of course be very limited at the start, but the child needs to know that even postcards in shop windows cost money. Not all advertising is expensive. Local newspapers, school magazines, photostating and delivering one's own leaflets may all be possible on a small budget.

It goes almost without saying that children should keep proper books of the business, noting all the income and outgoings. It is unusual for a child to make a great success of a business while he or she is still at school, but it has been known—and anyway keeping books is good practice for later on. If the child is successful, there may be tax to pay as well, so it is important to know what expenses can be offset against tax.

Parents should of course provide all encouragement for their children— *but that is all*. They should resist all temptations to interfere with the conduct of business unless matters are clearly getting out of hand.

Spotcheck

When your child is born, have you

- already thought about whether you will seek private education?
- decided how to finance the cost, if you have settled for private education?
- looked to relatives and friends who might help?
- checked that your life assurance is adequate to protect your spouse and children if you die?
- considered a friendly-society life policy to mature for your child's benefit?

When your children are able to understand, have you

- started them off on a regular savings habit?
- given them an allowance as soon as they are able to use money?

As the children get older, have you

- discussed with them how they might earn money or establish their own business?

Throughout the child's dependency, have you

- used the annual tax exemption to transfer funds and assets to them, thereby not only saving tax but also providing funds for education in later years?

FIRST JOB TO MARRIAGE

At the age of 16, when the first option to leave school arises, important financial decisions have to be taken by individuals themselves, as opposed to their parents. It is the time at which individuals become taxpayers and first realize that working life is finite and that they must start contributing to their pension, even though the day they receive it may be 45 or 50 years away.

Our first job means disposable income of our own and the ability, if we wish, to begin lifetime financial management. We can begin saving, even investing—we can open a bank account. Of course, we may not get a job immediately, but there are steps we can take to ensure that we get work at the earliest possible opportunity. This part of the book looks at the financial implications from the time we first get work until we marry.

5 First Job

The vast majority of Britons still leave school at the age of 16. Decisions taken immediately prior to our 16th birthday have implications for the rest of our financial lives. In general, job prospects and therefore earning potential are greater the more skilled we are. That can mean we should opt for further training after leaving school, even if we decide not to go on to higher education. A decision to continue in full-time education and training may mean that for several years our friends are earning money—in some cases good money—while we are scraping along on a grant, or being subsidized by our parents. It should not be forgotten, however, that the salary levels of people with training or university degrees very quickly catch up with and then pass those of their less qualified contemporaries.

It will be well worth spending some years in higher education. If that cannot be done, everyone should try to go into a job which has good long-term prospects and which will train you in a skill. You should have no regrets later. This applies whether you are male or female. Of course, we are concerned here only with the financial aspects of your pay packet; you will make the decision about your career on many considerations apart from the financial ones—your interests, skills, the opportunities available in your neighbourhood, and so on.

Entering the workforce

The first statement of your earnings that you receive in paid employment can come as something of a shock. You may have thought that you were earning £80 a week—and so you are. But that is not what you will actually receive—whether you get it in cash (increasingly rare) or have your pay put directly into your bank (see pages 36ff. for discussion on getting yourself a bank account). You will see that you have become a taxpayer. You have also become liable for National Insurance contributions. Both tax and National Insurance are deducted from your wages by your employer, who remits the withheld money to the relevant authorities. There are certain allowances which can be set against tax, but there are none against National Insurance contributions. These are today compulsory for all workers, employed or self-employed, although they are levied at different rates and depend on how much you earn.

National Insurance contributions

National Insurance contributions are a form of tax, even though they are not described as such. The difference is that they are, at least in theory, intended to contribute towards an eventual pension at retirement age (currently 60 for women and 65 for men, although equal retirement ages

24

CLASS I CONTRIBUTIONS (From 6 April 1987)

		Employee rate	
		Not contracted out	*Contracted out*
Contributions on all weekly earnings if they reach but do not exceed	£39.00 £64.99	5.00 per cent	2.85 per cent*
All weekly earnings if they reach but do not exceed	£65.00 £99.99	7.00 per cent	4.85 per cent*
All weekly earnings if they reach but do not exceed	£100.00 £149.99	9.00 per cent	6.85 per cent*
If weekly earnings exceed	£150.00	9.00 per cent up to £295.00	9.00 per cent on the first £39.00, 6.85 per cent thereafter

		Employer rate	
		Not contracted out	*Contracted out*
Contributions on all weekly earnings if they reach but do not exceed	£39.00 £64.99	5.00 per cent	0.90 per cent*
All weekly earnings if they reach but do not exceed	£65.00 £99.99	7.00 per cent	2.90 per cent*
All weekly earnings if they reach but do not exceed	£100.00 £150.00	9.00 per cent	4.90 per cent*
All weekly earnings if they reach but do not exceed	£150.00 £294.99	10.45 per cent	6.35 per cent*
If weekly earnings exceed	£295.00	10.45 per cent on all earnings	10.45 per cent on first £39.00 and on earnings in excess of £295; 6.35 per cent on earnings between £39.00 and £295.00

*Contracted-out contributions are payable on earnings between the lower (£39.00) and upper (£295.00) earnings limits. In addition, the first £39.00 of weekly earnings attracts contributions at the not-contracted-out rate for the appropriate earnings band.

25

are inevitable in the long run and there is already great pressure to allow men and women to retire at the same age).

This means that, from our very first week's work, we are contributing towards the pension we will get at the end of our working life. Pension arrangements are discussed in more detail later in this book (see chapters 16 and 20); here it is enough to say that the contributions go towards a flat-rate basic State pension as well as, very often, to an additional pension which is related to the level of our earnings. It is not compulsory to participate in the earnings-related part of the State scheme. From January 1988, employees will be able to make their own arrangements for any pension above the basic level. Some companies run their own private schemes and at present contract their employees out of the earnings-related scheme. Some contract out their male employees and not their female. When it comes to very young employees, there may be a qualifying working period or age before they can join the company pension scheme.

To a young person starting a first job, planning for a pension to be paid more than 40 years later is virtually impossible, and there is no reason why young people should begin to make arrangements quite so early: that will come later, after marriage or after the age of 21 or 25. However, it is as well to be aware that, whether you like it or not, contributions towards the basic State pension have to be made as soon as you start work. The self-employed do not escape contributions, but theirs are lower and they never qualify for more than the basic State pension; as a self-employed person, you cannot contract in to the earnings-related part. However, as we shall see later (see page 164), the self-employed get generous tax allowances which enable them to build up their own private pension rights.

For employed people, the contributions to pension come from both employee and employer, and there are two scales of payment. Those for the tax year from 6 April 1987 to 5 April 1988 are shown in the box.

You will see that, at the lower levels of income, the employee pays the same as the employer, but that there is a limit of 9 per cent for employees, levied only on the first £295 of each week's earnings, whereas, for employers contracted in to the earnings-related part of the pension, there is no limit: on any amount in excess of £150 a week 10.45 per cent is paid. A sliding scale applies to higher earners who are contracted out.

Taxation

Most people who start work at 16 or after full-time education do so as employees rather than as employers, so we shall concentrate here on taxation as it concerns the employee. There are various kinds of taxes levied on individuals, as we shall see, but the one payable on our wages or salary is *income tax*. Depending on when you start work, you may have a few weeks or months when you pay no tax at all.

First, a few general points:

● Taxation is levied in particular 'tax years'. These run not with the calendar year, but from 6 April in one year until 5 April the next. Taxpayers are required to make a *tax return* to the Inspector of Taxes every year, giving details of all their income from whatever source. For young people, the income will mostly be earnings plus, possibly, some interest on savings. If your affairs are very simple and you have only earnings, you may not receive a tax-return form every year. Do not worry if you don't: your employer is required to inform the tax authorities of the level of your earnings and your tax coding may not change significantly every year. Occasionally the amount of tax you should have paid may be different from that which you have actually paid, in which case you will get either a bill or a rebate, but usually what you are paying each month is what you actually owe.

● Everyone is potentially a taxpayer—even a child. As a general rule, although it is not invariable, anyone under 18 has their income lumped together with their parents' (usually the father's) until they start work. As soon as you begin earning, however, you are responsible for your own tax.

● Income tax is payable on *all* forms of income—wages and salaries, bonuses, interest on savings, dividends on stocks and shares, rents, pensions, etc. There are, however, certain allowances which can be set against income before we start paying tax; this is to ensure that very low earners do not pay taxes at the same level as higher earners. In addition, a variety of necessary expenses connected with our employment can be set against our income before it is assessed for tax. Further, the rate at which we pay tax rises with income; the better off and higher-earning we are, the higher, it is assumed, our ability to pay taxes. Here are all the personal tax rates for 1987/88:

Taxable income £		Rate %	Tax £	Cumulative income £	Cumulative tax £
First	17,900	27	4,833	17,900	4,833
next	2,500	40	1,000	20,400	5,833
next	5,000	45	2,250	25,400	8,083
next	7,900	50	3,950	33,300	12,033
next	7,900	55	4,345	41,200	16,378
Excess over	41,000	60			

All employees pay tax under what is called the pay-as-you-earn system (PAYE). The British government does not trust employees to pay their own taxes personally and is mindful that, if the tax owed is allowed to accumulate, people may not put aside enough of their earnings to pay the bill when the day of reckoning comes. The government has therefore given employers the responsibility for collecting the tax each month, or each week, from their employees.

This does not mean that the employee does nothing about his or her income tax. Everyone has allowances, if not expenses, and employers need to know these so that they can deduct the right amount of tax. After you have filled in your tax return, the tax inspector will issue you with a notice of coding. This has a number on it, and that number (although not details of how it has been reckoned) is passed on to your employer. From this, and from tax tables issued by the government, the employer knows what tax to deduct. Broadly, everyone gets a personal allowance except married women, and married men get extra just for being married (for taxation and married people see page 131). Married women get what is called an 'earned income allowance', which is at the same level as the personal allowance, but unlike the latter cannot be set against income from investments, rents, properties and so on. Then there are a variety of other small allowances.

Here are the levels of the main allowances for the tax-year 1987–88. These are increased with the level of inflation each year, and sometimes by rather more than it, if the government is feeling generous. The announcement is made by the Chancellor of the Exchequer in his annual March budget, shortly before the end of the tax year.*

- Single person allowance — £2,425
- Married man's allowance — £3,795
- Wife's earning allowance — £2,425
- Additional personal allowance — £1,370
- Widow's bereavement allowance — £1,370
- A new personal allowance was introduced in the 1987 Budget. In future, any profit-related pay (PRP) up to a maximum of £3,000, or 20 per cent of the employee's pay whichever is the lower, will qualify for 50 per cent earned income relief. The new system is hedged about with qualifications and each scheme will be considered separately by the Inland Revenue. Broadly, a link must be proved between the PRP and the audited profits it has generated. The relief will go to anyone working in an 'employment unit'—the whole business or a section of it—though new recruits and part-time workers can be excluded, the first group for three years and the latter completely.

There are some other minor allowances which, apart from the blind person's allowance, have remained unchanged for some time. These will not normally affect first-time employees, but for the record they are:

- Housekeeper relief — £100
- Dependent relative relief
  - Some women claimants — £145
  - Other claimants — £100
  - Relief for services of daughter or son — £55
  - Blind person's allowance — £540

For most young people, the only allowance they will be able to claim is the personal allowance, which is given automatically. There is no need to claim it in writing: it will be deducted from your *gross earnings*; i.e., the full amount you earn before National Insurance contributions are deducted. There is no allowance against tax for NI contributions although, if you are paying money into a private pension plan, that is fully chargeable against tax.

Let us assume that in your first job you earn £80 a week and are paid weekly. Your payslip will show that amount and also the amount you are actually getting. First of all, if you are not contracted out of the earnings-related part of the state pension scheme, 7 per cent of £80 (£5.60) will be taken off for National Insurance. £80 a week comes to £4,160 per year, against which you can set your personal allowance of £2,425, leaving £1,735 which is liable for tax at the standard rate of 27 per cent. That means your annual tax bill will be £468.45 (27 per cent of £1,735). Divide

28

*Age allowances are dealt with on page 216.

that by 52 and you get a weekly tax bill of £9. So what you get each week will be not £80 but £65.40 (£80 minus £5.60 National Insurance and £9 income tax).

Although you are unlikely to have any further allowances at this early stage of your working life, you may have some expenses which are essential to your work. It is likely that some or all of these can be deducted from your gross earnings before your tax is calculated. (See tax-saving hints in chapter 19.)

Points to remember

Everyone must fill in a tax return, but the form comes in several varieties to suit different circumstances. P1 is for the simplest cases; 11P is for more complicated ones; and 11 covers the self-employed.

When you start a new or first job, your employer will give you form P46. After you have filled that in, your employer can start charging you tax. In a first job, you will be able to work off the tax-free bit of your pay before tax is charged. If you think you are entitled to other allowances or expenses, ask your employer for Coding Claim Form P15 and do not delay in filling it in and sending it off to the taxman. If you have been overpaying because you have been slow in sending off your P15, your employer will eventually make an adjustment.

When you leave a job, your employer should give you form P45. You should immediately give this to your new employer, so that he or she can start deducting tax at the correct level. If you do not have P45, you will be taxed under an *emergency coding*, which assumes that you have used up all your tax-free allowances and taxes you at the standard rate immediately on *all* your earnings. An adjustment will eventually be made, but you could be short of money until the new coding comes through.

If you become unemployed you may have paid too much tax—because the payment is averaged out over the tax year. If you are claiming unemployment benefit, your tax refund will come to you via the local DHSS office. If you are not claiming unemployment or other benefit, you will need Form P50, which you can get from the tax office. You can reclaim overpaid tax on this after you have been unemployed for four weeks—although if you go on strike you cannot reclaim any tax until you have returned to work. Working short-time creates a rather more complicated situation, and the taxable nature of the benefits you get may mean that they cancel out any tax rebate to which you might have been entitled; also, it takes rather longer to get the tax relief.

Your tax return

Do not be afraid of your tax-return form. You are required in law to fill it in (the penalty for failing to do so can be £50), but it is not complicated. Returns used to be written in 'officialese' and many people quite justifiably found them daunting. However, great efforts have been made in recent years to simplify them, and you should have no problem. If you are not sure, write a letter to your tax inspector setting out what is bothering you. He or she is likely to be very helpful. They are not ogres aiming to take more tax away from you than you owe; they just want to ensure that

CAR BENEFIT SCALES

The fixed-rate assessments for 1987–88 in respect of the provision of motor cars where business use is more than 2,500 miles.

	Cars under 4 years old	Cars over 4 years old
Cars with original market value up to £19,250 and having a cylinder capacity* of:		
1400cc or less	£580	£380
1401cc–2000cc	£770	£520
Over 2000cc	£1,210	£800
Cars with original market value of £19,250 or more		
£19,250–£29,000	£1,595	£1,070
Over £29,000	£2,530	£1,685

Fuel Benefit Scales

The fixed-rate assessments for 1987–88 in respect of provision of fuel for private mileage of a motor car are:

Car cylinder capacity*:

1400cc or less	£480
1401cc–2000cc	£600
Over 2000cc	£900

*Separate scales are applicable for cars without a cylinder capacity.

you pay the taxes for which you are liable. Many will meet you and help you fill in your form.

Company cars and other perks

It is not all that uncommon for first-time employees to have cars supplied to them by their companies. These are a taxable benefit, according to the tax inspectors, because they reason that you will use the car for private purposes (which include travelling to and from work) as well as for business (travel on behalf of your company from your place of work to contacts, and so on), and so, if you did not have the company car, you would have to buy one out of taxed income. A scale of benefit has been worked out, however. Unless you count as 'higher paid' (which means earning at least £8,500 a year—not a particularly large sum these days), the taxable value of the car is counted as nil, provided that it is directly paid for by the employer. If the car is regarded as a taxable benefit, the taxable value is worked out depending upon

CONSUMPTION TAXES

Apart from income tax, there are other taxes which we pay everyday. Two particularly affect us: they are consumption taxes which we pay only if we use particular services or buy certain goods. For this reason, they are often called indirect taxes. They are:

Value Added Tax (VAT): this is levied on a wide range of goods and services. Some items like postal services and insurance premiums are exempt from VAT. Others are zero-rated and no tax is paid on them at the present time, although this could change. They include essential foods, children's clothing and fuel.

Most goods and services are, however, taxed at 15 per cent. The tax is levied on all transactions, including second-hand goods and all services such as hairdressing and restaurant bills, or solicitors' and accountants' fees.

Customs and excise duties: these are levied on a variety of goods, including some imports and tobacco and alcohol. The rates charged vary and the goods affected are also liable for VAT.

- How long you have the car.
- How much business travel you do in it. For anyone covering at least 18,000 miles a year on business, the benefit scales as shown in the box on page 30 are halved. By contrast, if you travel less than 2,500 miles on business a year, the inspector takes the view that the vehicle is basically for your own personal use, rather than business use, and ups the value 1.5 times.
- Whether you have two company cars and whether you actually pay your employer some money to allow for your personal (i.e., non-business) use of the car.

There can be no arguing about the taxable benefits, which are at a fixed rate for various sizes of car and their particular age. The box shows the rates for 1987–88.

In addition to the car, there are similar fixed rates of taxable benefit when your employer provides you with petrol for your private use. If you pay for petrol for the business use of your car and cannot reclaim it from your employer, you will be able to claim it as a business expense in your tax return. If you claim the full bill, there will probably be some balancing sum to allow for your private use.

The use of a car from a pool of office vehicles is not a fringe benefit, even if you are occasionally allowed to take the car away for private purposes. Such use, however, must be incidental to business use.

Other fringe benefits

Cars are not the only non-monetary benefit which employers may make available to employees. The general principle is that such benefits are taxable, but there are exceptions. First of all, the exceptions:

31

- Luncheon vouchers up to a value of 15p a day. Any excess over that is taxable.
- Working clothes.
- Board and lodging, unless you receive it in the form of cash.
- Interest-free loans.
- Employees' outings.
- Subsidized staff canteens.
- Any company assets at the disposal of the employee.

These are all rather small benefits, apart from interest-free loans. It is the bigger benefits which are taxable:

- Company houses in which the employee lives rent-free are taxed on the annual value of the benefit, which is the open market rental plus any other expenses paid by the employer, unless the house is needed for the employer to carry out his or her job. Then the benefit is tax-free.
- Suits and clothes are taxed on the estimated second-hand value.
- Private sickness or medical insurance premiums when these are paid by the employer.
- Cash vouchers.

Companies also give varieties of share options to employees. As long as these fulfil certain rules, any gains on them are tax-free.

Company directors are treated slightly differently as far as fringe benefits go. They are, for example, taxed on the full value of any suits and clothing and on any assets at their disposal.

When You Cannot Get a Job

6

Unfortunately, many people fail to get a job for some time after they leave school. When this happens, they should sit down with their parents and discuss what can be done about the situation. There are two basic options:

● To continue further training, either at school or in a college of further education, or under the Youth Employment Scheme run by the Manpower Services Commission
● To sign on as unemployed and available for work.

Further training

If you have planned to stay on at school and then go to college or university, you will have no problems at this stage, as long as you have the required qualifications. But not everyone wants to stay on at school after the minimum school-leaving age, and indeed it is not a suitable option for everyone. Unless you have good educational qualifications, it is unlikely that you will be able to go on to take 'A' levels and then move on to a university or polytechnic. Taking a degree will involve years of study, and you are unlikely to be earning anything until you are 21 or even older. Such a prospect is not attractive to everyone—even to some who have the necessary qualifications.

The family also has to consider whether it can any longer afford the burden of supporting you. While you are still at school you cannot normally claim supplementary benefits from the Department of Health and Social Security—although your parents may be able to if the total family income is low. If you are still in full-time education at a school after the age of 16, your parents (usually your mother) will still be able to claim child benefit for you until you reach the age of 19. That stops, however, if you go on to higher education at college or university, if you start full-time working or take up a training course, or if you get supplementary benefit.

You may decide that you want to take part in one of the Manpower Services Commission's Youth Training Schemes (YTS). You may work in a company, or on one of the special schemes in a training workshop, or on a community project. You do not get a wage as such, but are paid a training allowance. While you are on the course you do not have to pay income tax (the pay is anyway below the minimum taxable level) or National Insurance contributions (although you are allowed credits as if you were paying), and your allowance continues while you are on holiday. You are not guaranteed a job at the end of your training course, but you may well be taken on on a permanent basis by the company when you have acquired some skills.

There is a great deal of debate about these schemes. One view is that they are just a constant supply of cheap labour: firms can take on a trainee and then replace him or her with another one at the end of the training period, and so on *ad infinitum*. It is certainly true that not every YTS work experience turns into a job, but the benefits of training are never lost and the jobs market may not always be so unpromising as it is today. The allowance is not high, but many young people find earning it preferable to queuing up for dole. If you 'unreasonably refuse' a YTS scheme, you may not get any benefits for a period.

Signing on

Not everyone wants to join a Youth Training Scheme. The only other option (apart from trying to set up a business—see page 21) is to sign on at the nearest unemployment office; it is then a wise move to go to the local Job Centre, although this is not compulsory. Signing on does not mean you automatically receive unemployment benefit: until you have paid sufficient National Insurance contributions you are not eligible for the benefit, so you will have to work for some time before you are able to get it. If you have a job and lose it, and if you have paid the basic contributions, go immediately to the unemployment office and sign on. Take form P45 with you (your employer should have given you this when you left). If you are under 18, take your P45 to your careers office. Do not delay, or you will lose benefit.

If you have never had a job, signing on merely gives notice to the unemployment office that you are available for work; you will be expected to take any suitable job which comes along. The rules about benefits for school leavers have been tightened up recently, and it is now far more difficult to claim than it was before. If you are not eligible for unemployment benefit, you may be entitled to income support (which in April 1988 will replace the old supplementary benefit). This differs from unemployment pay in that it is not related to any National Insurance contributions you may have paid but is means-tested—in other words, based on your income and assets. You do not have to be unemployed to get it; many wage-earners on very low incomes qualify for income support. However, a school leaver is not likely to get it immediately. You cannot normally claim income support while you are still at school, or before you are 16. To qualify after that you must

- be looking after your own child, or
- be an orphan and have no one to look after you, or
- be disabled in such a way that you are unlikely to be able to get a job, or
- be living away from home and not in touch with your parents or kept by them.

Otherwise, if you are under 19 and have left school and are unemployed, you cannot claim income support until the first Monday in January, the first Monday after Easter Monday, or the first Monday in September— whichever comes first.

If you are eligible for income support you will have to call in at the unemployment office every fortnight to sign on. The money is sent by girocheque, which can be cashed at any post office.

What to do

The decisions you make about your job when you leave school are important for the whole of your life, and getting them right is vital if you are to establish a reasonable standard of living. This is true whether you are a boy or a girl. There is a general understanding today that education and training is just as important for girls as for boys, and that in the average home the financial contribution made to the total family income by a wife and mother is often absolutely necessary if the family is to achieve and maintain a good standard of living. It is also true that in today's difficult job market there are often positions available to women which men either cannot or do not want to do. The reverse is, of course, true.

If your family is one of the few that thinks that after leaving school girls are just marking time until they get married and give up working, remind them that today almost all women continue working after marriage: although many women give up work for a period, especially when there are small children to look after, as many as 60 per cent of all married women are at work at any one time. Today, married women rarely stay at home for more than five or seven years. Moreover, only 10 per cent of families today follow the traditional pattern of working husband, non-working wife and dependent children.

For all these reasons, both boys and girls should consider very carefully how they can acquire working skills which will serve them throughout their lives, and not just take any job to get their hands on ready cash.

The first step starts before you leave school. Most schools today have a teacher responsible for advising pupils about careers. If you know what you want to do, get the school to find out the best prospects. If you are not sure, talk all the possibilities through at school.

If you face opposition from your parents, get them to go and talk to your careers adviser. It is always better to have the support of your parents. If they are reluctant, talk to them calmly and try to convince them that what you want to do is sensible and has good long-term prospects.

Conversely, do not allow your parents to dissuade you if you are certain about what you want to do. Be firm but reasonable about it: parents usually come round in the end. If you are going to need their financial help, it is even more important to be tactful and, if you know that they cannot really afford to go on supporting you, make some offer of future recompense to be made once you have established yourself in your chosen career.

You may well find that, if you want to get a job at all, you will have to work away from home. If so, you may get some financial help from the Job Centre or unemployment office; this can include fares to attend interviews and allowances to visit the other areas in which you might want to work. If you succeed in getting a job, your fares may be paid and you may also receive some help with removal costs.

7 | Opening a Bank Account

As soon as we start working, the question arises as to whether we need a current bank account. It suits many employers to pay us by bank draft rather than in cash, if for no other reason than that they do not need to have too much cash on the premises. It certainly suits the banks to catch us as customers early because, although people can and do move their accounts from one bank to another, we in the United Kingdom exhibit a considerable amount of 'brand loyalty' to our particular banks. So far, the banks have managed to persuade around 70 per cent of us that we need an account with them.

Banks today are anxious to have young customers, although they may well insist that, until your 18th birthday, your account is held jointly with a parent. The reason for this is that minors are not responsible for their debts; the bank therefore wants a parent named in the account so that it has some recourse should the young person overdraw. You can usually persuade the bank to agree to send statements only to yourself, so that your parent is involved only if the account runs into an overdraft; in other words, as long as the account is run properly, in effect it belongs to you. After your 18th birthday the account can then be made over into your name alone.

Banks are particularly keen on signing up students. Students may be impecunious today, but many of them will be tomorrow's big customers.

Whether you should allow the sales gimmicks used to influence your choice of a bank with which you may spend a lifetime is debatable. When choosing your bank, you should look first of all to convenience, although in these days of cash cards and cheque-guarantee cards this is less important than it was. Family connections with a bank can be useful: if your family is well known to your bank manager, the chances are that he or she will look with more sympathy on any of your special needs than if you are completely unknown to him or her.

There are many types of bank account available to the young today, and the era of 'free banking' for current-account holders has greatly increased the attractions of current accounts to the young. Not everyone, however, needs a current account. The accounts offered by the building societies and by National Giro (via post offices) suit many of us very well.

The only remaining unique feature of current accounts is the overdraft facility. An overdraft is not the same as a loan, which can easily be fixed up today without recourse to an overdraft. An overdraft simply allows one to go on cashing cheques when there is no money in the account. Overdrafts are not automatic. If you have a current account and overdraw without the permission of your bank manager, it will not be very long before he or she will insist that you stay in credit; moreover, you will be charged interest on the overdrawn amount, and even the letter of complaint from the bank manager will be charged for. If you do not need an overdraft and never expect to, you can be as well off having a building-society account, which today may provide you with a cheque book and with a cash card for withdrawals from an ATM (automated teller machine) either inside or outside the premises, which will pay standing orders for you, and which will on top of all this not only give you free banking but pay you interest as well.

There is an almost bewildering choice before us when we decide to open our first account, so it is helpful to run through all the different types to explain and assess the relevance of the differences between them. Broadly, they break down as follows:

- bank current accounts
- interest-earning accounts from the high-street banks and licensed deposit takers
- building-society accounts
- bank accounts linked with building societies

Current accounts

Current accounts offer every variety of banking service. The owner of a current account is entitled to a cheque book and cheque-guarantee card (which at the time of writing guarantees cheques up to £50, and allows you to draw two cheques for £50 cash each day) and a cash card for immediate withdrawals from automated teller machines (ATMs). Depending on your financial circumstances, your ATM will have a weekly limit on withdrawals. Direct debits (which can be altered on instruction from the payee) or standing orders (which cannot be changed except by the account holder) can be paid from the account. Eurocheque and foreign-exchange facilities and overdraft and other loan facilities are also available. What current accounts do not do is pay interest (at least not straightforwardly—see below). In fact, they charge for the services you use.

As long as you stay in credit there is no charge for the services. Or, at least, that's the way it looks: as there is no interest payment, you are in fact paying a charge in another way. Banks offer what they call 'notional interest' on an account. It is called 'notional' because it is never in fact paid out, even if you have thousands of pounds in your current account: if you have plenty of cash it is better to keep most of it in a deposit account, switching funds to your current account when needed to make sure it stays in credit. The 'notional interest' on your current account is deducted from any bank charges you might incur when your account is overdrawn— colloquially known as 'going into the red'. If you stay in the 'black' (that is, in credit) you get as much benefit from being one penny in credit as you do from being £1,000 in credit.

If you are overdrawn, the charges can be high. In each 'charging period' you will pay for every transaction, whether it is the writing of a cheque, the operation of a standing order, or the withdrawal of cash from an ATM. The charging period may be one month or three; depending on the frequency with which you have to overdraw, the differing lengths of the charging periods can greatly affect the total charges you pay in any one year.

The banks change their charges from time to time. The box on page 40

CHEQUE-GUARANTEE CARDS

The introduction of the cheque-guarantee card has taken much of the difficulty out of paying bills by cheque. Anyone who has a card can cash two cheques of up to £50 each every day by presenting the card at any bank branch when cashing a cheque. Banks generally make a charge for cashing the cheques of other banks—it is worth finding out which other banks will cash your bank's cheques without charge, especially if you are travelling outside your own region. You can also use the card to cash a cheque at a post office, but you will be charged for this.

Payment for purchases of up to £50 each are also guaranteed. The card number is written on the back of the cheque and payment is assured.

If this runs you into overdraft and you do not have your bank's agreement to overdraw, the cheque will still be honoured, although the bank may withdraw your card if you are a persistent offender.

There is one snag. As payment is guaranteed, you cannot cancel the cheque for any reason at all. This means that, if you later decide you do not want to pay, you will first have to let the cheque go through and then try to reclaim your money. It may take some time, so, before signing a cheque which is guaranteed, be sure that you will not want to cancel for *any* reason.

sets out the details as for spring 1987 immediately after the March Budget.

With a little care, even if you have very little money to spare from your salary, you can achieve free banking on your current account and maximize your funds by leaving them on deposit until needed.

The first step is to get a credit card. (You may find this difficult if you are under 18.) It is almost always a good idea to have a credit card, as long as you are not tempted into overspending. You can use it for a variety of purchases during the month, settling up with just one cheque at the end, thus using far fewer cheques. There is always plenty of time given to settle the bill, so you can time your payments to some extent to suit yourself if you do not want to carry some of the debt on from month to month (see pages 121–2). Delay payments a few days, if you can, if you are coming to the end of one charging period on your current account, so that at least it is clear of charges. If you need cash and your account is running low, consider drawing money on your credit card.

If you know that you are certain to be overdrawn, ask your bank if you can have a loan account. This is not the same as a personal loan and it may well be the cheapest way to borrow. The system is that you have your loan account and then transfer money from it to your current account when you need it. That way you can keep your current account in the black.

If you do overdraw, use your account as little as possible during the charging period concerned. Also, if you think you have been overcharged or are perplexed about some of the charges that appear on your statement, tell the bank. Managers have some discretion in bank charges and you may get some money back. Frequently the very fact that you have brought the subject up will mean that future charges are reduced. The manager would rather reduce the charges than go to all the trouble of detailing all of them to you.

In summary, you should choose a current account for your first bank account if you have a regular salary and can more or less cover your outgoings each month, but have little left over which would build up in the account.

Interest-earning accounts at the banks and LDTs (licensed deposit takers)

These are a relatively new development and can be divided into two basic types: accounts which are current, but pay interest, and deposit accounts which have some current-account facilities; of the latter, some issue cheque books and others do not.

Current accounts which pay interest are generally offered not by the high-street banks but by smaller banking concerns—although the Co-operative Bank's cheque-and-save accounts come into this category. The amount of interest paid may vary with the amount you have in credit, and below a certain level there may be no interest at all. Similarly, charges may be nil, or there may be a monthly or quarterly charge or a charge for withdrawals. Some of these accounts require no minimum initial investment; others require an initial investment as high as £2,500.

Deposit cheque accounts are far more widespread among the bigger banks than are current accounts that pay interest, although many smaller banking institutions—who must be licensed deposit takers (LDTs)—are involved here as well. They will provide a cheque book (although a cheque-guarantee card is unusual, as is a cash card) or a direct debit and standing-order facility; some accounts offer all these. Although there is sometimes no minimum deposit, it may be as high as £2,500 or even £5,000. Similarly, there may be no minimum withdrawal, although the figure of £250 is quite common. The banks may offer these facilities, but they do not like the account to be too active and they impose restrictions. Paying interest is quite enough for most of them, and the charge for cheque withdrawals may be as high as 50p a cheque, although once again there may be no charge for this. The rate of interest paid may vary considerably, with much more being paid on larger amounts.

You will obviously not consider one of these accounts as your first bank account unless you have an unusually large amount of capital and yet do not want to use your account—particularly its cheque-book facility—very often.

Deposit accounts with some current-account facilities are less common, but are offered today by the major banks. They tend to have a cash-card rather than a cheque-book facility, but that is enough for many people. Some allow direct debit and standing orders; others do not. Most allow instant access to funds without any loss of interest, and the initial investment is never more than £100. Charges vary. The amount of interest is generally higher for larger amounts—deposits over, say, £1,000 may earn a percentage twice as great as deposits of £100 or even £500.

These accounts do not seem to have much attraction, except perhaps for people who have too little capital for a deposit cheque account and who have no need of a cheque book, but would welcome a cash card.

BANK CHARGES AT THE MAJOR BANKS*

Bank	Minimum for free banking	Charges for each cheque drawn	Charges for each credit	Charges for each ATM transaction	Charges for each standing order/direct debit	Fixed account charge	Charging period
Bank of Scotland	In credit	30p	nil	20p	20p	nil	Quarterly
Barclays	In credit†	29p	nil	29p	29p	£3 a quarter	Quarterly
Clydesdale	In credit	32p	20p	20p	32p/20p	nil	Quarterly
Co-op	In credit	36p	36p	36p	36p	nil	Quarterly
Lloyds	In credit†	20p	20p	20p‡	20p	£1 a month	Monthly
Midland	In credit	28p	nil	25p	28p/25p	£2.50 a quarter	Quarterly
National Girobank	In credit	75p	nil	nil§	75p	nil	Daily
Nat West	In credit†	28p	nil	28p	28p	£3 a quarter	Quarterly
Royal Bank of Scotland	In credit	32p	32p	20p	32p/20p	nil	Quarterly
TSB (England & Wales)	In credit	27p	nil	27p	27p	£2.75 a quarter	Quarterly
TSB (Scotland)	In credit	35p	nil	20p	35p/25p	nil	Quarterly
Yorkshire	In credit	24p	nil	24p	24p	£3 a quarter	Quarterly

Source: *Guide to Bank Charges*, issued by Save & Prosper.

Notes: *Early 1987. †or on average balance of £500 or more during charging period. ‡20p each day a dispenser is used. §no withdrawals allowed if overdrawn.

Building Society accounts

The majority of building-society accounts are still simple deposit accounts paying interest at varying rates and terms. This is all changing, however, as the Building Societies Act (1986) has given societies the power to extend their activities into more direct competition with the banks (see box on page 58). So far the most common facility offered is the cash card; as yet (1987) the societies do not normally issue cheque books and cheque-guarantee cards, or allow overdrafts, but these will come. At the time of writing, building societies will pay standing orders and perhaps direct debits. Many will make out a cheque for you to another person, or to pay your bills; in this case you may feel that you have no need of a cheque book, particularly if you have a credit card and a cash card. Very few building societies impose charges; those that do are generally the ones that issue cheque books. These latter accounts may also require some initial minimum investment, but there is no 100 per cent rule for these accounts. Interest may be fixed at any particular time, or it may rise quite substantially for larger amounts. If you are considering such an account, you should visit a few building societies, get details of all the accounts on offer, and then check that you are getting exactly what you need.

Building-society accounts are attractive to many people as an alternative to having a current account run alongside a deposit account of some kind. Interest is earned on all the money all the time that it is in the account, whereas money in a current account (as opposed to the deposit account) is simply saving charges. Building-society accounts are particularly suitable for tax-paying pensioners who do not need a very active account and who have relatively few bills to pay.

Bank accounts linked with building societies

These are a relatively new development, and there are still only a few of them about. They are bound to grow in number as the building societies improve their competitive position in the banking market. The banks are certain to want to develop links with societies to ensure that they do not lose out too much on business. So far such accounts have required a minimum initial investment of £500.

What happens with this system is that you put money into your building-society account and, when your current account falls to a level less than a certain amount—£100 is common—an automatic transfer takes place from the building-society account. This means that your current account is always in credit and that you do not have to worry about your credit balance being eliminated so that you incur charges. Of course, you *can* become overdrawn, if you make a sudden large withdrawal, and then there will be charges to pay, but you can watch out for this kind of thing. If it does happen, the charges are the usual ones for current accounts. It is important to make sure that the money goes into the deposit side of the linked account, because the automatic transfer works only one way—that is, out of the interest-earning account, not into it.

It is too early yet to say how these accounts will develop and how popular they will become. But banking is competitive and getting increasingly so, so further refinements seem likely. So far, the big high-street banks have not linked with the major building societies in these accounts, and they may continue for some time to run the normal current account, which is more profitable to them. But, should there be developments, do not hesitate to consider switching your account to the linked variety.

Changing your bank

Most of us—around 80 per cent—stay with the same bank or building society all our lives, although many of us move from one branch to another. Changing your bank is your prerogative. If you are really discontented with the service you get, make the change. Tell your bank why you are changing, because the manager will be expected to explain to head office why an account has been lost. Be careful, however, not to get a reputation for changing too often. If you go along to a new bank and it is clear that you have previously held an account elsewhere, the new manager will want to know why you are changing; the validity or otherwise of your reasons will have a major effect on his or her assessment of you as a customer.

It is at the time of starting your first job that you will first seriously consider opening an account. But, whatever the stage of your life, the arguments for and against certain accounts are always the same:

- Will it provide the services you want? We all have slightly different needs.
- Will it provide them at a minimal price? There is no point in running a current account and losing deposit interest if you have little use for your current account. On the other hand, if you need an active account and from time to time an overdraft, your activities will be curtailed if you always have to seek a personal loan rather than simply make a quick phone call to your bank manager to arrange a temporary overdraft.

It is worth taking a little time and trouble to select the sort of bank account you need right at the start: doing so can save you money. The array of accounts available today can be quite bewildering.

First Savings

8

With luck, by the time you start your first job, your parents will have already established you in the habit of saving and, if at all possible, you should continue to save regularly as soon as you start working. It really does not matter how much or how little you are able to save: it is the continuing habit which is important. Even a pound or two a week mounts up and, as wage and salary increases come along, you can add a little more. It is unlikely that at this point you will be taking a long-term view on your savings: they will probably be for a specific project, like a holiday or a car.

Later on, when you think about buying a home of your own, your savings will become important in building up the sum of money you may require for a deposit. We shall see later (see pages 58ff.) how such savings can guarantee a mortgage and possibly qualify you for a small grant and loan from the government to help in the purchase of your first home.

As we become employees we also become taxpayers, so there is a change in the type of saving that suits us. It is at this point that tax-paid savings come into their own. These are various kinds of deposits which pay interest net of tax, compared with National Savings, which pay gross. The tax deducted in tax-paid savings cannot be reclaimed back from the Inland Revenue by the individual, so these savings are not the best for non-taxpayers. But the level of tax paid by the financial institution on behalf of the saver is 25 per cent. This is below the level of standard-rate tax, so that the savers are getting some marginal benefit. If they put the money into National Savings and then eventually had to pay tax at the full standard rate they could be worse off. But, in money, things are rarely what they seem, and whenever you deposit money you should compare one interest rate with another and see what they mean in real terms. Say the National Savings Investment Account is paying 10 per cent and you are fully liable for tax. You will have to take 27 per cent off that (tax year 1987/88), so that the net interest will be 7.3 per cent. If a bank or building society is offering a scheme which pays anything more than that, tax-paid, this is obviously a better deal for standard-rate tax payers. Anything below that and the Investment Account is better.

If you are a higher-rate taxpayer, particularly if you are paying tax at the highest rate of 60 per cent (1987–88), tax-free savings become more attractive. These are available only in National Savings and in the government's Personal Equity Plans (PEPs) (see page 51).

Anyone with tax-paid savings who pays tax at the higher rates will eventually have to pay the difference between the standard rate and his or her marginal (top) rate of tax. This means that tax-paid savings eventually become less attractive as income rises. However, as you do not move to the 40 per cent tax level until you are earning over £20,000 per annum, it is unlikely that you will be in this category in your early working years; but the point is worth making to show how your investment and saving strategy and that of your family should change as the years go on. You should keep a close eye on interest rates and switch your savings accordingly. There are other things you should know about interest rates, which are not always what they seem (see also pages 119–20 for discussion of credit and hire purchase). Interest which is credited daily (although it will not actually be written into your account daily, but monthly, quarterly, or even annually) is worth more than that credited monthly. The reason for this is that a small daily addition to interest mounts up more quickly than if it is added only monthly. Ten per cent per year added each day to £100 means that your savings have become more than £110 by the end of a month; but if interest is added only at the end of the month your savings remain at £100 until then.

Further, what interest is really worth is related to the level of inflation at any time, because the value of your money is eroded as prices rise. Let's say you are offered an interest rate of 5 per cent in a period when inflation is only 2.5 per cent. You will then be getting a real rate of interest (i.e., an increase in the real value of your savings) of 2.5 per cent. Conversely, although a 12 per cent interest rate may look far more generous, if inflation is running at 10 per cent the real interest rate will be only 2 per cent—i.e., less than in the first example. Indeed, it is not unknown for there to be a negative rate of interest—that is, although you are getting interest the real value of your savings is falling. This happened sometimes in the 1970s, when interest rates were as high as 12 or 15 per cent but inflation was even higher.

The particular level of interest rates at any time is determined by what is called the *minimum lending rate*. This is the lowest level of interest that the banks are prepared to charge borrowers. Interest paid on savings will be 1–2 per cent below that: the lower the borrowing rate, the smaller the gap. Banks are generally free to fix their own interest rates, but they get strong hints from the Bank of England, which is banker to the banks in the United Kingdom. Control goes back from it to the Treasury, which imposes monetary and financial policy according to the policies of the government of the day.

Building societies are not required to keep their interest rates exactly parallel to those of the banks—and indeed they do not, although the two move fairly closely together. If the banks raise interest rates, building societies are forced to follow, or they lose savers to the banks. You might argue that the reverse need not happen when interest rates fall, but that would be to forget the borrowing side of the equation: if the banks lower interest rates, the building societies have to follow—because they must also lower their borrowing rates: they simply could not afford to lower rates to borrowers without also lowering them to savers. These fluctuations in interest rates are one reason why savers should always be on the alert for changes, because there are inevitably small time lags which make one form of saving temporarily better than another. And such fluctuations are also an argument against tying your money up too firmly. Whatever form of saving you choose, it will have certain withdrawal terms. If you tie your money up at a particular rate for a whole year, for instance, and then interest rates generally rise, you will be missing out on the increase. On the other hand, of course, you could see interest rates fall, and in that case you would be better off than those who had their money on shorter notice.

Which to choose

There are no absolute rules in saving and investing, but it is generally true that a good beginning for the saver in first-time employment is a building-society account. These come in various guises, some specially tailored to regular savers. If you agree to put aside a fixed amount each month, the chances are that any building society will offer you better terms than on a lump-sum account—assuming that both are on fairly short withdrawal terms. Regular savings are very useful to building societies, and the higher rate is to encourage them.

Look at the tables on pages 237–9 and decide which saving scheme might best suit you. Check to see which ones can be registered as savings under the government's 'Homeloan' Home Purchase Scheme. If you think that there is any chance at all that you will want to buy a home in the fairly near future (the account must be held for at least two years), register under the scheme. You have nothing to lose if in the event you do not use the savings as a contribution towards the purchase of your home, and much to gain if you do. (See page 59.)

If, on the other hand, you know that you are saving specifically for (say) a holiday, there is more choice for you between the banks and building societies, or other LDTs (licensed deposit takers). In banks and building societies, your savings are as safe as they can possibly be. In theory, there may be marginally more risk among LDTs, who may offer slightly higher interest, but that risk is so remote today under the rather stringent rules for LDTs (who may actually be banks but not part of the clearing system, or be foreign-controlled) that it can realistically be discounted. Under the new (1986) rules for self-regulation in financial services, even these minimal risks have been reduced.

What you have to remember is that if you do not stick to the rules for withdrawal you are likely to lose interest. This is not invariably the case, as financial institutions are prepared to take small risks to get their hands on large sums of money. They may offer high rates of interest on sums in excess of, say, £10,000 or be prepared to offer the same rate of interest as they pay on sums below that level but not require the same three months' notice of withdrawal. Generally, however, if your money is on three-months' notice you will either have to give that notice before withdrawing or sacrifice the whole or part of the interest you would have earned during the three-month period. The simple rule is that, the greater the chance you think you will need the money suddenly, the shorter with-drawal terms you should choose. There is not a lot of difference between the interest rates for small amounts, and it would be a mistake to tie up your funds for three months for the sake of a few pounds.

A savings plan

There is no reason why you should not work out a savings plan as soon as you begin working, even though (a) it may be many years before you can fulfil it and (b) you may have to abandon it from time to time when your financial commitments are such that you cannot save at all.

To make a plan, you must understand what you are doing. First, be clear in your mind about the difference between saving and investment. The two words are frequently used in the same context and are often substituted for one another. There is, nevertheless, a subtle difference. Strictly speaking, when you are *saving*, your capital is deposited in some financial institution and then earns interest at a rate depending on interest rates generally and on the terms under which you have made your deposit. The safety of the money you put on your deposit should be guaranteed in fact, if not actually guaranteed in law. *Investment* is different in that the safety of your original capital cannot be guaranteed. You are taking a risk. That risk may be rather small, but nevertheless it is there. You may put your money into stocks and shares quoted on the stock exchange or into unit trusts, which are several investments in shares grouped together and bought and sold by expert managers. These investments should pay an annual dividend; in essence, this is the same as an interest payment, but it is not fixed or guaranteed in any way and depends on the level of profits in a company, or, in the case of a unit trust, the varying profitability of the group of companies.

Investment extends beyond the stock market. You might buy property and let it out for rent; in that case, the rent would be the equivalent of interest or dividends. But investment has another aspect. As well as paying a dividend, an investment may—and should, if it has been chosen wisely—increase in value. If a company's profitability improves it will raise its dividend and the price of its shares may also rise, so that investors get not only a dividend but also a capital profit. Similarly, the value of a property could rise and yield a profit that way, or you might buy paintings or antiques at one price and sell them later at a profit.

All these are investments and, as there is a possibility of profit, there is also the possibility of loss. A company may do badly and cut its dividend or even omit it altogether. You may buy a property whose value decreases because an airport or motorway is built close by or because of job losses in the area. You might buy a painting which is overpriced or whose artist falls from favour. The element of risk in all these purchases is very clear, and you should not start investing, as opposed to saving, unless you can afford to take that risk. (See chapter 17.)

The first rule when starting out on life-time financial planning is, obviously, to get together a reserve for emergencies. This will be money that you can get at quickly if you have to. Even in the best ordered financial lives things can go wrong, and 'rainy day' money can help you get over short, sharp financial shocks. How much you will need for emergencies is something only you can work out. If you are young, single and still living at home, the amount you will need is probably very small— maybe just £100 or so. Once you start to live alone, the reserve fund should be increased, unless you are in the fortunate position that your parents are prepared to help you out if need be. Later on, when you marry, you will need a bigger reserve.

This money should be available to you for immediate withdrawal ('at call') or at least on very short notice. The National Savings Ordinary Account or Investment Account, building-society share accounts, and ordinary bank deposit accounts are all suitable, as are some regular monthly-saving building-society share accounts. Check with your local building society or one of the larger national ones. Make them explain carefully what is involved in their various accounts. Do not forget that it's your money they're after! They can afford to spend some time with you.

Once you have your reserve fund you can start to put your extra money where it may earn a little more interest, although the withdrawal terms are likely to be longer. You may be able to have interest credited to your account and thus see the amount of capital gradually increase, or have it paid out to you as a monthly income. The latter choice is not really suitable for small savers or for young people in employment, but it is an option for later. Gradually you will build up your second line of defence against financial disaster.

Investment

Many of us never move beyond this phase in saving and investing. As our responsibilities increase, so do our financial commitments; it becomes necessary, as we will see in the next chapter, to provide for our homes and to protect our dependants. Even so, an increasing number of us are able to extend our financial activities from the realm of saving into investment. In the investment field there are stages to follow, just as there are in savings. Investment in the stock market involves payments other than those necessary for the shares themselves. Stockbrokers charge commission for dealing (buying and selling) on our behalf, and so we need to buy quite large parcels of shares to make the whole enterprise possible without a very sharp increase in the selling price of the shares we buy. We also may need patience.

Building up a portfolio of shares usually comes rather late in life, so the subject is discussed in detail not here but in Part Five (see chapter 17).

Unit trusts

The fact that we may have only small amounts of money to save does not mean we cannot consider investment—and this is where unit trusts (known in the United States as 'mutual funds') come in. They are largely a development of the years since the end of World War II. They are an excellent vehicle whereby the beginner can get into the stock market, because initially very small amounts can be purchased; not only that, as each unit trust is made up of a considerable number of stocks and shares in different enterprises, the risk is spread among them all and therefore, overall, reduced—although at the same time, of course, the chance of a sharp *rise* in value is also rather reduced. Unit trusts combine the prospect of moderate-to-good growth with a dividend in good times and a cushion when share prices are falling.

A unit trust enables individuals of moderate means to get together and purchase shares on the same terms as the big individual investor. The managers of the trusts—who are investment experts—buy and sell the shares depending on the view that they are taking of them at the present time. They value the whole lot each day and then divide them into what are called units—each unit containing a tiny bit of every share in the trust's portfolio. The prices of the units are quoted daily in the financial press, just like individual shares, but they are bought not through stockbrokers or banks but through the unit-trust managers. The price is worked out not arbitrarily but according to a formula fixed by the Department of Trade. There are two prices—bid price and offer price. The offer price, which is the higher (usually by about 6 per cent), is the one at which the managers are selling the units; the bid price is the one at which the managers will buy.

Unit trusts are 'open-ended'; that is, there is no limit on the value of the trust. If more people are buying into the trust, the managers simply purchase more stocks and shares; if people are selling their units, the managers eventually sell some shares. Such deals will have an influence on share prices eventually, of course, because unit trusts are big dealers—if people were to panic out of unit trusts on bad economic news the price of

POUND-COST AVERAGING

£20 invested each month	price of units	number bought	average cost per unit
month 1	100p	20	100p
month 2	100.46p	19.91	100.23p
month 3	100.34p	19.93	100.27p
month 4	100.30p	19.94	100.26p
month 5	102p	19.61	100.61p
month 6	99p	20.20	100.34p
month 7	99.50p	20.10	100.22p
month 8	100p	20	100.19p
month 9	101.66p	19.67	100.36p
month 10	102.50p	19.51	100.57p
month 11	102.88p	19.44	100.77p
month 12	103.11p	19.40	100.96p

At the end of the first year, 237.71 units will have been bought for £240, at an average price of 100.96p, while the price has fluctuated between 99p and 103.11p. There will not be a profit yet on the investment, because the buying price will need to rise to around 107p before the selling price betters the average.

month 13	103.20p	19.38	101.13p
month 14	105p	19.05	101.39p
month 15	106.50p	18.78	101.17p
month 16	105p	19.05	101.92p
month 17	106.34p	18.80	102.17p
month 18	107.50p	18.60	102.46p
month 19	107.75p	19.56	102.44p
month 20	107.78p	18.56	102.70p
month 21	108.67p	18.40	102.97p
month 22	109p	18.35	103.22p
month 23	108.80p	18.38	103.46p
month 24	110p	18.18	103.72p

At the end of the second year, the investor would still not be making a profit, if he or she sold the units, but is very close to it. The average buying price of the 162.80 units which have been purchased for a total investment of £480 has risen rather more slowly to 103.72p than the buying price and very little further increase will be necessary for the investor to break even. Pound-cost averaging means that anyone investing in unit trusts is unlikely to see any fireworks, but over the long term a substantial investment can be built up.

the units would eventually fall—but as a rule unit-trust prices move only fractionally compared with the prices of single shares.

Because of the way unit prices are calculated, the managers will usually allow the investor to buy quite a small number of units—a minimum amount may be stated, but it is rarely high—and many allow the investor to buy on monthly plans. Unit trusts are good for new investors who have got their reserve fund together and may now be feeling rather more adventurous about their savings, if not exactly reckless. The money can, after all, be withdrawn from the plan at any time, subject of course to the difference between the buying and selling price.

The problem with unit trusts is one of choice. There are over 1,000 to choose from in the United Kingdom today. All are completely separate, even when they are run by the same managers. Many are similar—there is a limit to the variety of trusts, after all. Every manager will want a general trust as well as some trusts specializing in particular industries or activities such as finance, mining, commodities, high technology or services. There are high-yielding trusts and trusts which have little or no immediate return, but which should offer good potential for capital growth as well as trusts which invest in companies overseas in, for example, North America or the Far East. It can be difficult for the novice to choose—and it has to be admitted that, over the short term at least, the difference in performance is only marginal. It is only over the longer term that the superiority of one particular manager or set of managers over another can be seen. It is also important to remember that, when we are looking at performance, we are looking at *past* performance, which is by no means always a good guide to the future. Nevertheless, the past is the only guide we have, so choose a trust from a group of managers which has a proved record. To help you choose, there are many articles in the newspapers about trusts, particularly at the turn of year when the performance tables are published.

The differences are even less marked if you choose a monthly plan, because you will buy in only very small amounts, perhaps as little as £10 a month. Each month you will buy at the current offer price, which may have moved only a fraction. Over the year, the price at which you buy is

---

UNIT TRUST INVESTMENT

Advantages
provides easy access to stock market investment
initial investment can be a small sum
portfolio is managed by investment experts
strict controls over trust managers
capital can be built up in monthly instalments
large portfolio lowers risk of loss
buying and selling is very easy

Disadvantages
large portfolio lessens possibility of large profits
not so exciting as investing in individual shares
in bigger trusts may be difficult to beat stock-market average
quality of management varies
protection against risk is not guaranteed.

averaged out—a process known as 'pound-cost averaging', which irons out even more the difference in prices over a period. You may pay more one month and less in another, but as the overall price averages out you need not be too concerned about temporary price fluctuations. You will make money as long as, over an extended period, the basic trend in price is upward. The box on page 48 shows you exactly how it works over a two-year period.

Buying unit trusts is very simple. You merely write to the managers and send them a cheque. The price of the units will be that struck on the day your cheque arrives. If you are making a one-time purchase, you will buy an exact number of units and the managers will return the excess. If you are buying on a monthly plan, you will buy in units and fractions each month, so that the trust avoids unnecessary administration. Monthly plans can be linked to life assurance and, later on, to mortgages, but these are details which need not concern the first-time young buyer. The *Financial Times* lists all trusts along with the names, addresses and telephone numbers of the trust managers; if you write or call the managers they will send you a brochure.

Is your money safe?

To the extent that share prices rise and fall, it cannot be said that your savings are utterly safe in a unit trust. Prices will fluctuate. Even in times when overall share prices are rising, there are day-to-day variations and, of course, there can be prolonged periods when prices fall. Do try not to be panicked into selling when this happens, but bear in mind that, because of these fluctuations (among other reasons), unit trusts cannot be used for your emergency fund. On the other hand, you need not fear that unit-trust managers are going to run off with your money. The only risk you take is that you may have chosen the wrong trust.

Unit trusts are not allowed to operate without the authorization of the Department of Trade and Industry (DTI), and there is legal protection for investors under the Prevention of Fraud (Investments) Act of 1948; this states that there must be a reasonable amount of money behind each management company. Indeed, most unit-trust companies today have some connection with banks or insurance companies, and, where manage-ment companies are independent, they are large and have many years of experience.

Each unit trust must have a trustee, usually a bank, who is absolutely independent of the business. This trustee's responsibility is to look after the unit holders' interests as laid down in the *trust deed*. Every unit trust must have this document, which states how the trust is to be run; the trustee deed must follow guidelines issued by the DTI. It will set out the formula by which unit prices are calculated, give details of management charges which, while they can vary, may do so only by a little, and some rules for the investment policy of the particular fund. There is some variation here, but no trust is allowed to put more than 10 per cent of its total funds into one particular stock, and a figure of 5 per cent is more usual.

Trusts can invest only in shares quoted on a recognized stock exchange. Add to this the fact that unit trusts cannot sell door-to-door, and you will realize that you are rather well protected against everything except your wrong investment judgement. However, not all investments which might look like unit trusts are protected in this way, and you should be aware of the existence of these other types of schemes—either to avoid them or, conversely, so that you can make use of them.

Other funds and bonds

DTI authorization goes only to unit trusts, but there are other funds which operate in a similar way. These funds, *property bonds*, are not subject to the same restrictions as unit trusts, and are not allowed to advertise in the same way for business. They very often invest in property and, to get around the advertising restrictions, are frequently sold alongside single-premium life-assurance policies, which can be advertised. As there are not the same legal controls as on unit trusts, it is possible for the unscrupulous to set up these investment funds. There are, however, many good operators in this field and, if you stick to well known companies or those which also run unit trusts, you have nothing to fear. However, these funds have to be regarded as rather more risky than unit trusts, if only because it is less easy—and perhaps impossible—to estimate precisely the value of a particular property at any particular time; this value is known only if a property is sold, any other valuations being at best good estimates.

You may also come across a *managed fund*. This combines a unit trust with a property bond. Once again, these are not authorized by the DTI. Your investment goes into properties, shares or sometimes fixed interest stocks. The money moves from one investment to another, depending on where the managers think the best prospects lie at any one time. The hope is that a managed fund will be able to provide more regular growth than a unit trust, which is limited to stocks and shares. Managed funds, like property bonds, may have life assurance attached to them. In both property bonds and managed funds, the value of the policy at any one time depends on the value of the total units you have bought.

Debatably, unit trusts (and possibly property bonds and managed funds) are the only form of investment, as opposed to saving, which should be considered by the young employed person—and then not until they have reached the age of 18. Investing in the stock market is a matter for later in life and anyway many companies do not allow people to be shareholders in their own right until they reach 18. However, it is perhaps worth mentioning here the government's Personal Equity Plan, by which, through tax concessions, it hopes to spread share ownership more widely.

Personal Equity Plans

In an attempt to increase private share ownership, the government introduced in its 1986 Budget the Personal Equity Plan, or PEP (effective from January 1987). Each year anyone over 18 (and in this case husband and wife are treated separately) can invest up to £2,400 in stocks and shares. The attraction is that, if the plan is kept up for a qualifying period of between one and two years, all the tax on dividends received or on profits made through increases in the share prices is free of income and capital-gains tax.

PEPs are run for individuals by plan managers, who charge for their services. There are of course also the normal broking charges to pay (these are usually written into the overall charges). The individual need not mention that he or she has such a plan when filling in a tax return: the manager deals with the taxman.

The annual sum involved would not be likely to run into capital-gains tax if it was the only investment a person had (the annual exemption would anyway take care of that), but on any investment in shares there would normally be income tax to pay. To someone who has not invested in the past, £2,400 is a relatively large sum, but in investment terms it is very small and, with average yields well below 5 per cent, anyone investing the maximum amount and paying tax at the standard rate would probably save something like £32 a year in tax. The price you pay for this benefit is that you are locked into the scheme for a period of at least two years, during which time you may not make a profit. It is tempting to think that share prices always move upwards, because that is what they have done for many years (albeit now with occasional hiccups), but this is not always so, and there have been prolonged periods when share prices have fallen sharply.

The attractions of PEPs are limited, and the schemes represent a raw appeal to the feeling many of us have that we would like to pay less tax. For this reason alone they are likely to be popular with the public and to shift some money from safe havens like building societies and banks, which pay higher-than-average interest, into risk-bearing stock-market investment. You should not take out a PEP unless you are fully aware of the risks involved.

With that warning, here are the rules:

- PEPs must be run by a person authorized to deal in securities and registered with the Inland Revenue for the purpose of acting as a plan manager.
- Investors must be over 18.
- The investor must pay cash.
- Investments made in one calendar year must be held for the whole of the following year to qualify for the tax exemption. This means that, if you bought on 1 January 1987, the date when the scheme first came in, you would have to hold at least until 1 January 1989. Any dividends received in that time would have to be held within the plan and not used as part of your income until the qualifying period is completed. But you could buy as late as the end of December 1987 and cash in your plan in January 1989 to fulfil the qualifying period. In that case, your period of obligation would be only one year and two or three days (allowing for public holidays).
- Investments are limited to ordinary shares in UK companies quoted in the stock market. This puts out investment in commodities, property, etc., and also those companies traded over-the-counter, but it does include shares quoted on the unlisted securities market (see page 172 for an explanation).
- Allowing for the above, 25 per cent, or a maximum of £450 a year, can be invested in unit trusts or investment trusts.

The owner of the plan must be the beneficial owner of the shares, which can be registered either in the individual's name or jointly with the plan manager. The manager must ensure that the investor receives all company reports and any other relevant shareholder information and, where the investor so wishes, must arrange for him or her to go to company meetings or exercise voting rights.

Plans come in two varieties: nondiscretionary, where the PEP owner decides what shares can be bought; and discretionary, where the choice is made by the plan manager. In the latter case, many investors will be buying the same plan and the same investments, although individuals may be offered a choice of portfolios. To that extent, the purchase is rather similar to buying a unit trust. Plans come to an end if the investor dies, but there is no income tax or capital-gains tax to pay when the plan is liquidated, although the cash raised forms part of the normal estate of the deceased person.

There are some attractions for the small investor who can afford to tie up his or her capital for up to two years, but the success of PEPs will depend to a large extent on the skills of the plan manager—and such skills will obviously vary. It is not possible yet to establish any track record for managers; the plans have not been going long enough. It is also worth mentioning that PEPs might not be regarded as desirable by future governments and could be stopped at any time, or the tax concessions could be withdrawn.

Employee-share schemes

One other way of beginning to invest in the stock market in a relatively inexpensive and easy way is through employee-share purchase schemes. These plans are sure to increase, because PEPs can be adapted for company schemes. At present, there are three basic kinds of schemes which might be preferred by people who have not got a spare £2,400 a year, or who disapprove in principle of PEPs. They are:

- Simple profit-sharing. In these schemes the company sets up a trust and makes tax-deductible contributions to it to buy shares for employees (assuming they want them). Such schemes must be open to all employees. The employee immediately owns the shares bought on his or her behalf, and gets all the dividends and other rights associated with them. Usually, such shares must be held for at least five years before they can be sold.
- Employees get an option to buy shares at some future date at a price specified now. These schemes, too, must be open to all employees. A regular savings account is set up for the employee to ensure that, when the time comes, the employee has enough money to pay for the shares at the contract price. This is fine if the price has gone up, but no use if it has fallen, in which case the employee would refuse the shares and instead take the money in the savings account.
- An option to purchase limited to certain employees—usually senior executives, although the company may extend the scheme. In such a system there is, however, no requirement to save for the purchase, and the amount of shares which can be bought is usually much higher than in a scheme which must be offered to all employees.

If you are offered an employee-share scheme, consider it carefully. They are usually good for employees, and you could be throwing money away if you refuse them. It is as well to remember that, whether we like it or not, we live in a capitalist society, and that we may lose out financially if we do not take up the opportunities which are available.

Spotcheck

When you reach 16, have you

- already discussed with your parents and your career adviser what kind of career you might have?
- decided whether to stay on full-time at school and, if so, discussed with your parents how this might be financed?

When you start working, do you

- understand how National Insurance contributions work?
- understand the basic tax system, the tax rates and how they are levied, and the system of allowances and expenses which can cut your tax bill?

If you cannot get a job

- have you signed on at the local unemployment office to register that you are available for work?
- considered further training, either part- or full-time?
- considered joining the youth training scheme?

If you are opening a bank account, have you

- thought carefully about what kind of account you need and want?
- thought how best to relate the use of the money for spending and that for saving?
- started to build up your funds to allow for emergencies?

When you have your emergency fund, have you

- considered investment as opposed to saving and understood the risks involved?
- considered the possibilities of a Personal Equity Plan (PEP)?
- checked to see if your company has an employee-share scheme?

THE EARLY YEARS OF MARRIAGE

If financial planning has not already started by the time we marry it should be delayed no longer—and it is as well to remember that money problems are a not infrequent cause of divorce. Marriage means that we are no longer simply individuals but half of a partnership, with responsibilities to another person. We need to set up a home or at least start saving towards it, if we have not already built up some funds towards a deposit or towards furnishings and fittings; to protect our spouse; to begin to look towards our later years when we retire; to save to protect ourselves against illness or even untimely death; and to maximize our financial resources. Regrettably, we must also consider how we will cope if we become unemployed. We need to look at the taxation of married couples, which differs from that for single individuals, and use it to our best advantage.

Marriage is still to most people in the UK a life-time commitment, and sensible financial planning from the outset can do much to make that commitment pleasurable and rewarding from both partners' point of view. It is axiomatic that all planning should be a joint effort between husband and wife: each should be open with the other, problems should be discussed and solutions should be found together. Both should understand the fundamentals of family finance, because one partner will eventually be left to carry on alone.

9 Setting up a Home

The first priority for most couples after marriage—or, ideally, as soon as the decision to marry has been taken—is the setting up of a home. It is almost always true in the long run that it is better to buy rather than rent, but this may not always be possible, especially at the start of the marriage. The couple may not have any savings to put towards a deposit on a house or flat, or sufficient income to sustain mortgage payments; there are occasions, too, when a move might have to be made shortly after marriage when money could be thrown away simply because of the buying and selling costs involved in property deals. Such instances apart, however, it is safe to say that home ownership is preferable to renting. In case you have any doubts about it, here are just some of the things to consider:

- Rent is almost never recoverable. In contrast, although you may be buying your home on a mortgage and paying interest only for the first few years or even throughout the loan period, the rise in prices usually makes up for the interest paid.
- The increase in property prices in recent years has in general far outstripped the increase in overall prices, so that home owners have seen a real as well as a paper profit when they sell.
- In later years, the money raised from the sale of a family home, when a couple often chooses to move to a smaller property, can be used to supplement income in retirement.
- The tax relief which is available on mortgages makes borrowing in this way relatively inexpensive. We shall go into this in more detail later on, but, briefly, any loan for home purchase up to a maximum of £30,000 is fully eligible for relief at all levels of tax for each individual or married couple. There is a further limitation: only one loan is eligible—that on the so-called 'principal residence'.

From time to time there are calls for the tax relief available on mortgages to be abolished, so that general income-tax rates can be lowered. It is true that the standard rate of tax could be reduced by about 5 per cent if mortgage relief were removed. All taxpayers would then benefit, not just those buying their home with a loan. Any further move towards abolition (there was a time in the past when the interest on loans to any level was fully allowed for tax), however, would be very unpopular with the public and no government has been prepared to take the risk of the loss of votes which would be sure to follow such a move.

Any couple planning to buy a home can feel fairly secure that their tax relief will not vanish without warning. This is not to say that the system of tax relief on mortgages and rent subsidies for local-authority tenants is preferable to generally lower rates of tax, but it is what the public wants, and increasingly so, as more and more people opt to buy their homes.

So much for the arguments in favour of buying your home. The problem for most people is of course how to get the money together. The early years of marriage, particularly if a couple chooses to have children fairly soon, are the ones when money is both most needed and least available. The purchase of a home is probably the single most important financial transaction a couple will make in their lifetime, involving the expenditure of many thousands of pounds. The purchase of the first home is especially important as it is usually the only way that a married couple can ensure that, when it comes to moving, they will be able to afford their next home from the proceeds of selling their existing one.

House prices in Britain have been rising steeply in recent years; by the end of 1986, the average price of a house had reached £42,000. Very few people, and particularly the newlywed, can afford that kind of cash purchase, so they have to borrow. Taking the same figure, the average amount borrowed on mortgage at the end of 1986 had reached £17,000, though the average new mortgage was approaching £30,000, the top limit for tax relief. These average figures mask regional differences: mortgages in the south and east of England are much higher than elsewhere in the United Kingdom.

There are, however, tremendous regional variations. London and the Southeast are by far the most expensive areas in which to live, while Northern Ireland is the cheapest. Similarly, the amount that has to be borrowed varies from region to region.

It is worth making the point here that, even if you can afford to pay cash, it is not a sensible thing to do, unless money is not a consideration in your life. It is a mistake, too, to tie up all your capital, or a very large proportion of it, in your home. Not only do tax relief and inflation make borrowing relatively cheap, but you can use any surplus capital you may have in various ways through savings schemes to increase your income and also have it available should you require it in an emergency.

You will have noticed that there is a gap between average house prices and the average mortgage, and anyone purchasing a home will have to find the difference between the two, unless they are lucky enough to get a 100 per cent mortgage—which, though increasingly offered, is still not the normal rule. For this reason, we shall first look at savings schemes to help you build up some capital before you buy, so that you can find any deposit required for the purchase and pay the other obligatory costs without overstraining your budget. If you want to buy a home as soon as you marry, or have it ready to walk into immediately after your marriage, it is clear that you will have to start saving well before the ceremony.

It may seem obvious, but until you are actually married or purchasing your home, it is sensible to make sure that savings are either made in separate accounts or that, if you are saving in a single account, you have agreed in writing how the savings should be divided in the event that you do not marry after all.

If you are both contributing the same amount to the savings, then it is clear that, on a break-up, the accumulated funds should be equally divided. However, if you are paying in different amounts, you should agree beforehand what proportion of capital and interest each should get.

You will probably want the highest interest possible from your savings, with the proviso that you can get at your money quite quickly when you need it. It is no use going for a high-interest account, which demands three months' notice of withdrawal, if you may need to put down a deposit within weeks or even days.

There are other considerations, however, apart from a high level of interest. When you find your home you will want to be fairly certain that you will get the full amount of loan you need. For the past few years getting a loan has been relatively easy, provided you fulfil the lenders' requirements, but this is not always so and you may have to shop around quite some time before getting your loan. During that time you could lose the property you want to buy.

Savings with building societies

There is great competition for mortgage business between the banks, insurance companies, and the building societies, which were set up solely for the purpose of financing private home purchase—although their freedom to move into other areas of financing has been greatly extended by the Building Societies Act (1986). As many as 70 per cent of borrowers, however, still choose building societies. If you are one of them, you should save in a building society scheme rather than anywhere else. Building societies like to lend to people who have already saved with them. A few will lend *only* to existing savers, although this policy is less frequent than it used to be; a great many more give their own savers priority for mortgages. The longer the period you have saved, the better are your chances of getting what you want. In particular, some building societies like people who save regular amounts with them—they show some discipline over their money—and they will guarantee a loan to such savers when the time comes. Naturally, even in this case there are limits on how much will be lent, and this depends on the couple's financial position, but you will be sure of as generous treatment as is possible.

NEW POWERS FOR BUILDING SOCIETIES

For many years, building societies were limited in their activities to lending first mortgages on private homes and paying interest on various savings deposits. From 1 January 1987, however, their powers have been greatly increased. All the following services may be offered by a building society. Whether or not they are available may influence your choice of a particular building society.

- money transmission
- unsecured personal loans (loans not attached to the building)
- estate agency
- conveyancing
- stockbroking
- personal equity plans
- insurance broking
- foreign exchange
- pensions
- house building

There are two choices open to you, either (a) a regular savings account, which can be specifically designated a mortgage account, or (b) if you are not able to save regularly, one of the other accounts, which will have various levels of interest for differing amounts and differing withdrawal terms.

The banks

Banks are less concerned than building societies about lending to existing savers, but naturally they too will look with more favour on their own account-holders, whether they have current or deposit accounts. The balance of advantage on interest-rate savings tends to go to building societies. If you happen not to be a taxpayer—which means that you are probably on a very low income and are therefore anyway unlikely to qualify for a mortgage—you should put your money into National Savings. The reason is that in this scheme interest is paid gross, before deduction of tax. Thus the advertised pre-tax interest tends to be higher than that available from banks or building societies. In all forms of savings apart from National Savings, interest is tax-paid; i.e., the financial institution remits the tax due to the Inland Revenue before crediting the interest to account-holders. This tax cannot be reclaimed by people who are not taxpayers. There are some circumstances whereby a couple may not have a high income at present—two students perhaps—and might not be taxpayers when they start saving for a deposit. They can maximize their interest payments by putting their money into National Savings and then switching to a building society or bank once they start earning.

The government home-purchase scheme

Whatever savings scheme you choose, make sure if (a) you are a first-time buyer and (b) you expect to be able to save for two years before you need your mortgage that you register your savings account with the government home-loan scheme. This costs you nothing, but offers you a tax-free bonus of up to £110 and an interest-free loan of £600. Not only is there no interest to pay on the latter, but none of the capital has to be repaid for five years. You simply fill in a form, HPA 1, which your building society or bank should be able to supply. It is all very simple. Twelve months before your application is made you must have saved at least £300, and you must always keep a minimum of £300 in your savings account. It need not be designated a mortgage account, nor even be the one in which you make your regular savings. This is how the bonus works:

minimum savings in the 12 months before applying	*cash bonus*
£300–£399	£40
£400–£499	£50
£500–£599	£60
£600–£699	£70
£700–£799	£80
£800–£899	£90
£900–£999	£100
over £1,000	£110

The rules concerning the interest-free loan are similar to those for the bonus, although there must be at least £600 in the account when the application is made. The £600 is added to the amount of the mortgage, but no interest is paid on it during the first five years of the loan; after that, it carries interest in the usual way. The scheme is designed to help the less well-off, and applies to homes which are bought for less than a certain sum—varying regionally from £20,400 to £38,000. Any first-time buyers purchasing in this price bracket are likely to find an extra £600 for five years very useful, and it has to be said that not enough people take advantage of the scheme, partly because it is not widely publicized. The financial institution in which you are saving ought, however, to mention it: if they do not, remind them. National Savings Income and Deposit Bonds and the Saving Certificates Yearly Plan can all be used for the government's home-purchase scheme. (See pages 216 and 237–9.)

It is also worthwhile bargaining with the seller of the property if a small reduction in the price of the property would bring it within the limits of the scheme. Most people find that mortgage payments are most difficult in the early years: every little extra helps.

This scheme is for first-time buyers only.

Savings in unit trusts

There is nothing to stop a couple from building up the money they will need for a home deposit by regular savings in a unit trust. Most trusts offer savings schemes; some start at £10 a month, although £25 is more likely. Saving towards a home purchase this way, however, is probably not a good idea for two reasons: (a) a unit-trust scheme is not eligible for the government home-loan scheme, and (b) the time you need the money for your deposit may coincide with a period of stock-market setback, so that the value of your units may have fallen. As we will see later in this chapter, unit-trust saving can be linked to mortgages.

How much deposit?

The amount of mortgage you will get depends on two factors: (a) the value of the property itself, and (b) your personal financial status.

When mortgages were first widely granted, it was impossible to get a 100 per cent loan. While this is not true today, lenders are still not keen to provide the entire purchase price: they tend to do it only for new properties, especially those which are part of a large-scale single development, or to first-time buyers. A 90 per cent loan is normal for modern houses, and 80 per cent or two-thirds for older properties. Flat-buyers usually find themselves less generously treated than house-purchasers; in fact, a few lenders are reluctant to lend at all on flats, although a lot of the resistance against them is breaking down.

A further point to bear in mind is that the 90 or 80 per cent which you may be offered is not necessarily a percentage of the purchase price: it is instead a percentage of the *value the lender puts on the house*, which is not necessarily the same as the purchase price. The lender will send round a valuer (for whose services you have to pay) and the loan you get will be a percentage of his or her valuation. That said, there may be no difference between the building-society or bank valuation and the purchase price on new properties, and in some developments the building company may have done a deal with a building society which guarantees that buyers will get a 100 per cent loan. On older properties, there may be a marked gap between the purchase price and the valuation, so be prepared for this.

Building societies, banks and any other lenders will not give loans to levels which they think are beyond the capacity of the individual or couple to pay back. As a general rule of thumb, they reckon that about 2.5–3 times annual income is about the limit for a mortgage. When it comes to married people, they will take into account the incomes of both husband and wife, but probably not the whole of the wife's income. Under the Sex Discrimination Act (1975), it is illegal to refuse a loan to a woman if a man in the same financial circumstances would get one, but so far, in dealing with the second income differently from the first, mortgage lenders have not run foul of the law. If the wife's income is the larger one it might be worth arguing with the lender about the level of the loan; but it makes sense, especially if you are planning to have children soon after your marriage, to leave yourself with some financial leeway in case the wife should stop working even temporarily. Children bring added expense to the family, and for their arrival to coincide with a sharp drop in the family income if mortgage repayments are particularly heavy shows a lack of sensible financial planning.

Other considerations

You will find it difficult to get a loan if you are under 18, because minors cannot be held responsible for their debts. (There are also upper age limits, although these are gradually disappearing.) Some lenders put a ceiling on the amount they are prepared to lend, but this is usually quite high (perhaps £75,000), and the restriction rarely affects first-time buyers; here again lenders have become more generous in recent years, so you may find there is no limit at all. Conversely, while building societies are usually prepared to lend quite small amounts, other lenders may be interested only in making larger loans.

Unmarried couples should have no problems in getting a joint mortgage, whether or not they intend to get married: in fact, they may be more generously treated, because they will be entitled to full tax relief to a maximum loan of £30,000 each.

Getting a mortgage

When you make your mortgage application you have to provide details of your income, and the lender will check with your employer that the information you have given is correct. If you are self-employed, the lender will want details of your recent earnings, probably for the last three years, as certified by an accountant.

The problem today is not getting a mortgage—lenders are fighting for the business—but choosing the right one to suit your circumstances. The level of repayments can vary considerably for the same amount of loan, and the eventual benefits even more so, depending on which type of mortgage you choose. Although there is a wide variety of mortgages available today, they boil down to two basic types: (a) the type where the

How mortgage payments break down

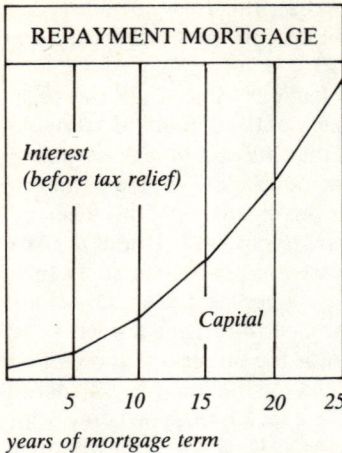

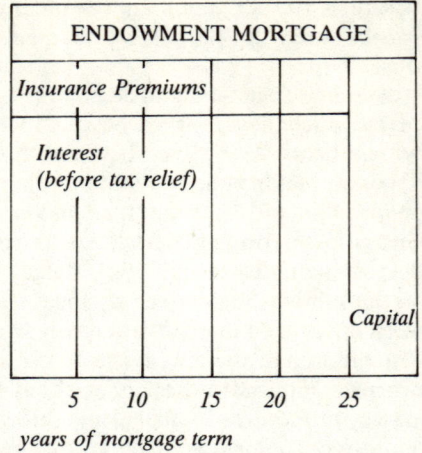

REPAYMENT MORTGAGE	ENDOWMENT MORTGAGE

Interest (before tax relief) — Repayment Mortgage, with *Capital* rising

Insurance Premiums, *Interest (before tax relief)*, *Capital* — Endowment Mortgage

years of mortgage term — 5 10 15 20 25

There is no life-assurance premium to pay with a repayment mortgage, but there will probably be a mortgage-protection policy attached to the loan. Such premiums are usually paid once a year.

borrower pays back a combination of interest and capital (repayment mortgages), and (b) those where only interest is paid during the period of the loan and the capital is repaid in a lump sum at the end (endowment-, pension- or unit-linked mortgages). Different mortgages suit different situations, and it is as well to remember that, although mortgages may initially be taken out for 25 or even 30 years, the average life of a mortgage is seven years, as most people move several times during their adult lives. This means that different types of mortgages can be chosen as one goes along.

Repayment mortgages

With a repayment mortgage, you start paying back some capital from the first monthly payment you make. At the beginning, only a very little is repaid: most of the money goes on interest. Gradually repayment of capital begins to dominate and the interest element falls. If the mortgage actually runs to the end of its life, the interest payment is practically zero by the time you make the last payment.

Repayment mortgages, which may or may not have an insurance element, come in two kinds. First there are the original level-repayment mortgages, in which the repayments themselves are constant throughout the life of the mortgage, subject only to changes in rates of interest and tax relief. These are the most common mortgages granted, a fact which is both important and unfortunate for many first-time buyers, who often have less disposable income at this stage in their lives than at any other. However, anyone in this position may be able to get instead what is called an increasing-repayment, or low-start, mortgage. In these mortgages repayments start off rather lower than in level-repayment mortgages but increase later (after allowing for tax relief, and quite apart from any changes in the rate of interest on mortgages in general).

There is no legal reason why any kind of life assurance should be attached to a repayment mortgage, but the lender, particularly if it is a building society, will encourage you to take out a mortgage-protection policy to cover the amount of your loan in the event of your death. These policies are known as decreasing term life assurance. (For more on term assurance see later in this chapter.)

Here is how the system works. Let us assume you have a loan of £20,000 which you reduce by £1,000 a year (this is highly unlikely, in fact, because of the way the repayments work). Your mortgage-protection policy would provide £20,000 if you died the day after the mortgage was taken out. In the second year, £19,000 would be provided, after ten years £10,000, and so on. If the mortgage goes its full term, the mortgage-protection policy is worth nothing, but you have provided protection for your family in the event of your untimely death.

Mortgage protection is cheap, particularly for non-smokers. Premiums vary slightly from company to company and also with age. It is best to take out a joint policy, which provides protection in the event of the death of either the husband or the wife. Although this is slightly more expensive than cover on a single life, an annual premium for a couple of non-smokers, where the husband is 25 and the wife two years younger, on a £20,000 mortgage over 25 years, would be somewhere between £43 and £50 a year; i.e., not much. (The premium over a single life would be in the region of £10–£20 a year.) The discrepancy is enough to make it worth your while to shop around rather than simply to accept the quote given by the insurance company suggested by the lender. These premiums are for

---

MORTGAGES—THE RELATIVE COSTS

Endowment versus repayment; monthly payments
A couple both aged 35 taking out a mortgage of £20,000 over 25 years at 11.25 per cent (the post 1987 Budget rate) interest, with tax relief at the standard rate of tax of 27 per cent:

	Endowment	*Repayment*
Net mortgage payments	£136.88	£158.98
Life assurance premium	£34.30	£5.90
Total monthly cost	£171.18	£164.88
Total cost over 25 years*	£51,354.00	£47,464.00

But, at the end of the mortgage period:

Basic sum assured	£8,580	nil
Reversionary bonuses†	£13,425	nil
Terminal bonuses	£14,955	nil
Total payable at maturity	£36,960	nil
Less mortgage loan	£20,000	nil
Cash sum available	£16,960	nil

*Assuming no changes in interest rates and tax. However, even if these do change, the relationship between the two figures will be constant.
†Not guaranteed, but average for 25-year policies maturing in 1986.

simple mortgage-protection policies for people in normal health and in regular jobs which do not carry any undue risk; such policies pay out only on death. By paying more, however, further benefits can be secured to cover the individual and the family in periods of illness, disability or redundancy.

Even in families which have planned their finances carefully, unexpected problems can arise due to redundancy and illness, and it can happen that, for a period at least, there is difficulty in meeting payments. This need not be a disaster as long as immediate action is taken to inform the lender. If a couple has not been profligate and there is a good chance that the situation will revert to normal, lenders are usually prepared to extend the loan-repayment period, permit the borrower to make interest-only payments for some time, or allow a period of grace to pay off any arrears which may have arisen. In a really bad situation, the borrower should apply immediately to the Department of Health and Social Security (DHSS), which will make the interest payments once the family becomes eligible for supplementary benefit.

Endowment mortgages

Although there may not be a great deal of difference in the actual monthly outlay between an endowment mortgage and a repayment one, the two types of mortgage are in fact very different. No repayment of the capital borrowed is made at all during the course of an endowment mortgage: the monthly payment to the building society, bank or other lender is simply an interest payment on the total amount borrowed. The loan is coupled with a life-assurance endowment policy which matures at the end of the loan; the tax-free lump sum available on this policy at the end of the loan period pays off the debt. Interest payments on the loan are affected by changes in interest and tax rates, but the monthly premiums you have to pay on the endowment policy is calculated on the basis of what kind of risk you are. This means that the younger and fitter pay less in monthly premiums. Once fixed, the premium does not change.

WHAT CHANGES IN MORTGAGE INTEREST RATES MEAN

Size of loan*	Gross monthly repayments at 11 per cent	Monthly increase in repayments on a mortgage rate rise of		
		1 per cent	1.5 per cent	2 per cent
£20,000	£197.92	£14.58	£22.00	£29.46
£30,000	£296.88	£21.87	£33.00	£44.19
£40,000	£395.84	£29.16	£44.00	£58.92
£50,000	£494.80	£36.45	£55.00	£73.65
£60,000	£593.76	£43.74	£66.00	£88.38

*Mortgage term assumed to be 25 years.

Depending on what kind of policy you take out and the success of the insurance company in its investments during the life of your mortgage, there should also be, in addition to the redemption of the debt, a lump sum due to you at the end of the mortgage's life. There is automatic life cover, so you do not need a mortgage-protection policy. When you go to the lender, he or she will probably suggest a particular life policy, but you do not have to accept this offer and you can also probably use any policies you have outstanding, rather than take out a new policy, as long as they cover the full amount of the loan.

Broadly, endowment mortgages are, like repayment mortgages, divided into two kinds, low-cost endowments and low-start endowments, which also incorporate low-cost endowments. You can in addition take out more expensive endowment cover, which will produce a large capital sum at the end of the mortgage period, but this is very costly and neither usual nor sensible for the average first-time buyer.

With *low-cost endowments* you have to be very certain that you know what you are buying. This type of mortgage pays off the loan at the end of the mortgage period and usually provides an extra tax-free sum to the borrower, which may be up to one third over and above the amount of the original loan. However, it is wise to recognize that there is no guarantee that anything more than the whole of the loan will be paid off. The minimum guarantee covers the loan only. Also, the possible extra tax-free sum could be of doubtful benefit, if you look as far ahead as the end of the mortgage. For example, if you borrow £30,000 now and the best hopes of the tax-free sum, 20 years from now, are £10,000, this might look great now but not so generous after 20 years' worth of inflation.

These points are worth mentioning, because superficially endowment mortgages look very attractive—and they are given the 'hard sell' by lenders trying to earn the commission paid to agents who sell life-assurance policies; the banks or building societies find these commissions a healthy contribution to their profits. However, endowment mortgages do not have the flexibility of repayment loans. What happens when interest rates change or you sell your home illustrates this. When interest rates go up, for example, a householder with a repayment loan can choose either (a) to make the higher payments or (b) to extend the period of the mortgage and keep payments level. Conversely, when rates fall, either the repayment period or the monthly repayments can be reduced. If you have a repayment mortgage and you sell your home you simply redeem the outstanding loan from the proceeds of the sale and stop paying the premiums on the mortgage-protection policy. With an endowment mortgage, however, you repay the loan but your endowment policy may still have years to run. Unless you want to transfer the policy to a new loan (and the lender will have to be prepared to accept it), you will be stuck with either (a) continuing to pay premiums on a policy you no longer want, (b) having it paid-up to avoid paying further premiums, but reducing your expected benefit from it, or (c) surrendering the policy on what may be rather poor terms (see page 107).

It is especially important to take these factors into account when you are buying your first home because you may move fairly quickly to another property.

Low-start, low-endowment mortgages have the built-in protection an endowment mortgage provides, but they are designed so that borrowers can make rather lower payments at the outset than in ordinary endowment mortgages. Although this means that there is some benefit to young people, there is some catching up to do later, and eventually the monthly cost is rather higher than on the normal low-cost endowment schemes. There is a two-way argument to these mortgages. A couple may expect their income to rise, so that when they have to make the higher payments there is no problem. On the other hand, both may be working at the start and the salary increases of the husband may not fully compensate for the loss of the wife's salary if for any reason she has to stop working. In such circumstances, the couple will find that in the long run they would have been better off choosing a normal low-cost endowment.

People with endowment mortgages of either kind face greater problems than those with repayment loans if for any reason they are unable to keep up their payments. They cannot extend the period of the loan, as that is linked to the life-assurance policy. The DHSS will pay interest on the same terms as on repayment loans, but will not pay the premiums: these will still have to be found, however much your circumstances are reduced.

The considerations when embarking on any mortgage, particularly a first one, are complicated, and certainly not as simple as they appear at first glance. Every couple's situation is unique to them, and the first rule with mortgages is to discuss the possibilities very thoroughly and to assess how the various options fit in with your short- and long-term plans.

Taking into account the fact that the purchase of the first home is not likely to be the last, the relative inflexibility of endowment loans, and the lack of a guarantee of profits, first-time buyers are probably wise to choose a repayment mortgage with a mortgage-protection policy. Life assurance, which can be attached to a later mortgage, can always be bought when there are more surplus family funds than is usual at the start of a marriage. There will always be some exceptions to this rule, and the lender will probably suggest an endowment policy, but this does not mean that it is the better choice: if you do not want an endowment loan, resist the pressure.

An overwhelming percentage of mortgages are either simple repayment or endowment loans, but there are all kinds of special deals which may be worth your consideration, and some new developments may become increasingly important in the overall mortgage market. These are pension mortgages and unit-linked mortgages.

Pension mortgages

Basically, these work on the same principle as endowment mortgages, in that interest-only payments are made for the life of the loan. They differ in that the contributions, rather than buying an endowment life policy, are made to a pension plan. Even more important, these payments qualify for tax relief if the purchaser meets certain criteria. At the end of the period (i.e., at the state retirement age) the plan provides a cash sum to pay off the loan as well as a pension (which is of course lower than it would have been had there been no loan to be repaid). These mortgages may become very popular and oust endowment mortgages, as individuals will become free to make their own pension arrangements from January 1988. The 1987 Budget effectively put a ceiling on pension mortgages; it set a maximum tax-free element available on retirement of £150,000. Pension mortgages are to be preferred to endowment because contributions to quite a large percentage of annual earnings get full tax relief—17.5 per cent of annual earnings for anyone born in 1934 or after. The percentage rises the older you are, but this would obviously not apply to young people setting up their first home. Pension plans are far more attractive—at the present time and assuming the government does not change the rules— because since the 1984 Budget new life-assurance policies have not normally been eligible for any tax relief. (For the rules on insurance and tax, see page 100.) If you are considering such a mortgage, you will also need to think about whether or not you will be able to live on the reduced pension which will be available after the loan has been repaid.

Pension mortgages are particularly good for earners who pay tax at the higher rates. Full tax relief is available on certain proportions of income ranging from 17½ per cent for those under 50 to 27½ per cent for those over 75.

It has to be remembered, however, that the plan must run to retirement age (although it can be moved from one property to another); that is a very long way ahead for a young couple to think, and it presupposes no change in circumstances over perhaps 40 years of working life. So, what if the home is sold before the plan matures? The loan would have to be paid off from any profit (assuming of course that there is one) on the sale. As a general rule you can move to a new plan, but you may find you have to produce funds to top up the loan if it is larger. Also, if you are already investing the full 17.5 per cent of your income in your existing plan, any increase in the mortgage loan will have to be funded in a different way. It is clear that there are quite complicated considerations involved in pension mortgages. Such mortgages should not be entered into, particularly if you are young, until you have thought through the implications properly.

Unit-linked mortgages

These, too, are interest-only mortgages, but because the price of units can rise as well as fall the repayments have to include premiums on some sort of life-assurance policy to ensure that the lender can guarantee that his or her loan will be repaid. Unit-trust prices are generally linked to stock-market prices, and these can rise and fall quite sharply, so that when you come to sell you could be showing a loss on your total investment. It is quite a long time since the stock market had a sustained fall (1973–4), but it is certain to happen again eventually.

To protect themselves against market falls and the possibility that the home buyer may have chosen the wrong unit trust in which to invest, lenders will insist that there is always enough insurance cover to pay off the mortgage. This means that, once you have chosen the unit trust, property bond or other investment, part of your monthly payment throughout the life of the loan will go not into units but towards life cover. When the trust or fund does well, however, there could be much more profit for the home owner than is likely to be available in low-cost endowment. Very few investments in unit trusts have failed to show a substantial profit over the theoretical 20- or 25-year period of the typical mortgage. The same cannot be claimed, however, for the average mortgage's actual life, which is about seven years.

HOW A PENSION MORTGAGE MIGHT GROW

Pension mortgages are usually not a good choice for first-time buyers. An appropriate age to take out this kind of mortgage would be 40. This example shows the monthly cost of a unit-linked pension mortgage of £50,000 at 11.25 per cent for a man aged 40; the loan will be repayable when he reaches 65, the present retirement age for men. The figures come from Target Life. No rate of growth can be accurately predicted, so the example assumes an average 10 per cent or 15 per cent rate.

	Cost interest on loan	Pension premium	Total	
Gross	£485.33	£147.98	£595.90	
Net	£378.58	£105.07	£475.05	(at 27 per cent tax)
	£348.33	£88.79	£429.21	(at 40 per cent tax)
	£293.33	£59.19	£345.86	(at 60 per cent tax)

Benefits after mortgage is repaid

Assuming 10 per cent annual average growth:		
Projected value of fund	*Surplus cash*	*Level of pension*
£166,426	nil	£15,123 pa

Assuming 15 per cent annual average growth:		
Projected value of fund	*Surplus cash*	*Level of pension*
£372,865	£62,021	£33,882 pa

As you can see, the higher the tax rate, the cheaper and more tax-efficient a pension mortgage becomes. At current rates, for example, the above mortgage would cost a standard-rate taxpayer £142,515.00 over 25 years, but only £103,758.00 for a 60 per cent taxpayer. It is normal, of course, for the higher rates of tax to be reached later in one's working life.

Mortgage swaps

If you have chosen one type of mortgage loan you may come to feel that you would prefer another kind, even if you are not selling your home. If you change to a different scheme you must be prepared to pay a small arrangement fee (not likely to be much over £100), legal fees of 0.5 per cent of the amount of the loan, a valuation fee (under £100 for any house worth up to £50,000), and land-registry fees, which are on a sliding scale. Over the longer term you may well benefit by changing your loan from, say, a repayment mortgage to an endowment mortgage, but because of these initial charges it will be some time before you do. On the whole, therefore, it is better to make the right decision at the start and then to stick with it. From time to time financial commentators will point out that one type of mortgage has distinct advantages over another, but, over the whole life of the mortgage, the gains often cancel one another out on the swings-and-roundabouts principle.

Index-linked mortgages

In this type of mortgage, part of the loan is linked to a cost-of-living index. Such mortgages enable young couples to borrow rather more than three times their incomes without having to pay crippling monthly payments at the beginning. The idea is that the rise in the level of repayments will be matched by the rise in the level of income, so the mortgage burden in terms of total income will stay relatively constant. Such mortgages may be fully index-linked—that is, with the entire loan valued annually against the way the index has moved—or, more frequently, partly linked, so that some of the loan is repaid in the normal way and some of it (say a half) is repaid on the index-linking principle.

The Retail Prices Index (RPI) is the index usually chosen. The valuation is normally done not monthly, when the index appears, but at the end of the year. What happens is that the interest charged on the index-linked part of the mortgage is very low, comparatively speaking, and remains fixed for the whole of the life of the loan. Interest on the other part fluctuates in the normal way. The borrower knows two things at the start of each repayment year: (a) that the index-linked element of the loan will have been upvalued by the amount of inflation in the past year, and (b) exactly what amount of interest will have to be paid on that part of the loan.

Let us take a very simple example. A £20,000 mortgage could be divided into two equal parts: half must be repaid in the standard way and half is index-linked, with the latter half carrying interest for the full period of the loan at 4 per cent (a quite common figure for 1987). At the end of year one, if prices have risen by 5 per cent, £10,000 of the total loan will rise to £10,500, 4 per cent of which is £420. If prices rise a further 5 per cent in the next year, the index-linked original £10,000 will have moved up to £11,025, and the interest up to £441. (Interest on the rest of the loan will vary with interest rates generally.) If prices do not rise at all, there will of course be no increase in the index-linked element; and, in the unlikely event that prices actually fall, the amount of the loan will be reduced.

In a period of low inflation these mortgages are rather attractive, but as always there are snags. The amount of the index-linked part of the loan

69

falls very slowly—much more slowly than does the other part. In times of very high inflation but when home prices are rising rather more slowly than other prices, a borrower might find that the loan was higher than the selling price of the home. Although it is very unusual for this to happen, the possibility could be enough to deter some people from borrowing in this way.

If we are to have a long period of relatively stable prices, index-linked mortgages seem likely to become more popular, but for the moment they must be regarded as somewhat experimental.

Protecting mortgages through insurance

As part of the extension of their activities, building societies are beginning to offer insurance packages which will guarantee that mortgage payments can be maintained in the event of accident, illness, redundancy or unemployment. If the mortgage is paid through two incomes, the loss of either one of them can be insured against. The cost is about £4 for every £100 of monthly payments. To qualify, applicants must usually take out the insurance at the same time as the mortgage, and normally the lender requires the applicants to be under 60 and to have been in continuous employment for the preceding six months. The policy covers repayment mortgages and also endowment life-assurance premiums.

As with all insurance, there are exclusions. Typically, these include illness incurred through alcohol or drug abuse, any self-inflicted injuries, illness resulting from childbirth, and any dismissal from work because of misconduct or crime.

Tax relief on mortgages

There are many points of difference between the taxation of individuals and that of married people. Here we look only at the tax relief available on mortgages. The broad rules are:

- Only one home per person qualifies for relief. In this respect, a married couple is treated as one person, not two. Each person is eligible to full tax relief on the interest paid on a mortgage up to a maximum of £30,000, so a married couple is entitled to relief on only £30,000, not the £60,000 which would be available to two single people buying a home together. If a married couple happens to have two homes, both mortgaged, they will get tax relief on only one, even if the total amount of the loan is within the £30,000 limit. They have to decide which one is their principal residence, and claim relief on that alone.
- If a couple have two homes at the time of marriage, they are allowed a period during which to decide which one will be their principal residence; both loans will continue to qualify for relief for 12 months. After that, though, they will have to decide on one or the other. If the two homes are, say, both in a major city, the couple will probably not want to keep both, so it is probably better to dispose of one before the marriage and thereby avoid any hassle with the taxman later—particularly as the principal residence does not only qualify for tax relief on the mortgage but is also the only one free of capital-gains tax should a profit be made on a sale. On the profits of the sale of a second (or any further) home the rate of capital gains

tax is 30 per cent, after allowing for expenses and the annual exemption the government gives on capital gains.

- The £30,000 maximum is allowed at all tax levels and, whatever the level of the loan, the standard rate of tax relief is included in the payments under a system which is called MIRAS (mortgage interest relief at source). What happens is that the lender deducts only the standard rate of tax from the interest repayments. This has the effect of reducing the payments by rather less than one third what they would be without tax relief (with tax at a standard rate of 27 per cent); if you pay tax at the higher levels, which range between 40 and 60 per cent, the amount of extra relief is allowed for in your tax coding. If the amount of the loan is more than £30,000, the MIRAS system is applied only to the first £30,000. Before April 1987, the tax relief due to those with very large mortgages was set out in their tax coding, and take-home pay was compensatingly higher than for those with loans of £30,000 or under.
- There are two occasions when tax relief is allowed on a second loan. One is when you buy a home for a dependent relative who does not pay rent for living there. The other is if you divorce or separate, a topic discussed in detail in a later chapter (see page 188 ff.). Here, however, we can note that the rule is that a husband can get relief on two mortgages as long as the total is not more than £30,000. If the total is higher than that, there is no tax relief on the difference. (There are ways around this, though—see page 191.)
- Other loans as well as mortgages qualify for tax relief, assuming the total does not go above £30,000, if the loan is specifically for home improvements; normal repairs and decorations do not count. You cannot get relief simply by saying you want the money for a home improvement: it must be for a permanent change to your home, such as building a swimming pool, a garage or an extension or installing central heating or insulation. If you are converting a badly run-down property, the expense involved is likewise eligible for tax relief, again up to the £30,000 limit. The home-improvements rule means that, if you think before you borrow, you can maximize your tax relief. For example, if you want both to build a garage and to buy the car to go in it, it makes sense to borrow for the garage, so that you get tax relief, and pay cash for the car.
- Not all loans for home improvement are eligible for relief, even if they are within the £30,000 limit. You must get the loan for a specific stated purpose. If you use a credit card or simply get a general overdraft, the loan does not qualify.
- The £30,000 rule may be suspended temporarily if you are moving home, have bought a new property, but have not sold your existing one. The old loan is ignored for the purposes of calculating the relief on the new one, and the relief on the old one can continue for up to 12 months (see page 72).
- In addition to tax relief on interest payments, our principal residence is normally free from any capital gains tax (CGT) if we make a profit on its sale. If you have two homes and there is little difference in the tax relief available, it makes sense to designate the one on which you expect to make the most profit when you finally sell it as your principal residence. You will have to make this decision eventually and, if you do not do it within two years of marriage or purchase of the second home, the taxman will make it for you. Note, though, that the home you designate your principal

residence need not be the one you spend the most time in, nor need you have a mortgage on it. Once you have made your choice, you can always change it later simply by informing the taxman. Any change you make can be backdated by two years.

You may lose all or part of your CGT exemption if you do certain things. The commonest of these is letting out part of your home; other possibilities are: converting your home into separate dwellings and selling some of them off; using part of your home exclusively for work and claiming the space against your income tax; and buying a series of homes, moving in but selling them again very quickly for profit, so that your activities could be justifiably described as your business. In contrast, you do not lose your exemption when you provide a home for a dependent relative, even if the relative pays rates and other bills, including repairs.

The whole question of tax relief and exemption is quite complicated, and you should try to understand it right from the start so that you are not landed with an unnecessary tax bill. Also, relatively speaking, the higher your income and therefore the higher the level of tax you pay, the cheaper it is for you to borrow on a mortgage. For example, a standard-rate taxpayer borrowing £25,000 over 25 years when interest rates are $11\frac{1}{4}$ per cent (the post 1987 Budget level) would pay a net £181.20 a month on a low-cost endowment mortgage under the MIRAS scheme. A 60-per-cent taxpayer, by contrast, would make the same payment to the building society or bank, but because of the additional tax relief in his or her coding would actually be paying less than £120.

Tax relief on bridging loans

So that people are not unduly burdened by payments when they move home, there are some temporary relaxations of the £30,000 rule. If a borrower finds himself or herself paying back two loans for a period, because the old home has not been sold by the time the new one is purchased, the interest on the old loan is treated as if it does not exist when calculations are made about eligibility for tax relief on the new loan. This means that, for a period, a borrower could be getting tax relief on as much as £60,000. The Inland Revenue normally sets a cut-off point of one year on the two loans, but it may, if it thinks you are a deserving case, allow the relief for even longer, although this is rare.

Where to get your mortgage

Raising a loan is no longer a matter of going to a building society and hoping to convince them that you are worth lending money to. The days when people felt it was a privilege to get a mortgage are over. Over the last few years, indeed, financial institutions of all kinds have been fighting for the privilege of lending money to us.

Building societies and banks

The days of periodic shortages of money available for mortgages may be over for good, because the new financial institutions offering mortgages are not directly dependent, like building societies, on depositors for their source of funds. Moreover, building societies themselves, the traditional lenders, are changing their business and moving more and more into banking and other financial services related to the purchase of homes. Until the 1986 Building Societies Act, they were allowed to lend only for the purchase of private homes, but the scope of their activities has now been widened so that, although they face increasing competition from other lenders, there is also growing use of new types of borrowing from their funds. Despite all this, building societies are likely to remain the dominant lenders when it comes to private homes. Their share of the market varies between 70 and 80 per cent, with the banks providing most of the rest. The biggest contrast between banks and building societies lies in the minimum they are prepared to lend. The banks are after the bigger mortgages and are more likely than building societies to insist on a minimum size of loan. The costs involved in putting a mortgage on the books are the same whether it is for £5,000 or £100,000, but nevertheless for a long time building societies were reluctant to lend larger amounts, and charged customers extra for doing so. With growing competition, however, this differential has slowly been abolished.

Among the very big banking institutions, only the National Giro does not offer mortgages; all the others do, although their enthusiasm varies with the economic climate. Although you do not have to have a current or savings account with the bank from which you borrow, obviously your own bank would be your first choice for a loan. By the time you marry and are looking for a mortgage, you should have built up a good financial relationship with your bank. If you find that it is not prepared to give you a mortgage, you may have difficulty in getting a bank mortgage anywhere else.

As well as putting a minimum on what they are prepared to lend (possibly £20,000), the bank may offer you a lower proportion of the purchase price the higher the loan. This is particularly true of those banks whose names are less familiar to the public than the Big Four (Barclays, National Westminster, Midland and Lloyds), and some may also insist on a minimum loan of £50,000 or even more.

Altogether, the banks are more interested in maximizing their profits than are the building societies. Banks are simply commercial companies whose business is money. Building societies, by contrast, were originally thought of as essentially benevolent institutions whose function was to help the average family without much capital to become home owners. The aim was not to make profits, but to balance income from savings with loans to home buyers, putting a little into reserve for safety and making a small surplus to cover administration costs. Building societies have become much more aggressive operators in recent years, but their activities are still controlled by the Registrar of Friendly Societies rather than by the Department of Trade and Industry.

Insurance companies

The next big push into the mortgage market seems likely to come from the insurance companies. Some of the bigger ones are already making efforts to break into the business, and are offering attractive packages. They can arrange any variety of loan to suit the customer, in the same way as the banks and building societies, and eventually may become the first choice for people who already have life assurance when they come to need a mortgage. The insurance companies do of course already provide many forms of insurance to protect loans. They may put some pressure on you to take out an endowment mortgage, as this brings them more profit than a repayment loan.

However, one insurance company is unlikely to accept another's policy as security for a loan. Building societies are less choosy, although they tend to have deals with a particular insurance company. They are prepared to let you make your own arrangements, or lodge an existing policy with them to cover the loan. They may make a small administrative charge for doing this.

Other lenders

Although well over 90 per cent of total lending is done by the banks, building societies and insurance companies, there are many other potential sources of mortgage funds.

The first to try is your employer. Some employers—the banks themselves, for example—are prepared to give loans on very favourable terms to employees.

Finance houses, which provide the funds for hire purchase and credit-sale deals, are also happy to lend in quite large amounts, although they may charge rather higher interest than building societies and banks.

Finally, there are local authorities. These do not have much to lend and will usually grant mortgages only to council tenants who want to buy the property in which they live; even then, they prefer that borrowers use them only as a last resort. Very few people getting married are likely to be council tenants. However, if their parents are, they can benefit from the 'Second Generation' Scheme, whether they want to become tenants or to buy from a general council-house sales list.

Joint names

Applications for mortgages by engaged or married couples should always be made by them jointly, and it goes almost without saying that the property, too, should be in the joint names of the couple or, alternatively, held in common: the difference is that, where a property is in joint names, it automatically goes into the sole name of the survivor should one of them die, but where it is held in common each partner can leave his or her share to whoever they want. A couple might choose the latter course if, for example, one or both had been married before and wanted to leave some or all of their share to their children by a former marriage. Some people, usually men, are reluctant to own their home jointly or in common with their spouse. Anyone who feels like this ought to ask themselves whether they should be getting married at all.

When a couple takes out an endowment or any other insurance-linked mortgage, the life cover can be on one or both lives.

If the marriage breaks down, a wife or husband will usually be entitled to some share of the home (perhaps only a cash sum), whether or not their name is on the title deeds. This applies even in cases where, say, a wife has never worked or made any financial contribution to the mortgage payments. (See page 189.)

Quite apart from finding the money for a deposit, furnishings, fittings and decoration, there are other expenses for would-be buyers. It is advisable to work out what these will be in some detail to avoid financially overreaching yourself in the early stages. It may be, for instance, that you will have to modify your furnishing and decorating plans, or temporarily to defer some purchases.

It is difficult to put precise figures on these extra costs but, to be on the safe side and to avoid any nasty surprises, it is better to assume the highest possible. Average buying costs range from 2.5 to 4 per cent of the purchase price. First of all, there are fees to solicitors, who deal with the legal aspects of the purchase; this process, *conveyancing*, can be perfectly legally done by yourself and is quite easy when you are selling, but it is rather more difficult when you are buying, and there is no guarantee that you will escape all the pitfalls. If you do not do your own conveyancing it has to be done by a solicitor, but soon firms specializing in conveyancing may be allowed to operate. Because of this possibility, conveyancing fees have been coming down recently, and some solicitors offer a flat-fee conveyancing deal, regardless of the price of the property—in some parts of the United Kingdom this may be as low as £200 (plus VAT). Where there is no such deal, the final bill for the conveyance will be related to the purchase price of the home and, for a £30,000 property, could be anywhere between £350 and £500.

The next charge is for the survey of the property which the lender will require before making the mortgage loan. This survey will not point up anything other than major defects; that is not its purpose. It simply tells the lender whether there is any danger of the loan not being covered by the value of the property in the event of a sale. A survey of this type on a £30,000 home should cost about £45. You may well be advised, especially if you are buying an older property, to get a full survey done to make sure you know exactly what state the property is in. Once again, there is a sliding scale: the more valuable the property, the greater the cost of the survey.

MONTHLY PAYMENTS AT VARIOUS INTEREST RATES

These payments are before allowing for tax, which at the standard rate would reduce them by a little under one third. They are for every £1,000 borrowed over a period of 25 years.

Interest rate	Monthly payment
8½ per cent	£8.25
10½ per cent	£9.54
11 per cent	£9.80
11½ per cent	£10.26
12 per cent	£10.63
12¼ per cent	£10.81
14 per cent	£12.13
15 per cent	£12.90

ADDITIONAL COSTS IN BUYING A HOME

This example is for a £30,000 home* with a £20,000 mortgage

All mortgages
Conveyancing, including VAT at 15 per cent	£345
Building insurance premium	£50
Land Registry fee	£73

With building societies
Building society surveyor, including VAT	£51.75
Building society solicitor, including VAT	£77.62

With banks
Mortgage arrangement fee, including VAT	£86.25

With repayment mortgages
Mortgage indemnity insurance	£80

*On homes costing over £30,000, there is a 1 per cent stamp duty to pay.

There may also be stamp duty for the buyer to pay, if the price of the property is £30,000 or more (no stamp duty is paid by the seller). If you find that you are just on the margin, it is worth negotiating with the seller to bring the price below £30,000. This does not necessarily mean that the seller gets less money, simply that some of it is ascribed to furnishing and fittings, which are not liable for stamp duty. At £30,000, the saving would be £300. Whatever the price of the property, an allocation for furnishings and fittings will bring down the cost of stamp duty, but care is needed here: they must be items worth the value put on them.

Finally, there is VAT to pay at 15 per cent on the solicitor's bill and any bills for surveys. If you use a removal company, there will be VAT on its bill, too. In total, on a £30,000 home, it is advisable to allow about £1,000 for the charges other than those directly involved in the transaction.

Running costs

Before making the final decision on a purchase, it is helpful to give yourself some idea of the running costs of your new property. This means finding out the current levels of general household rates and water rates and assessing gas and electricity costs as well as those of any insurance necessary for the fabric of the building or its contents. If you have chosen to move to an area further away from your work, travel expenses should be considered as an additional running cost.

Rates

House ownership brings with it the liability for some other compulsory bills. The most important and heaviest of these are the rates levied on owner-occupiers by local authorities. Rates are a tax on property owners and, depending on where you live, they can be a major item in your expenditure. The bill you pay is based on the *rateable value* of your property, and each year local authorities fix a payment of so much per pound of rateable value; for example, if the rate is £1.50 in the pound and your property's rateable value is £350, your total rates bill will be £525 a year, but if the rate is only 70p in the pound your bill will be only £245. Legally speaking, rates are due at the beginning of the financial year, but you are allowed to pay in instalments. Many people pay in two halves, and most councils allow you to pay your rates in ten equal instalments. If you do not pay, the council will eventually sue for the money.

There are several ways of getting a cut in your rates bill.

- People on low incomes or who are disabled can often get a rates rebate (or housing benefit, as it is now called). This does not cut the actual bill, but eases the burden of paying. The rules are quite complicated, depending on the rates bill itself, your income, and the number of people in your family. If you think you may qualify, make an application: it costs nothing. Successful claims are backdated to 1 April of the relevant year.
- The rateable value of your home may be too high compared with similar properties. Beware, though: the opposite can be true, so before you make your application check that your property is not undervalued compared with others. Any reduction you get is likely to be small.
- Even if you have been correctly valued, a change in your environment can qualify you for a rates reduction; for instance, a new motorway close to your home could greatly increase noise levels and make your home less attractive. Rates levels are based not on the sale value of your home but on the rent a tenant might be expected to pay. It is arguable that living close to a motorway could mean that you would have to cut the rent to any prospective tenant. Similarly, the siting of a new airport close to your home could have a negative effect on rental values. Here are a few of the kind of changes in your immediate environment which could bring you a rates reduction: excessive noise which was not there when you purchased the property; new industrial or commercial buildings; loss of local services like a railway station or school; paradoxically, the building of a railway station or airport; bad quality of surrounding properties; poor amenities, such as lack of main drains, electricity or street lighting; danger of flooding or subsidence; rooms which have little natural light; difficulty of access to your home. It is clear that, if one property is adversely affected by some of the above factors, neighbouring properties are likely to be similarly affected. If so, it is a good idea for you to combine with your neighbours to make a general claim. If only you find the presence of a new road a nuisance and your neighbours find it quite acceptable, it is unlikely that you will succeed in a claim to have your rates reduced.

It is important to remember that any improvements to your home can increase its rateable value. It may not seem fair to you that, if you build a garage, swimming pool or extension at your own expense, you increase the amount of rates you have to pay. But it all comes back again to what a tenant would be prepared to pay, and obviously the existence of, say, a swimming pool would increase the rental value and hence the rates which have to be paid.

Domestic rates are to be abolished in Scotland at some time between

1989 and 1992, and this move signals the abolition of the whole rating system. It is planned to replace rates by a 'community charge' paid by everyone living in a local area. This will spread the burden of the tax from 16 million householders to some 37 million adults (1987 figures). The only people to escape this tax will be those under the age of 19, convicted prisoners and long-term hospital patients.

There will be rebates, as there are in the present system, but everyone, no matter how poor, will have to pay some proportion of the charge, which will be fixed by local authorities. In effect, the financial burden for the average family may well be the same as under the present rates system and high-spending councils will make correspondingly high community charges. Home-owners living alone will benefit, but those living in rented accommodation, who at present do not pay rates (at least not directly), will be caught in the net of the tax.

To make sure that no one escapes it, local authorities will be able to apply to the courts to deduct the charge from earnings; anyone who fails to register for the charge will face an automatic fine of £20 for the first offence and £200 for the second. Those who live in rented accommodation will have to pay a special 'collective charge' directly to the landlord with the rent. Local councils will check all through the year on who should be paying, and a 'responsible person' at each address will be required to supply details to the register.

Buildings insurance

The additional insurance cover which will be required by anyone giving you a mortgage is for repair of the fabric of the building should it be damaged or totally destroyed. As a rule, the lender will suggest an insurance company, but you can refuse the suggestion and arrange your own cover, if you can get something better. The policy must be acceptable to the lender, who will want what he or she regards as satisfactory cover in the event of damage. The lender will usually insist on an amount of cover far above the level of the mortgage you have taken out, and therefore far more than the sum you would owe if, in the event of damage, you decided not to rebuild or repair and simply took the insurance payment (as is your right) and paid off your loan. However, you will not have any choice about the actual amount involved in building insurance: the lender will make it a condition of the loan.

The Association of British Insurers works out every year what it reckons it costs completely to rebuild properties of various types and sizes in different parts of the country. The updated figures are usually released in March. Check them against the amount you are asked to insure your property for and, if it is way out of line, argue about it. Your insurance premium will rise each year in line with any increase in rebuilding costs.

If you do not have a mortgage and are trying to work out what level of rebuilding insurance you should have, look not at the price you could sell your home for (because that includes some value for the land) but at the actual costs of rebuilding, which may be very different. Rebuilding and repair costs may not vary very much in a particular district, regardless of the price of the property, but the number of times you may claim on your policy can vary a great deal—if some risks are greater than others, such as frequent flooding or subsidence. That sort of cover may be excluded from the standard policy, and you will have to pay more if you want it.

You can work out the approximate cost by measuring up your home and applying the measurements to the prices set out by the Association of British Insurers. If you do not have a mortgage there is no legal requirement to insure your home against damage. To neglect to do so, however, could involve you in considerable cost if your home is damaged or, worse still, destroyed. The policy will allow for the complete replacement of your home, but will also cover other things such as burst pipes and the damage they do and leaking roofs. Claims may not always be met: insurance policies cover accident, not normal wear and tear. Many policies stipulate today that the holder pays the first £15 or £50 of any bill; this is to deter people from making lots of small claims. If you do keep making these, the insurer may well put up your premium.

The standard rates themselves are not expensive: the risk of a house totally burning down is, after all, slight. You should be able to get a year's cover for between £1.50 and £1.90 for each £1,000's worth. For a normal family home insurance companies generally put a lower limit on these policies of £10,000 and an upper one of £250,000.

It is vitally important to check what your policy covers: do not pay the first premium until you have done this. It is too late to look at the small print in the policy when you come to make a claim. Make sure, too, that the insurer knows if your property is subject to any particular risk. The insurer may not charge you any extra premium, but he or she will probably not meet any claim you make—or at least not meet it fully—if you have failed to tell him or her about it. Here are some of the risks which can occur in Britain:

- Fire, lightning, explosions, or earthquakes or—more likely in Britain—earth tremors.
- Escape of water.
- Damage from aircraft or cars. Be warned, however, that there have been problems in proving aircraft damage.
- Theft. Although it is very rare, parts of houses have been stolen.
- Subsidence. Cover against this has become more common in standard policies since 1976, when the very dry summer brought many claims for subsidence damage and many householders found they were not covered.

The risks the homeowner faces vary all the time; for example, the opening of the Thames Barrage has meant that homes once in risk of flooding are no longer under threat, but houses below rather than above the barrage are unaffected and there the risk remains. Danger of malicious damage varies a great deal both over time and by area. Product development can reduce, for example, the risk of burst pipes or fires in the home. For all of these reasons and many more, policies should be checked periodically, because the risks covered may be either (a) inadequate or (b) overstated because of the passage of time. Adjust the cover if necessary.

Contents insurance

Whether or not you decide to insure the contents of your home and any valuables you may have is no business of the organization giving you a mortgage, although you may well be offered a combined buildings and contents package. These packages can be attractive, but there is rather more flexibility for the home-owner if the two are kept separate. Contents insurance is something which many people ignore until it is too late and they have actually been burgled, lost an expensive watch, or had their carpets damaged by fire. The buildings cover, while it will deal with any necessary repairs to the fabric of the building, will not pay for the carpets, furniture or curtains which may be damaged accidentally.

Contents insurance usually comes in two forms: new-for-old and ordinary contents. The first covers you against rising prices. The second pays you the original cost of the contents, after allowing for wear and tear, and this may be far less than the replacement value. Such a policy might also put a 'life' on some items, after which the insurance company would not be prepared to offer anything at all if they were destroyed or damaged. New-for-old policies, however, although they replace your goods at current prices, may make some deduction for wear and tear. In either type of policy you may have to pay anything between the first £10 and £100 loss yourself; the higher the figure, the lower the premiums will be. These policies may have a minimum level of cover set by the insurance company.

Whatever kind of insurance you choose, its cost will vary considerably depending on where you live. If you live in an inner-city area (particularly Central London) you may not damage your carpets or suffer a burst pipe more often than someone living in a country area, but you are far more likely to be robbed and so your insurance will be more expensive. New-for-old cover might cost £2.50 per £1,000 in the country and £15 per £1,000 in London and other inner cities, with the suburbs and smaller towns at various levels in between. Ordinary contents, which is a poor bargain, costs between £1.50 and £6 per £1,000, although the scheme run by Age Concern charges £3.50 per £1,000 throughout the country.

Even though ordinary contents insurance is a poor bargain—because you will never get back the full value of what you have lost—it is better than nothing. If you want to include cover even for things damaged when you are travelling, you will have to take out an additional all-risks policy, which can cover all your possessions or simply those items of particular value. Such policies may be called 'new-for-old accidental damage', and they cost £4–£11 per £1,000's worth of cover, the rate again varying according to the area in which you live. If you do not have an all-risks policy to cover such items as expensive cameras or jewellery, do not take them on holiday or leave them in cloakrooms where they may be vulnerable to theft. An ordinary new-for-old policy, if it covers such losses at all, will limit them to a certain level—for example, a top value of £500 per item.

It is perhaps worth mentioning here that, when you buy certain items of equipment, you can get an extended guarantee on them. These guarantees are simply insurance policies that extend the guarantee on your purchase from the usual one or two years to five years, ten years, or however long you pay for. You buy the policy with a single premium paid at the time you purchase the goods.

If you have a number of really valuable but small things, you can cut the cost of your contents insurance by putting them in a safe-deposit box at a bank. The cost varies with the items' value, but generally speaking it is about £1.25 per annum per £1,000's worth outside London and £1.50 inside.

When you first embark on contents insurance, go through your home checking what everything would cost to replace. Rough averages are: £2,500 for the living room, £2,000 for each bedroom, and £1,500 for the dining room. This means that the average family home with three bedrooms needs insurance cover of about £10,000, even if there is nothing especially valuable.

When you could lose your home

Before you go ahead with a mortgage, be absolutely sure that you can afford the repayments or interest payments and life-assurance premiums. Your financial resources should not be completely stretched: there should be some leeway, because if you cannot pay and run into arrears the lender will eventually go to court to repossess your home. Remember, you do not own your home until you have completed your mortgage payments.

Banks and building societies are very keen to lend at the moment, although some people in the business are getting worried as there are increasing signs that home-buyers are borrowing more than they can really afford. Many people working in the building societies feel that they have been going too far down-market and have lent to people who really should not be in owner-occupation. Repossession is very much a last resort, but every year since 1980 has seen a rise in the numbers of repossessions enforced. By the end of 1986 around 3 of every 100 homes mortgaged had been repossessed.

This is not the whole story: many other borrowers are 6–12 months in arrears—close on 67,000 of them. So check your total outgoings very carefully to see what you can afford, however much someone might be willing to lend you.

Structural defects

The work we pay to have done on our homes is not always satisfactory, and defects may take a while to appear. Today we have some long-term redress against—and can seek compensation from—builders, architects, surveyors and solicitors.

The Latent Damage Act of 1986 extended the period during which proceedings can be taken. Before this Act the period was six years after the job had been done, but this has now been extended to allow claims to be made within three years of a defect being discovered, which can obviously be very much later. The act also gives a new right to people who find they have bought an already-damaged property, when the damage is (a) not known and (b) could not have been known. There is now a final time-limit of 15 years.

Gazumping

When you have chosen the house or flat you want and your offer is accepted by the seller, it is normal to pay a deposit 'subject to contract'—in other words, until the conveyancing goes through. A 10 per cent deposit used to be normal, but as house prices have risen, a nominal deposit of a few hundred pounds is becoming increasingly accepted. This deposit can be reclaimed at any time until contracts are exchanged, a process which takes a month or two, but if you withdraw after that you will lose your deposit. However, until contracts are exchanged, either side can back out without forfeit. This all applies only in England and Wales: in Scotland a contract is made as soon as the offer is accepted. The Scottish system avoids the unfortunate habit of 'gazumping'—i.e., accepting a higher offer after one has previously been accepted. Gazumping is quite common when house prices are rising and there is a shortage of the kind of properties that are in high demand. It is, nevertheless, an undesirable practice, although obviously it is tempting for sellers.

Buying a council home

The right to buy the local-authority-owned property you live in is laid down in the Housing Act of 1980; the right extends beyond the actual property you live in to other properties which the authority may own and which are available. To qualify at all, you must first be a 'secure tenant'—i.e., you must have been living in local-authority housing for at least three years. The law states that:

- You can buy the home of which you are the tenant.
- You can buy it alone or jointly with members of your family, as long as they live with you.
- Depending on how long you have been a local-authority tenant, you can buy at a discount price between 33 and 50 per cent less than the current market value as set out by an independent valuer. You have the right to a valuation by the district valuer. He or she is an independent arbiter and his or her decision is binding in cases where the potential purchaser and local authority do not agree. To get the maximum discount, you must have been a tenant for 20 years.
- You have a right to a mortgage from your local authority, or New Town, although you may be encouraged to seek one from one of the normal mortgage lenders.
- If your salary does not qualify you for a mortgage of the amount you need, you are given a two-year option to buy at the current price.

Housing Associations

Another way into the property market is to join a housing association. For a period, these were very popular, but are less so now, though here and there they are still being set up. No two are exactly the same, but they all involve a number of people collaborating to build new or improve existing properties. A joint mortgage is raised and every tenant pays a rent which goes to servicing the mortgage.

Naturally people move and at that time they receive a capital payment from the association, which is their share so far of the increased value of the total property. This means that tenants are able, without having to find a deposit, to build up some capital, which can later go to the purchase of a home. In some cases, particularly London, these capital amounts have been substantial.

Housing Associations are covered by the Housing Act of 1980, which gave tenants in some housing associations the right to buy their homes on the same basis as the purchase of a council property. This facility is available in those housing associations which are *not* registered as charities, have received any public funds towards the development, or are co-ownership or fully mutual co-operatives. Eligible housing associations should be registered with the Housing Corporation.

Renting out your home

One way of purchasing a home when funds are low is to get a contribution to costs by renting out part of it. There are obvious advantages for some home-owners in this, but there are pitfalls. It is wise not to consider letting, unless you are fully aware of them. They include:

- Any home which is let out for rent ceases to become completely free of Capital Gains Tax (CGT) on sale. If a part is let out, a formula is applied to cover the proportion of the home rented and the period of the rental. CGT is payable on that sum when the home is sold, on any gain over the annual exemption from CGT (£6,600 in 1987/88).
- If you have a mortgage, you will need to have permission from the lender before letting out part of your property.
- Tax is payable on any rentals.
- Care needs to be taken to make sure that when you want the house totally for your own occupation, or to sell it, that the tenant does not have a right to stay on in the property.

Freehold or leasehold?

Properties are sold either freehold or leasehold. Freehold means that the owner has full rights in perpetuity to the house or flat and the land on which it stands (in the case of a flat, the owner will probably share the freehold with other owners in the block); in England or Wales, most properties come freehold, although it is much less common with flats. In contrast, if you buy a leasehold, someone else owns the freehold and the lease will eventually end and revert to the freeholder, who may or may not have the right to refuse to grant a new lease, depending on the status of the leaseholder.

Leaseholders used to have very little protection, but today their rights have been extended, and in some cases they have the right to purchase the freehold whether or not the freeholder wants to sell.

Some leases are very long—99 years and even 999 are not uncommon—so they are virtually the same as owning the freehold. The only difference is that there is some annual rent, generally called 'ground rent', to be paid for the lease. This may be only a nominal amount, but in some cases it is quite substantial. Anyone buying a lease should check the terms carefully.

In Northern Ireland and Scotland it is more common to live in leasehold rather than freehold property.

Spotcheck

Have you

- decided where you want to live?
- decided what sort of property you want and need?
- decided on the size of the property?
- worked out exactly what you can afford?
- matched up the running costs with what you can afford?

Beforehand, have you

- saved regularly or intermittently for a period, so that you have enough to pay any deposit required?
- registered your savings account under the government's home loan scheme?

Before making your mortgage application, have you

- looked in detail at all the types of mortgage available and chosen the one which suits you?
- decided what sort of repayment period you want and can afford?
- checked the costs of borrowing from different sources?
- understood the tax position vis-à-vis mortgages?
- worked out the costs of the purchase apart from the mortgage?
- made certain that you can afford the running costs?
- thought about what would happen if either one source of income dried up or one or both of you were to be made redundant?

Finally, have you

- decided on the question of ownership—in one name, joint, or in common?

Protecting Your Spouse

10

Making a will

When they first marry, a couple rarely thinks about what will happen should one of them die unexpectedly. There is, however, one thing which they should do before anything else and that is to make a will, each protecting the other. The importance of this cannot be overstressed. Any previous will is invalidated by the marriage contract. Until a new will has been drawn up, the surviving spouse inherits everything—with certain legal limits.

On marriage, a couple may not have a great many assets, but what they have they will probably want to leave to each other. They are also likely to have more assets than they realize, particularly if they are buying a home (probably with a mortgage loan). The untimely death of one of them would mean that the mortgage would be repaid, through either a mortgage protection policy, an endowment policy or a pension policy. These are assets which form part of what is called the deceased's 'estate' on death.

Many people do not make a will, although there are no good reasons for not doing so. They often assume that their husband or wife will automatically get all they leave, but this is not always the case. What is more, even if the survivor does eventually get his or her hands on the assets, he or she will have to go through a long and laborious process before receiving them. If you leave more than the equivalent of £1,500, your assets cannot be distributed without a will until what is called a 'letter of administration' has been granted to the claimants. This can take some time. When a will has been made, there is also a process, *probate*, which must be gone through before the distribution of assets. Probate and letters of administration are more or less the same thing, but probate is much easier and faster to complete.

People who do not make a will are said to have died intestate, and the law sets down precisely how the estate must be distributed. The figures are updated occasionally by the government. At present, the surviving spouse gets everything if there are no children or close relatives. The same applies if the total estate, which must be valued whether there is a will or not, is worth £40,000 or less.

Where the estate is worth more than £40,000 the spouse will receive all the personal effects, such as the car, household furniture and jewellery, as well as the first £40,000. Then he or she gets a life interest in half of anything else left over. The other half goes to the children, and this is where it becomes complicated. If a husband and wife leave everything to one another, there is no inheritance tax (IT) to pay, but if someone dies intestate the whole cannot in law be given to the wife unless it is £40,000 or less. This means that a person who makes a will leaving, say, £140,000 can make sure that no tax is payable on any of that amount by leaving it to his or her spouse, whereas someone else who died intestate would leave his or her heirs with a tax bill of £3,300, because of the way the estate must be distributed by law.

This is how it works. If a husband or wife wills his or her whole estate to their spouse, there is no IT to pay, although there will be eventually when the survivor dies. (We shall look at how to minimize that tax bill later—see page 198). In contrast, if there is no will, the wife gets only £40,000. This leaves £100,000. Now the first £90,000 (1987–88 tax year) of any estate left comes tax-free. So IT has to be paid on the surplus over and above the wife's £40,000, and the exempt £90,000. In this case, that is £10,000 to be divided equally among the children. It attracts IT at the lowest rate of 30 per cent, so immediately there is a tax bill of £3,300. That is not much, of course, in terms of the figures we're talking about, but just look how the tax rates rise as the value of the estate rises (1987–88):

Proportion of value	*rate (per cent)*
0–£90,000	nil
£90,000–£140,000	30
£140,000–£220,000	40
£220,000–£330,000	50
£330,001 and above	60

It is quite common in a family where no will has been left for children to say that they do not want to benefit until the surviving parent dies. Unfortunately, they cannot save tax that way. Unless there is a will leaving everything specifically to the surviving spouse, the wheels of the law start turning. Where there are no children, settling the estate of someone who has died intestate becomes even more difficult.

Where there are close relatives, the widow or widower will get up to £85,000 (this figure is increased periodically) and half of everything else which is left. The rest is divided among the relatives in a quite complicated way, although they may not get it until the surviving spouse dies, as he or she gets a life interest on the money. Problems can then arise if the ultimate beneficiaries think that the money is not being invested to provide them with the maximum possible when they eventually inherit. Without going into any more detail, it becomes quite clear that a great deal of time and trouble—not to say argument—can be saved by people making wills.

Quite apart from the legal and tax implications (and if you have a great deal of money consult a tax lawyer before making your will) there are many other reasons for making a will as soon as possible in your life, and certainly immediately you marry, if not before. One of these is quite simply that you will get used to the idea of disposing of whatever assets you have at a particular time in whatever way you want. It is also certain that you will want to make several wills in your lifetime, and getting into the habit early is a good idea. Here are just some of the reasons for making a will:

● You will be able to control where your money goes after your death.
● By using professional advice, you can reduce the amount of money which goes to the taxman.

- You can decide who will see that your wishes are carried out. To ensure this, you appoint executors who have the responsibility of carrying out your wishes. You can have only a single executor, who may be your spouse if he or she is the sole beneficiary, but if the will is at all complicated you may prefer to have two or more, including a professional (perhaps the solicitor who draws up the will for you). *Do not appoint anyone as your executor without asking them: after you die they can refuse to take the job unless you have asked them and received their consent.*
- You can tell your executors exactly what you want them to do. Either (a) you can give them wide powers to dispose of your money in what they think is the best way, or (b) you can leave precise instructions which they must follow.
- If you have children and you want to leave them something, you will need a trustee to see that they get their entitlement (see page 157).

All a will need contain is a statement of your wishes and the date. It must then be signed by you in the presence of two witnesses, who must also sign. It is a good idea to start with the words: 'This is the last will and testament of [your name], dated [whatever the date might be].' *You need not show your will to the witnesses: they are there simply to verify that the signature at the end is yours. You are quite entitled to keep its contents secret.* You must take care, however, about whom you choose as witnesses, because in law they cannot be people who benefit under your will. Incorrect witnessing is one of the commonest reasons for a will being deemed invalid.

Although a solicitor is not essential when you make your will, it is nevertheless a good idea to use one. Simple wills are not expensive, and the fee we pay the solicitor is usually money well spent, because we are unlikely to write down our wishes absolutely clearly unless we have the aid of a solicitor. Things do not always mean, in legal terms, what we think they mean. So, if you decide against using a solicitor when making your will, it is wise to read one of the books on the subject to ensure you get things right. It is better, however, to put everything into your own words rather than use one of the standard forms for wills, which you will sometimes see around. If you have used a solicitor, lodge the will itself in his or her offices and ask him or her to do a photostat for you to keep at home. If you decide that you do not want to leave everything to your spouse—e.g., if you want to protect your children by a former marriage, or even a former spouse—discuss the matter fully with your current spouse to make sure that you do not leave financial as well as other grief behind you. Some husbands and wives make joint wills, and there is nothing to be said against this as long as they are agreed on the contents, but on balance it is better for each to make a separate will.

A final point. Do not decide against making a will because you see it as some sort of death sentence. One of the reasons for getting into the habit of making wills early in life is that doing so will then become a normal part of everyday financial planning.

The role of life assurance

As soon as we marry our responsibilities extend not just to ourselves but also to one other person, our spouse, and later on usually to more than one other person—i.e., to our children, too. This applies both to men and to

THE DUTIES OF EXECUTORS AND TRUSTEES

An executor:

- Arranges the funeral. For this reason, it is a good idea to choose as one executor someone who is part of your family or who knows them well.
- Becomes the legal representative of the dead person, taking on their rights and responsibilities. This means collecting together all the assets, paying any taxes due and any other debts, and distributing the net assets in accordance with the wishes of the deceased.
- The first step is to get probate. This means preparing a statement for the Inspector of Taxes of the value of all the assets at the point of death. Next, an executor's oath must be sworn, then the original will (not a copy or photostat) and the probate papers must be sent to the Probate Registry. After all this has been completed and probate granted, the estate can be divided up between the heirs. Remember, an executor can benefit from a will. He or she can also charge for doing the job.

A trustee:

- May also be an executor.
- Is responsible for dealing with a 'trust' which will be set up, generally (a) when a person does not leave an estate outright to another adult, but leaves them only the interest on capital for their lifetime, or (b) where there are dependent children. The income and sometimes the capital is used for their benefit as they are growing up, and full right to the capital usually reverts to them when they reach a certain age (which need not be 18).
- Must balance the interests of the tenants (the people who get income during their lifetime) and the remaindermen (the people who will eventually get the capital). This can require some skill if family quarrels are to be avoided.
- Must know exactly what investment powers he or she has. These can be as wide as the person making the will wishes, but, if no such statement is made in the will, the Trustee Investments Act states broadly that half the investments can go into certain companies quoted on the stock market and unit trusts. The other half must go into fixed interest stocks or savings.

women. Probably the most important event couples will want to protect one another against is untimely death of one or other; both will want to know that the spouse and any children do not suffer any more than they have to. Most people will already have taken two steps before they turn to the subject of general life assurance: they will, if they are purchasing a property, have protected the home by means of a mortgage-protection insurance policy or endowment life assurance, and they will have made a will ensuring that any inheritance tax payable on their estate is minimized or eliminated altogether. However, more protection than that is needed, and a couple should turn as soon as possible to the question of life assurance. It is not only the home which needs protection: so does the family's standard of living, which could be drastically hit were one or other spouse to die (especially if there are small dependent children). It is important to remember that these remarks apply to both husband and wife: it is often forgotten by couples that today wives often make a valuable, even a vital, financial contribution to a family's standard of living, whether they work outside the home or not. The financial contribution a so-called working wife makes is easy to quantify, but it should not be forgotten that a woman who stays at home looking after children is making just as positive a contribution to the family's standard of living. She, after all, is prepared to work for nothing: in contrast, employing a cleaner, nanny and cook would be expensive.

For this reason, a couple should look together at their life-assurance needs and, wherever possible, take out joint or separate policies on both lives. Although awareness of the value of life assurance is growing, most people have yet to grasp its importance for wives and mothers. About 75 per cent of men carry some life assurance (often, it is true, attached only to their home), but only about 25 per cent of women have similar cover.

For a variety of reasons, life assurance is one of the most neglected aspects of family financial life. The most important of these reasons is that it can seem expensive and its benefits vague and very long-term. It is cheapest when we are young, but even then it may make demands on the family budget which are too heavy in relation to the total amount of money available: the car, the home, family holidays and possibly school fees all seem to have a much greater priority.

It is also true that in no other area of our financial lives are we as subject to high-pressure sales techniques used by salesmen who often do not really know what they are doing. Although the insurance industry and the government are taking steps to see that these high-pressure approaches are minimized, it is easy to make a mistake when buying life assurance—to buy too much or too little, or to buy the wrong kind. The reason is the way the selling of insurance is organized. Companies sell either (a) through their own sales staff, (b) through brokers and agents, or (c) through advertisements. Policy documents are not always easy to understand, and very often we may not be buying the benefits which we think we are simply because we have failed to read the policy's small print.

There are snags involved in all the approaches taken by insurance companies. Policies vary from company to company, but salesmen and saleswomen will, naturally, offer only the product of their own company, which may well not suit the particular customer.

Where brokers and agents are used, there is just one word to describe the eagerness with which they sometimes sell unsuitable policies: 'commission'. Commission levels used to be controlled by the Life Offices' Association (along with the Associated Scottish Life Offices), but after several prominent members left the associations the maximum commission levels were dropped, though they are now being re-imposed and must be disclosed by anyone selling insurance. There is a natural temptation for a broker or an agent to try to earn the maximum commission possible, with the result that he or she may suggest policies with an eye to commission levels rather than to the needs of the customer. Then again, brokers and agents quite often have links with particular companies, and will suggest only those products to the customer. Very few brokers are likely to suggest that their clients take out policies with those few companies which do not pay commissions (such companies use either sales staff or advertisements, or a combination).

Buying life assurance straight off the page is not to be recommended. If you like the look of a policy you see advertised, do not simply fill in the form: insist that the company explains the benefits and payments clearly to you.

Commission to salespeople is eventually paid for by the customer, and insurance companies make sure that the customer does so with the first premiums, so that the company does not lose out if a policy is later dropped. There are also administration costs involved in putting a policy on the company's books and these, together with commission, make up what is called 'front-end loading' on a policy. This loading can mean that almost the whole—and occasionally even more—of the early premiums paid by the policy-holder go simply to covering initial costs. The policy-holder gains no benefit from the premiums paid in this period, unless he or she dies during it—which most of us would rather not do! So, should you avoid those insurance companies that use agents and therefore pay commission? The answer has to be no, because sales staff and advertisements likewise have to be paid for, and over the years experience has shown that policy-holders in commission-paying companies do no worse than those in others.

Because of the sales techniques employed throughout the insurance industry, it makes sense when first buying insurance, particularly life assurance, to know what you are buying and what benefits it will bring. There are codes of conduct for insurance practice: see below. Make sure that these codes of conduct are followed by anyone trying to sell you insurance cover of any kind.

Before we go on to look at the types of policies available, bear in mind that life assurance has two possible functions: (a) to provide a financial cushion when a family is facing disaster, because one of the parents has died; and (b) to be an integral part of long-term family financial planning and saving. For most young couples, cover against a time of financial crisis is probably the main priority. Nevertheless, it is convenient to look at all life-assurance policies together, to see how they relate to each other, what different functions they have, and the protection they provide.

Code of conduct for insurance salesmen

All insurance brokers must in law follow the code of conduct set out below, but in practice not all of them do. If you feel that a broker has fallen short of this ideal, write to or phone the Insurance Brokers' Registration Council, 15 St Helen's Place, London EC3A 6DS (tel. 01–588 4387).

1. This Code of Conduct shall serve as a guide to insurance brokers and other persons concerned with their conduct but the mention or lack of mention in it of a particular act or omission shall not be taken as conclusive of any question of professional conduct.

In the opinion of the Council the objective of the Code is to assist in establishing a recognized standard of professional conduct required of all insurance brokers who should, in the interests of the public and in the performance of their duties, bear in mind both this objective and the underlying spirit of this Code.

Matters which might relate to acts or omissions amounting to negligence will be dealt with, if necessary, by the Courts but the Council acknowledges that gross negligence or repeated cases of negligence may amount to unprofessional conduct.

2. The following are, in the opinion of the Council, the acts and omissions that breach the fundamental principles governing the professional conduct of insurance brokers set out in paragraph 3 below.

3. The principles mentioned in paragraph 2 above are as follows:

Insurance brokers shall at all times conduct their business with utmost good faith and integrity.

Insurance brokers shall do everything possible to satisfy the insurance requirements of their clients and shall place the interests of those clients before all other considerations. Subject to these requirements and interests, insurance brokers shall have proper regard for others.

Statements made by or on behalf of insurance brokers when advertising shall not be misleading or extravagant.

The following are some specific examples of the application of these principles:

1. In the conduct of their business insurance brokers shall provide advice objectively and independently.

2. Insurance brokers shall only use or permit the use of the description 'insurance broker' in connection with a business provided that business is carried on in accordance with the requirements of the Rules made by the Council under sections 11 and 12 of the Act.

3. Insurance brokers shall ensure that all work carried out in connection with their insurance-broking business shall be under the control and day-to-day supervision of a registered insurance broker and they shall do everything possible to ensure that their employees are made aware of this Code.

4. Insurance brokers shall on request from the client explain the differences in, and the relative costs of, the principal types of insurance which in the opinion of the insurance broker might suit a client's needs.

5. Insurance brokers shall ensure the use of a sufficient number of insurers to satisfy the insurance requirements of their clients.

6. Insurance brokers shall, upon request, disclose to any client who is an individual and who is, or is contemplating becoming, the holder of a United Kingdom policy of insurance the amount of commission paid by the insurer under any relevant policy of insurance.

7. Although the choice of an insurer can only be a matter of judgement, insurance brokers shall use their skill objectively in the best interests of their client.

8. Insurance brokers shall not withhold from the policy-holder any written evidence or documentation relating to the contract of insurance without adequate and justifiable reasons being disclosed in writing and without delay to the policy-holder. If an insurance broker withholds a document from a policy-holder by way of a lien for monies due from that policy-holder he shall provide the reason in the manner required above.

9. Insurance brokers shall inform a client of the name of all insurers with whom a contract of insurance is placed. This information shall be given at the inception of the contract and any changes thereafter shall be advised at the earliest opportunity to the client.

10. Before any work involving a charge is undertaken or an agreement to carry out business is concluded, insurance brokers shall disclose and identify any amount they propose to charge to the client or policy-holder which will be in addition to the premium payable to the insurer.

11. Insurance brokers shall disclose to a client any payment which they receive as a result of securing on behalf of that client any service additional to the arrangement of a contract of insurance.

12. Insurance brokers shall have proper regard for the wishes of a policy-holder or client who seeks to terminate any agreement with them to carry out business.

13. Any information acquired by an insurance broker from his client shall not be used or disclosed except in the normal course of negotiating, maintaining, or renewing a contract of insurance for that client or unless the consent of the client has been obtained or the information is required by a court of competent jurisdiction.

14. In the completion of the proposal form, claim form, or any other material document, insurance brokers shall make it clear that all the answers or statements are the client's own responsibility. The client should always be asked to check the details and told that the inclusion of incorrect information may result in a claim being repudiated.

15. Advertisements made by or on behalf of insurance brokers shall comply with the applicable parts of the Code of Advertising Practice published by the Advertising Standards Authority and for this purpose the Code of Advertising Practice shall be deemed to form part of this Code of Conduct.

16. Advertisements made by or on behalf of insurance brokers shall distinguish between contractual benefits, that is those that the contract of insurance is bound to provide, and noncontractual benefits, that is the amount of benefit which it might provide assuming the insurer's particular forecast is correct. Where such advertisements include a forecast of noncontractual benefits, insurance brokers shall restrict the forecast to that provided by the insurer concerned.

17. Advertisements made by or on behalf of insurance brokers shall not be restricted to the policies of one insurer except where the reasons for such restriction are fully explained in the advertisement, the insurer named therein, and the prior approval of that insurer obtained.

18. When advertising their services directly or indirectly either in person or in writing insurance brokers shall disclose their identity, occupation and purpose before seeking information or before giving advice.

19. Insurance brokers shall display in any office where they are carrying on business and to which the public have access a notice to the effect that a copy of the Code of Conduct is available upon request and that if a member of the public wishes to make a complaint or requires the assistance of the Council in resolving a dispute, he may write to the Insurance Brokers' Registration Council.

This Statement of General Insurance Practice is a voluntary Code of Conduct. Complaints should go to the Association of British Insurers, Aldermany House, Queen Street, London EC4N 1TP (tel. 01–248 4477). The Code applies to personal insurance only, not business insurance.

Proposal forms   The declaration at the foot of the proposal form should be restricted to completion according to the proposer's knowledge and belief.

Neither the proposal form nor the policy shall contain any provision converting the statements as to past or present fact in the proposal form into warranties. But insurers may require specific warranties about matters which are material to the risk.

If not included in the declaration, prominently displayed on the proposal form should be a statement:

- drawing the attention of the proposer to the consequences of the failure to disclose all material facts, explained as those facts an insurer would regard as likely to influence the acceptance and assessment of the proposal;
- warning that if the proposer is in any doubt about facts considered material, he should disclose them.

Those matters which insurers have found generally to be material will be the subject of clear questions in proposal forms.

So far as is practicable, insurers will avoid asking questions which would require expert knowledge beyond that which the proposer could reasonably be expected to possess or obtain or which would require a value judgement on the part of the proposer.

Unless the prospectus or the proposal form contains full details of the standard cover offered, and whether or not it contains an outline of that cover, the proposal forms shall include a prominent statement that a specimen copy of the policy form is available on request.

Proposal forms shall contain a prominent warning that the proposer should keep a record (including copies of letters) of all information supplied to the insurer for the purpose of entering into the contract.

The proposal form shall contain a prominent statement that a copy of the completed form:

- is automatically provided for retention at the time of completion; or

- will be supplied as part of the insurer's normal practice; or

- will be supplied on request within a period of three months after its completion.

An insurer shall not raise an issue under the proposal form, unless the policyholder is provided with a copy of the completed form.

Claims Under the conditions regarding notification of a claim, the policyholder shall not be asked to do more than report a claim and subsequent developments as soon as reasonably possible except in the case of legal processes and claims which a third party requires the policyholder to notify within a fixed time where immediate advice may be required.

An insurer will not repudiate liability to indemnify a policy-holder:

- on grounds of nondisclosure of a material fact which a policy-holder could not reasonably be expected to have disclosed;

- on grounds of misrepresentation unless it is a deliberate or negligent misrepresentation of a material fact;

93

- on grounds of a breach of warranty or condition where the circumstances of the loss are unconnected with the breach unless fraud is involved.

These do not apply to Marine and Aviation policies.

Liability under the policy having been established and the amount payable by the insurer agreed, payment will be made without avoidable delay.

Renewals Renewal notices shall contain a warning about the duty of disclosure including the necessity to advise changes affecting the policy which have occurred since the policy inception or last renewal date, whichever was the later.

Renewal notices shall contain a warning that the proposer should keep a record (including copies of letters) of all information supplied to the insurer for the purpose of renewal of the contract.

Commencement Any changes to insurance documents will be made as and when they need to be reprinted, but the Statement will apply in the meantime.

Policy documents Insurers will continue to develop clearer and more explicit proposal forms and policy documents whilst bearing in mind the legal nature of insurance contracts.

Disputes The provisions of the Statement shall be taken into account in arbitration and any other referral procedures which may apply in the event of disputes between policy-holders and insurers relating to matters dealt with in the Statement.

EEC This Statement will need reconsideration when the Draft EEC Directive on Insurance Contract Law is adopted and implemented in the United Kingdom.

Life assurance selling

The Association of British Insurers, the Associated Scottish Life Office and the Industrial Life Offices Association have a code for their own agents and salesmen which is separate from that of insurance brokers. Complaints should be made to your local Trading Standards Officer or Citizens' Advice Bureau.

Code for intermediaries
A: General sales principles It shall be an overriding obligation of an intermediary at all times to conduct business with the utmost good faith and integrity.

- The intermediary shall:

1. Where appropriate make a prior appointment to call. Unsolicited or unarranged calls shall be made at an hour likely to be suitable to the prospective policy-holder.
2. When he makes contact with the prospective policy-holder, identify

himself and explain as soon as possible that the arrangements he wishes to discuss could include life assurance. He shall make it known that he is the agent of one or a number of offices (as the case may be), one or more of whose policies he may wish to discuss.

3. Ensure as far as possible that the policy proposed is suitable to the needs and not beyond the resources of the prospective policy-holder.

4. Give advice only on those matters in which he is competent to deal and seek or recommend other specialist advice if this seems appropriate.

5. Treat all information supplied by the prospective policy-holder as completely confidential to himself and to the life office or offices to which the business is being offered.

6. In making comparisons with other types of policies or forms of investment, make clear the different characteristics of each policy/investment.

The intermediary shall not:

1. Inform the prospective policy-holder that his name has been given by another person unless he is prepared to disclose that person's name if requested to do so by the prospective policy-holder and has that person's consent to make that disclosure.

2. Make inaccurate or unfair criticisms of any insurers.

3. Attempt to persuade a prospective policy-holder to cancel any existing policies unless these are clearly unsuited to his needs.

B: Explanation of the contract

The intermediary shall:

1. Explain all the essential provisions of the contract, or contracts, which he is recommending so as to ensure as far as possible that the prospective policy-holder understands what he is committing himself to.

2. Draw attention to any restrictions applying to the policy, such as statutory restrictions applying to individual pension arrangements.

3. Draw attention to the long-term nature of the policy and to the consequent effects of early discontinuance and surrender.

4. In the case of a policy qualifying for life-assurance premium relief, draw attention to the fact that the relief may be varied by the government from time to time.

Where a policy offers participation in profits, or otherwise depends on variable factors such as investment performance, descriptions of the benefits shall distinguish between fixed and projected benefits.

Where projected benefits are illustrated, it should be made clear, where applicable, that they are based on certain assumptions, e.g. about future bonus declarations, and hence are not guaranteed, and these assumptions should be stated.

In the case of with-profit business, it should be made clear that bonuses declared in the future may be lower or higher than those currently quoted.

95

Thus past performance may not necessarily be a guide to future performance.

● In the case of unit-linked business, it should be made clear that unit values, and hence the value of the policyholder's benefits, may go down as well as up.

● Where an intermediary has been supplied with an illustration by the life office, he shall use the whole illustration in respect of the contract which he is discussing with the prospective policy-holder, and no other, and shall not add to it or select only the most favourable aspects of it. If the intermediary is authorized by the life office to prepare illustrations himself, he shall prepare them in accordance with the recommendations in the appendix attached to this Code.

C: Disclosure of underwriting information   The intermediary shall in obtaining the completion of the proposal form or any other material:

1. Avoid influencing the proposer and make it clear that all the answers or statements are the latter's own responsibility.
2. Ensure that the consequences of nondisclosure and inaccuracies are pointed out to the proposer by drawing his attention to the relevant statement in the proposal form and by explaining them himself to the proposer.

D: Accounts and financial aspects   The intermediary shall:

1. Keep a proper account of all financial transactions with a prospective policy-holder which involve the transmission of money in respect of insurance.
2. Acknowledge receipt (which unless the intermediary has been otherwise authorized by the office shall be on his own behalf) of all money received in connection with an insurance policy and shall distinguish the premium from any other payment included in the money.
3. Forward without delay any money received for life assurance.

Code for introducers

● The introducer shall:

1. Give advice only on those matters in which he is competent and seek assistance from the life office when necessary.
2. At the earliest opportunity call upon a qualified representative from the life office whose contract he wishes to be presented to the prospective policy-holder, to explain the contract to the prospective policy-holder.

● The introducer shall not:

1. Solicit life-assurance business outside the terms of his agency appointment.

2. Attempt to influence the prospective policy-holder with regard to the completion of the proposal form.

Life quotations, recommendations for bonus and yield illustrations In preparing bonus and yield illustrations for use in life-assurance policy quotations, the following guidelines should be observed.

Non-linked business
1. The prospective policy-holder should be as aware of the nature and purpose of the illustration as he is of its content. He should understand what he is reading while he is reading it—or at least should be given a clear opportunity to do so.
2. The illustration shall not be based on unrealistic assumptions and should either be preceded by a suitable (and suitably prominent) cautionary statement or alongside the bonus projection there should be clear reference to that part of the illustration which contains the cautionary statement. This statement should:

- make clear the assumptions on which the rates have been projected, for instance that the continuance of present rates in the future has been assumed,
- warn that future bonuses depend on future profits and cannot be guaranteed.

3. To emphasize that there is no guarantee attaching to the benefits quoted, there should be used some expression such as 'assumed bonus rates' or 'projected bonus/maturity proceeds' or 'maturity proceeds based on . . .', etc.
4. The illustration of bonuses based on similar policies maturing at the date of illustration without suitable qualification must be questionable, having in mind continuing uncertainties in the economic and social outlook. Where terminal bonuses are illustrated, they should be shown as a separate item and the assumptions underlying the calculation must be stated. Illustrations of total emerging benefits, however constituted, shall not be unrealistic or create a misleading impression.
5. The spirit underlying the above provisions applies equally to pensions policies, for example in the use of current immediate annuity rates to illustrate projected benefits and again in the relationship assumed between salary growth and investment returns.

Linked business
1. Here again the prospective policy-holder should be aware of the nature and purpose of the illustration while he is reading it, and so there should be clear references, within the body of the illustration, to the possibility of decrease as well as growth in the investments and to what the assumed rate(s) of growth include or exclude. To avoid overelaboration, reference may also be made to a brochure describing the contract more fully.
2. Illustrations should, if possible, be provided on the assumption of more than one rate of growth and should show clearly the rates assumed. It is recognized, however, that in the case of some complex quotations it may be impracticable to do this.

3. Where several rates are used, it should be made clear that these do not represent the lower and upper limits of possibilities that may occur.

4. For the same reason as for nonlinked policies, there should be used some expression such as 'assumed additions', 'assumed growth', 'projected result', etc.

5. As regards the actual levels of growth assumed, illustrations of emerging benefits shall not be unrealistic, whether they are based on rates of growth of unit values, bonus rates or interest rates. Where the value of a policy depends on the value of the underlying units, it should be stated whether the value of the units includes the reinvestment of income and whether allowance has been made for capital-gains-tax liability or whether any deduction is made from the policy proceeds.

The types of life assurance available

Although there are literally thousands of life-assurance policies on sale in Britain today, they can be broken down into three basic kinds: (a) whole-of-life, (b) term, and (c) endowment. Each kind comes in two basic varieties—with and without profits. The difference between these two varieties is very simple. If you take out a with-profits policy, you will insure your life for a basic sum of money (the 'sum assured'), but as the years go on you will share in the profits made by your insurance company, so that the eventual payout either on your death or when the policy matures may be much higher than the sum assured. The profits come in the form of bonuses, which are declared annually. (See box.) In a without-profits policy, by contrast, you will get only the sum assured or a little more—although you may not have paid in as much as you get out if the policy runs to maturity or you die. Naturally, pound-for-pound of life cover bought, a without-profits policy costs less than a with-profits one.

There are other differences in the costs of life assurance. All premiums paid on insurance are related to risk. The higher the risk of the company paying out sooner rather than later, the more it will charge for the insurance cover to protect itself against an unacceptable level of claims. This means that, generally speaking, the younger you are when you take out life assurance the less it will cost. There are exceptions to this overall rule where people are in dangerous jobs or have certain health conditions, in which case either their premiums may be 'loaded' (which means they have to pay more for life assurance than a person of the same age in a routine job, or in normal health) or they may not be covered if they die at work or of that particular medical condition. Men's premiums are effectively loaded simply because they are men, because the average man pays more in premiums than an average woman of the same age. It is well known that men have an average life expectancy seven years less than women, so the risk of paying out on a man's death when fewer premiums have been paid is rather higher than in the case of a woman. Insurance companies recognize this risk, but rather than calling it loading they simply treat a man as if he were four years older than a woman of the same age (not seven years: women do not get the whole benefit of their longevity). This means, for example, that a 21-year-old man would pay the same premiums for the same policy as a 25-year-old woman.

It is worth pointing out here that, if you are taking out life assurance and you knowingly lie about an existing medical condition, and you then die of

BONUSES

The with-profits element in life-assurance policies is announced every year, and policy-holders receive a statement early in the new year setting out the previous year's bonuses and earlier accumulated bonuses.

Not all companies deal with bonuses in the same way, and it is worth asking what the bonus policy generally is before taking out a policy. If the policy runs to death or maturity, there may not be much difference in total value, but if it is surrendered early for any reason the value can vary considerably.

Bonuses come in two kinds, reversionary and terminal. Reversionary bonuses are those which are declared each year. The terminal bonus (it may sometimes be called the additional bonus) comes as the policy matures. Once a reversionary bonus is declared, it is written into the value of the policy and guaranteed, and is added to the basic benefit. A terminal bonus, by contrast, remains an unknown quantity until it is actually paid.

Some policy-holders prefer to go to companies which are generous in their reversionary bonuses and which may not pay much in terminal bonuses. But, where reversionary bonuses are not large, terminal bonuses can be very generous and bring a sharp boost in value right at the end.

Unfortunately, companies are not always consistent in their bonus policy, so it is wise to be as sure as possible—regardless of bonus policy—that you will be able to run a policy to its full term to make sure you do not lose out.

that condition, your heirs will not get the money. This does not apply if you develop the condition later. The same goes for your job, although that will be implicit in the company's decision when you state what you do. It is also worth voluntarily mentioning to the company, if they do not ask, if you are involved in a dangerous leisure pursuit which has a high accident and death rate.

Companies have become much more relaxed in recent years about the medical information they require from potential policy-holders; they are also prepared to consider quite a wide range of medical conditions at 'normal' premium rates. As a general rule, few companies today demand a medical for anyone who is under 50—although, if the application is marginal as far as health is concerned, or a very large amount of life cover is requested, one might be required.

The proposal form will usually ask a few simple questions about health—e.g., have you currently got a medical condition which is being treated, or have you recently had an operation? If you have to answer 'yes' to any of these questions you will be asked to elaborate. Even then, it is by no means certain that you will be refused cover at the normal rates. If you are, and if you are determined to have life assurance, it is worth shopping around a few companies or getting a broker or agent to do it for you, because different companies take different views of the level of risk in various medical conditions. If there is no escape from loading, you may be asked to pay higher premiums, which will treat you as if you are older than you actually are, or you may be offered a smaller sum assured than available to those in normal health, at least at the start of the policy.

Once you are over 50, you will probably be asked to take a medical, particularly for a whole-of-life policy. These policies are very useful in minimizing any inheritance tax payable on your estate when you die (see page 198). Loading against the sum assured can be as high as 90 per cent, but if this is all you are offered you are a very bad risk indeed and are lucky to be offered anything! In many such cases, if you are seen to have recovered as time goes on, the company may gradually increase the sum assured towards the normal level, eventually giving you 100 per cent cover.

A recent development in life assurance has been the large discounts offered to nonsmokers. Insurance companies are concerned with risk, and they are uninterested in the arguments about health and smoking. What they look at is the statistics on mortality of smokers and nonsmokers. Although there may not be much difference in the level of risk of death from smoking-related diseases when people are quite young, nonsmokers over 50 may be offered a policy with premiums at less than half the level of those offered to smokers.

You will often see life-assurance policies described as 'qualifying policies'. These are policies which are taken out initially for a period of at least ten years. In such cases, the lump sum available on death or when the policy matures is tax-free under present British law. It used also to be a requirement when there was 15 per cent tax relief on the regular premiums paid on policies. That relief ended with the April 1984 Budget, which abolished tax relief on new but not existing policies except for Section 226 policies, which qualify for full tax relief to certain levels. These policies are currently available only to people who are not in a recognized pension fund at their work, or who are self-employed. They are part of pension planning, and are discussed more fully in chapter 16. After January 1988, everyone will be able to buy them.

Remember that all policies can be on the lives of individuals, or at some extra cost jointly on both husband and wife, but the higher premiums are generally well worth paying if you can afford them. Even though it is generally true that wives live longer than their husbands, every year in Britain over 7,000 women die under the age of 45 and with dependent children.

When you are sold a policy, make sure that you know exactly what it is that you are buying. All sorts of fancy names are thought up for policies; and you must be sure that, if you want endowment, for instance, that is what you are getting.

It is now time to look at the three basic kinds of life cover and the most important variations within them.

Whole-of-life

Whole-of-life policies assure that a sum of money will be paid to the beneficiaries on the death of the person whose life has been covered—this is called the life assured. They do not have maturity dates as such when the

RELEASING LIFE-ASSURANCE FUNDS

You may find as you get older that you have a whole-of-life assurance policy which will eventually produce a substantial sum assured, but that you have no one to leave it to or you need the money now.

You may have asked for a surrender value which has not satisfied you. All is not lost, however. You can auction the policy. Although this means that you or any heirs lose all rights to the policy, you get your hands on the money now.

H. E. Foster and Cranfield of Cheapside, London, specialize in this sort of business. You can make sure that you get at least the amount of any surrender value that you have already been offered by setting a reserve price on your policy of that level, plus something for the auctioneer's fee.

person who has taken out the policy might collect the money. They can remain in force for many years and premiums may have to be paid right up to the time of death. Many whole-of-life policies do have a cut-off date, after which no further premiums need be paid, but this may be when you are as old as 90 (75 or 80 is more common).

There is little point in taking out a whole-of-life policy very early in married life, particularly if it is without profits. Insuring your life for £20,000 when you are 25 may sound reasonable, but if your heirs do not collect for another 50 years that sum of money is not going to look like very much. Whole-of-life policies which simply pay a lump sum, either with or without profits, are most suitable for the middle-aged, who may be thinking about what will happen to their assets when they die. Such policies can help avoid much of the pain of inheritance tax, and we shall look at them again (see page 199). Whole-of-life policies are clearly for protection against untimely death, or form part of long-term tax planning.

A whole-of-life policy need not be just a simple policy. It can be linked with the purchase of units in a unit trust run by the insurance company. What happens is that premiums are paid, as a rule monthly, with part going into life cover and the rest into the purchase of units. There is a choice about the level of insurance cover in the plan, with maximum and minimum limits. To begin with, insurance cover is guaranteed for ten years. What happens after that depends upon how well the units have done. Most people cash in their policies after ten years, sacrificing some or all of the life cover, especially if the units have done well, but there is no need to do this. After the first ten years, the policy will be reviewed at five-yearly intervals, and in some policies of this type premiums on the insurance part of the plan may be increased. The cost varies with age and health, and this form of whole-of-life policy has more appeal to the young than the conventional type. Even so, there are better avenues than this for the relatively young newly married. What can be particularly beneficial for those seeking high insurance cover at low cost is term assurance.

As with whole-of-life assurance, in term assurance the sum assured (or alternatively an income for one's heirs for a number of years) is paid only on death. The difference between it and whole-of-life assurance is that a term policy runs for a certain number of years; and if you live longer than that the policy lapses and there is no benefit. These policies are designed primarily for financial protection.

A mortgage-protection policy (see page 63) is a form of term assurance, as are the policies which are available at airports which provide cover for us when we are travelling. To qualify for a tax-free lump sum or income, term assurance must of course be taken out for a period of at least ten years. At first glance term assurance does not seem very attractive, but it is one area of life assurance which is growing rapidly and for a very good reason: it is extremely cheap in comparison with any other life cover.

Term assurance is the one means whereby a young couple can, without crippling the family budget, protect their family in the event of the death of one of them. If a 25-year-old man, for instance, wanted £100,000 life cover, it would cost him only about £10 a month for straight term assurance for 25 years. The same cover in a whole-of-life policy would cost around £30 per month without profits or £150 with, and an endowment policy with profits (see below) could cost as much as £320 per month.

Basic term assurance comes in two varieties, level term and increasable renewal term. The policy can cover the person who takes out the policy, or their wife or husband, or both. Level-term assurance is in essence without profits. A fixed sum or income is paid out if death occurs during the life of the policy. In an increasable-renewable-term policy there is the option of increasing the amount of cover—every three or five years, perhaps. If you go for the higher cover, the premiums will of course increase; but most of us do not die during the period of a term policy.

Insurance companies do not take undue risks and they tailor the premiums accordingly. They are well aware, however, that many people are put off term assurance by the knowledge that there will be nothing if they survive. They also know that, generally speaking, people can afford higher premiums as they grow older, so recently the companies have incorporated into the policies the option of converting a term policy into a whole-of-life or endowment policy, should the policy-holder so wish. This way, term offers very cheap cover when funds may be low with some protection of the premiums paid later when there is more disposable income. You can, if you wish, take out a term policy which on death pays not a lump sum but a regular income. There are two terms involved here: the life of the policy, and the number of years for which the income is to be paid.

You may want to consider quite early in life such a life policy—perhaps immediately after the first child is born, when the knowledge that there is another person in the family who will be dependent for up to 20 years usually sinks in. These policies are usually not called term policies (although that is what they are) but family income benefit policies. The income may be fixed for the period—or, even better, may rise by 5 or 10 per cent a year (although in this case the premiums will probably be about one third higher than if the income were fixed). If a man aged 30 were to seek an annual income of about £15,000 for his wife and/or children for 20 years after his death, he could expect to pay around £12 a month for fixed family income benefit, about £18 a month if he wanted the income to rise by 5 per cent a year during the 20-year period, and about £24 a month for a 10 per cent annual increase. The income is tax-free, just as is the lump sum available on any life policy. What is happening is simply that, instead of the benefit coming to one's heirs in one lump, it is spread out over a period and either allows or does not allow for inflation.

Endowment life assurance

For many people, endowment life assurance represents the ideal, although when we are young, when there are so many calls on our limited resources, it may be prohibitively expensive. It offers the prospect of a payment whether the person assured in the policy survives or not. Either the policy will mature and the tax-free lump sum will be paid to the policy-holder, or he/she will die and the payment will be made to the heirs. When endowment comes with profits, the payout after, say, 20 or 25 years can be well over twice the original sum assured. So endowment life assurance represents a means of providing a family with hefty amounts of capital at particular stages in their life.

This means that endowment life assurance has two functions: (a) it provides cover against untimely death, in the same way as a whole-of-life or a term policy, and (b) it also plays an important role in family financial planning through providing tax-free lump sums, which can be timed to be paid according to the needs of the policy-holder. Such lump sums can then be reinvested to supplement the family's income, particularly in retirement, when income tends to fall. It must be remembered, however, that no particular level of profits can be guaranteed. The with-profits element, often called the bonus, is announced every year, and for the past few years policy-holders have done very well indeed. The most reputable companies, however, do not make exaggerated claims for the profits which can be made. As a general rule they suggest in their promotion a profits growth of seven per cent a year. Most companies have beaten this level by a handsome margin in recent years. This is partly due to the investment skills of the people who manage the funds of insurance companies; but it has not taken that much expertise in recent years to do well in the stock market—from 1974 to 1986 world markets rose steadily, with very few hiccups—but we may well now be entering a period when investment managers of all kinds will need to show far more skill than in the past if they are to continue to beat the seven-per-cent growth forecast.

Anyone buying with-profits life assurance gets the benefit of these skills, whatever type of life assurance they buy. So, if you have time, it is worthwhile when you are choosing your insurance company to try to find out how its recent level of bonuses compares with those of other companies. Looking simply at the last year will not do: you need to know performance over a few years. And, having said that, you have to remember that what you are looking at is the past, and that there is no guarantee that a company will perform as well—or indeed as badly—in the future. Investment managers change jobs and retire, so it is better to assume the seven-per-cent profits element than to expect rather more.

Endowment life assurance has become increasingly popular as mortgages linked to life assurance have grown in appeal. A great deal of the

DEALING WITH SALESMEN

Do not negotiate any insurance deal with someone who just turns up on the doorstep without an appointment.

● Do not let salesmen wander about your house. They could be taking notes of your belongings.

● Make every salesman identify himself and the company for which he works.

● Be very suspicious if anyone starts off by saying they are doing a 'survey' and then goes on to try to sell you some life or other insurance.

● Do not sign on the spot. Ask for literature and study it when you are alone, or discuss the matter with members of your family.

● Insist on written details of any policy you are offered.

● Ask the salesman what commission he is getting. If he refuses to tell you, be suspicious. You will have to pay his commission and any administrative charges in setting your policy on the books before your policy will start earning bonuses. He is now required to reveal the level of his commission.

● Remember that, if you have failed to follow the above rules, there is always the cooling-off period during which you can change your mind. It is not unusual for people to sign under pressure; the cooling-off period is for their protection.

attraction went out of these mortgages when tax relief on insurance premiums was abolished in 1984. To regain momentum, most building societies abolished the small extra interest charge they made on endowment mortgages to bring them to the same level as repayment mortgages.

The fact that endowment policies have a set life (the 'maturity' date as well as the death benefit) has a price: this form of life assurance, particularly where there is a with-profits element, is by far the most expensive. However, in their efforts to increase the business, insurance companies have developed a form of low-cost endowment which is specifically linked to mortgage loans. A further refinement is the low-start low-cost policy (see page 65). If you are thinking about life assurance quite aside from your mortgage, endowment does not really offer good value for money when you are very young. In particular, the non-profits variety is a poor choice. The premiums paid in the life of such a policy are not as much as the total sum which will be paid out at the end of the period, but even so, allowing for inflation, which over a 20- or 25-year period is likely to average at least five per cent a year, most people would do better to put the same amount of money into a savings scheme and let the capital accumulate. For instance, it would cost a 30-year old man about £29 a month for a £10,000 endowment policy on his own life (a little less on that of his wife, assuming she is the same age). Over a 20-year period, this would mean a total cost of just under £7,000 to get the £10,000 benefit. If instead (although it is unlikely that anyone would go on so long) he were to save £29 a month in almost any way for the same period at, say, an average rate of interest of seven per cent, the accumulated capital at the end would be £12,000. What is more, the saver would have access to the money in case of need. In an endowment policy, the money would be tied up for 20 years unless the policyholder chose to surrender the policy; as we shall see, that is a costly thing to do.

With-profits endowment is a different matter, and policies can be tailored to mature at certain stages in life—e.g., when the children go to secondary education or university, when they marry, or when we retire. Even so, you really need to be sure that you can afford it. A with-profits endowment for £10,000, to use the above example, would cost the 30-year old man over £43 a month, or £10,300 over 20 years. True, the lump sum payment would be more in the region of £23,000—in comparison with the £10,000 in the case of a non-profit policy—but this is still a lot of money to tie up for 20 years. Taking on such a policy is a matter for careful consideration.

On balance, endowment assurance is best avoided at the early stages of married life, apart from low-cost endowment policies linked to mortgages. There are far better places to put your money under schemes which are more flexible and which can be altered as family needs change.

Joint life

Life assurance policies need not be in just one name. As noted (see page 100), married couples can have joint cover for their mortgages for less than double the cost. Partners in a business or co-directors can also buy joint life or last-survivor policies (these can be an important element in protecting a business, but are not worth considering here). There is, incidentally, nothing to stop friends or brothers and sisters from taking out such policies. Both parties will have to fill in the proposal form, and the premium level will be calculated from the answers given. Most joint life policies pay out the benefits on the first death, but there are also last-survivor policies, which are particularly useful if they are whole-of-life policies, because they can be used by a husband and wife who have left all their assets to one another to pay any inheritance tax to which the total estate may be liable on the second death. We will look at these in detail later (see page 199).

Unit-linked policies

We saw when looking at mortgage options that unit-linked policies are beginning to be used for mortgages (see page 67), with the attendant risk of unit trusts being eliminated by setting minimum levels of insurance cover. It is of course possible to take out any form of unit-linked policy, and these have become increasingly popular in recent years, providing people with a regular saving scheme protected by insurance, with the possibility of quite large profits over the years if stock-market prices rise. Most life-assurance policies have a cash (surrender) value which grows each year (see later, page 107). In a unit-linked policy, the value at any time is linked directly to the value of the units in the fund into which the balance of premiums goes after the life cover is paid. As with all types of life assurance, it is essential to take a fairly long-term view of such a policy: the profits will not come early. Ten years is a popular length of time, and monthly premiums can start quite low if you search around, although a £20 or £25 minimum monthly payment is quite usual. The level of life assurance guaranteed will normally be 75 per cent of the total premiums you pay over the term of the policy. You choose which unit trust you want, and you can usually switch to a new fund for a small charge during the course of the policy if you are not satisfied with your current one.

At the end of the period, you have a choice of taking a tax-free lump sum (this is a qualifying policy under the rules), or you can go on paying premiums to build up your capital further, or make the policy *paid up*; this means that you no longer pay any premiums but the units you already have are not sold, and go on accumulating value (assuming stock prices rise, of course).

Some of these plans allow a tax-free income rather than a lump sum to be taken at the end of the policy. Such an option is probably attractive only to people with plans maturing on retirement.

Although these plans have a life-assurance element, they should not be thought of as a major means of providing life cover. They are basically a savings plan with added protection in the event of the death of the saver during the term of the plan.

Single premium policies

Insurance companies also offer policies known as single premium bonds, which are linked to unit trusts or other investment funds.

What happens is that the investor pays a sum of money, usually a

ANNUAL COST FOR £50,000 SUM ASSURED*

| Man† of Age | Whole-of-life insurance | | | Term Assurance[1] | | Endowment |
	With-Profits[3]	Low-Cost[4]	Unit-Linked[5]	Level	Increasable[2]	With-Profits[1]
20	£804	£144	£180	£60	£72	£1,956
25	£924	£192	£180	£60	£72	£1,968
30	£1,104	£264	£180	£96	£72	£1,980
35	£1,260	£360	£228	£145	£84	£2,016
40	£1,488	£492	£360	£240	£132	£2,076
45	£1,764	£696	£612	£324	£204	£2,736
50	£2,112	£984	£900	£432	£336	£3,744
55	£2,544	£1,056	£1,320	£564	£564	£5,652
60	£3,228	£2,004	£2,296	—	£948	—
65	£3,828	£2,904	£3,312	—	—	—
69	£4,560	£3,432	£4,764	—	—	—

*Standard rates.
†Women pay the same as a man four years younger.

[1]25 years or to near age 65 (i.e., 20, 15, 10 years for age 45 and over). [2]Premiums rise every 3 years over age 34; sum insured can go up by 30% every 3 years. [3]Sum insured will rise with bonus additions. [4]Premiums stop at age 75 (at 80 for age 69). [5]Sum insured or premiums can rise after 10 years.

minimum of £500 (although it may be £2,000) to buy the bond. A certain number of units in a chosen fund are allocated to the bond. Later, additional investments can be made, normally in multiples from £250 to £1,000.

It is the bond which holds the investments, not the bond-holder directly. There are buying and selling prices for the bond—a gap of about 5 per cent between them is usual—and this is quoted in various newspapers.

The insurance companies normally pay any Capital Gains Tax on the bond, although not invariably, and when they do the bond price is adjusted to take account of it. Before buying, check how CGT is dealt with, as this may have an impact on the annual exemption you are allowed (see page 201).

There are a great number of bonds on offer—some general, some specializing in different areas and industries, and some more risky than others. Seek advice if you are not sure what to choose.

Most insurance companies allow you to have a limited change of mind about your investment if you think you can do better elsewhere. One switch a year is usually free, but £10 or £20 per switch may be charged for further switches.

The bonds carry life cover, which varies from company to company and declines with age, and there may also be a penalty if bonds are cashed during the first four or five years of their life.

An attractive feature of the bonds is that, for basic-rate taxpayers at least, they can offer a potentially tax-free income. This can be useful as a contribution to school fees (see page 11), if a bond is held for some years.

Check on all the possible features before buying a bond.

Surrender values

One should never overlook the long-term nature of life assurance. Before you take out a policy it is wise to look carefully at your budgeting to be sure that you can afford it, because, if you cannot, defaulting may cost you dear. Insurance companies do not like to lose money on policies, and setting-up and commission costs can be high and must be cleared before the insurance company is willing to give the policy-holder any money back. Thereafter, the company will work out a surrender value if the policy-holder asks for it. Surrender values are never generous. Straight-term policies never have a surrender value, and the best figures come from with-profits endowment. A non-profits policy will probably be worth nothing if the policy is surrendered in less than four years, and even most with-profits policies do not start to have a surrender value until two years' premiums have been paid. A 20-year endowment policy with profits would probably have to run for about seven years before anything more than the total premiums paid would be repaid on surrender, because the with-profits element grows most rapidly during the latter half of a policy. Whole-of-life policies may not have a surrender value at all until they have been running for about ten years.

If this all sounds somewhat vague, it is because companies have different approaches to surrender; and it might be worthwhile, before you take out a policy, to find out what the company you are considering does in this respect. If you are thinking in terms of surrender before you start, however, you should ask yourself whether you ought to be considering life assurance at all—at least that particular type, if you are not going for the cheapest available. Think very carefully about the commitment you are making: you may think that your planning cannot go wrong, but insurance companies say that almost half the policies taken out are surrendered within seven years for one reason or another, so clearly people are either overextending themselves or are simply buying the wrong policies in the first place.

This may be because of high-pressure salesmanship by agents more concerned to make their commission than to sell you the right sort of policy to suit your circumstances. So, once you have worked out as carefully as possible whether you can afford the long-term commitment involved in life assurance, make sure that the company, broker or other agent selling the policy to you explains it fully to your entire satisfaction. You may lose some of the money you have paid in if you surrender, but the agent's commission, once paid, will not be called back in by the company.

If you simply cannot afford any future premiums but would like to retain the life cover you have already paid for, you can ask the company to have the policy 'paid up' instead. When this is done, you pay no more premiums, but you do not claim the surrender price. The money stays with the company until the date when the policy would have matured or until your death, if it is a whole-of-life or term policy. During that time, it continues to share in profits, although at a lower level than it would have done had you gone on paying premiums. This means that eventually there will be some tax-free payment. Unless you absolutely have to get your hands on some cash, a paid-up policy is often a better option than a surrender.

Life-assurance surrender values may be increased by the new commission deal worked out by the insurance industry. Previous attempts to reach such an agreement have not been particularly successful, but the Financial Services Act (1986) has made it imperative.

Until the act was passed, companies had no need to reveal commission levels to customers, but the new City watchdog—the Securities and Investment Board—decreed that, unless enforceable agreements could be agreed, all commissions paid on any life-assurance or investment deals would be disclosed.

Commissions differ not only from company to company but also from policy to policy within the same company. They are commonly part of the so-called 'front-end loading', the total charges which must be paid on a policy before it starts earning profits or bonuses.

From January 1988 front-end loading will be abolished, and commissions will be spread over the first few years of a policy. A ceiling of 25 per cent on the amount of commission which can be paid on any premium has been imposed. This means that the overall commission earned by the salesman will not fall, but will be spread out over a period. The move should raise surrender values quite substantially without putting the insurance broker, agent or salesman out of business.

Temporary financial difficulties

If you expect your financial problems to be short-term and do not want to give up your policy—for example, you may become temporarily unemployed—tell the insurance company. Today various arrangements can be made to tide the policy-holder over temporary difficulties. It is as well to let the company know immediately a problem arises.

Because of previous high-pressure sales techniques, the government has gone some way towards protecting the potential purchaser of life assurance from making a mistake. The Insurance Companies Act of 1974 gave people who had recently bought life assurance a 'cooling off' period during which they could change their mind and cancel the contract. Virtually all life policies are covered by the Act, including unit-linked policies which are taken out on one's own life or that of one's spouse. Not covered are nonconvertible term policies which are taken out for a period of seven years or less (these include policies to cover a holiday or a specific journey, for instance) and any life cover which forms part of a personal hire-purchase or credit-sale agreement.

The cooling-off period does not last very long. It lasts until the latest day of the following:

- the date on which the policy-holder knows that the first premium has been paid,
- the date on which the policy-holder knows that the contract has been entered into, or
- ten days after the statutory notice has been received by the potential policy-holder from the company.

Of course, policy-holders and companies may argue about the exact date in the first two instances, although it is difficult to argue about the third. Companies tend to be generous about the cooling-off period; if someone is arguing about it too much at the outset they are obviously a potential surrenderer, and short-term policies are simply not worth the companies' while. Cooling-off, incidentally, does not apply in law in the Channel Islands, although companies generally do allow a similar cooling-off period there.

Read the statutory notice carefully. It will tell you what your rights as a policy-holder are, as well as the level of premiums to be paid, the frequency of them, and the length of time for which they have to be paid. It will set out the benefits which are guaranteed to accrue either when the policy matures or on your death, or, in the case of those whole-of-life policies where premiums cease at a particular age, when the policy is in effect paid up. The notice will not mention any level of bonus which will be made, but, in the case of a low-cost endowment policy or a low-start low-cost policy, it will quote the minimum amount to be paid out on death.

A statutory notice is required in law (except in the Channel Islands), and does not vary from company to company in what is required, so you should check what it says against what you have been offered. It will have something to say about surrender or paid-up values, which do vary between companies. Unless you check around, you will not be able to tell whether the company is being generous in this respect or not.

Protection against sickness

Of course, many disasters other than death can strike at a family's financial stability. It is very difficult, for instance, to maintain your standard of living if unemployment suddenly hits one or both wage-earners. The social-security system provides a safety net, but not such that a family is completely protected. (For invalidity allowances etc., see pages 212–214.)

One thing a family can do is to provide itself with cover in the event of the breadwinner(s) being taken ill. Various forms of insurance have been developed over the years, and the costs are not prohibitive. It is only right to say that this form of insurance comes further down the list than mortgage and life cover, and it should not be undertaken until a check has been made with your employer to find out what he or she will provide in cases of long-term sickness. And, as with unemployment, the state provides some help to people too ill to work. At present, the weekly rate for any person paying full National Insurance contributions (the few remaining married women who pay only industrial injury benefit cannot claim) is £30.05, and an additional £18.60 comes for a wife or any other adult dependant. The rates change each year, as do most social security benefits, with the upgrading coming each April. For a family with a couple of dependent children, the total (including child benefit of £7.25 which is paid directly to the mother) is £63.15 which is usually not enough to provide a family with its basic necessities, particularly if the illness is a long one. The employer is responsible for paying the first 28 weeks of benefit in any tax year; after that the state takes over. State sickness pay applies to the employed, the unemployed and the self-employed, although the self-employed do not get the earnings-related part of the payment, so it is very important for them to provide themselves with extra cover against being taken ill.

Most illness is short-term, of course, and many families can cope with this—particularly since employers do not normally deduct any wages or salary for just a few days off, or even a few weeks if the company has a sickness fund. Such funds may be entirely noncontributory on the part of employees, or there may be a contribution rate which varies depending on how much is in the fund at any one time, and the benefits may vary likewise. Many employers today take out a group policy to cover sick employees. Claims on this will be paid to the employer, who can then pass the money on to the employee as part of earned income. If someone is ill for a very long time, the insurer may insist on a medical examination by its own doctor to ensure that the case is genuine.

Permanent health insurance

Employees and the self-employed—for whom it is even more important—can take out insurance to provide them with a regular income if they suffer a long-term illness. This cover is good, because once it has been taken out the insurer cannot cancel or alter the terms, no matter how ill the policy-holder is or how long the illness lasts. Premiums naturally rise with age, on the basis that, the older you are when you take out the cover, the more likely it is that you will soon suffer serious illness. Women, too, are disadvantaged in this type of insurance—in three ways: (a) they cannot get cover at all for absence from work through pregnancy and childbirth; (b) they usually have to pay much more than a man of the same age for the same cover—as much as 80 per cent extra; and (c), if they are married women working at home, they may find it extremely difficult to get cover for a period when they might be too ill to take care of the family and need

ANNUAL PREMIUMS FOR £10,000 A YEAR PHI*

Starting after sickness of:

Age†	1 month	3 months	6 months	1 year	2 years
20	£192	£120	£96	£72	£72
25	£216	£120	£96	£96	£72
30	£240	£144	£120	£96	£96
35	£288	£168	£144	£120	£96
40	£336	£216	£192	£120	£120
45	£408	£264	£216	£192	£168
50	£480	£360	£288	£240	£216
55	£624	£456	£384	£336	£288

*Premiums will vary, sometimes considerably, from company to company.
†Men: women's rates may be up to 80 per cent higher.

to hire someone to do this. So punitive are the terms for women that they should not take out this type of insurance unless they are very high earners.

These kinds of policies differ greatly and, depending on the terms you seek, their cost can also vary a great deal. What the policy-holder gets if he or she is unable to work because of sickness or an accident is a weekly payment which goes on as long as the person is unable to work, or reaches a particular age (perhaps the state retirement age) which is agreed beforehand. Generally payments start not immediately but 13 weeks after the absence from work commenced. By varying the terms and conditions of the policy one can bring down its cost. If, for instance, you are prepared to defer the start of payments until you have been away from work for six months or even longer (whether you can do this will depend to some extent on what arrangements your employer makes), the policy will be much cheaper. Rates in this type of insurance vary enormously, so it is well worth shopping around. Try not to pay more than the average. Rates rise sharply with age, so it is as well to take out cover as soon as possible. Remember that, once the premium has been fixed, the company cannot raise it or cancel the cover. Remember also that the cover is provided only for conditions which develop after you have taken out the insurance, so you must be certain to come clean about any medical condition you may have when you first buy such a policy; otherwise, your claim will, quite rightly, not be met. If you are in poor health, you may have to take a medical and your premiums may be loaded to take account of your condition.

If you are considering this kind of insurance—called Permanent Health Insurance (PHI) because it assures that, whatever your actual medical state, your financial health is assured to some extent—get several quotes from different companies before deciding. If you are a woman, it is worth arguing about the premium: it may not get you anywhere, but some women have been taking PHI cases to the European Court, alleging that they are discriminatory, and eventually one of them may win their case. Similarly, of course, a man could perhaps eventually also bring a successful case on the grounds that the premiums on standard life-assurance policies discriminate against him because he is a man.

Medical expenses

Fortunately most illnesses, particularly when we are relatively young, do not last long, but they do occasionally require specialist treatment and hospitalization. The question then arises whether we use the facilities of the National Health Service or opt instead for private treatment. This can be prohibitively expensive for most people, so insurance policies exist to cover many of the costs. It has to be admitted that medical-expenses cover is not cheap, but even so the number of people taking it out each year in the United Kingdom is rising. One reason is that people fear that treatment under the NHS is not as good as 'going private'. This is not so: NHS hospitals offer full and comprehensive treatment, and quite often people using private medicine find they are paying for NHS facilities which they could have had for nothing. Most doctors say that you are better off under the NHS. Nevertheless, many people prefer private medical care. As a result, a lot of companies offer it to their more senior executives—and it is certainly worth bargaining when you start a new job to see if you can be included in any scheme (although, if you are, it is a fringe benefit which will eventually be taxable). It may be possible to have your spouse included in your cover and even, although this is much less likely, your children.

There are distinct benefits in having private medical treatment. Perhaps the most important is that you can choose when and where you have your treatment. This can be extremely important for the self-employed: waiting lists in the NHS are sometimes very long, and if for any reason you are forced to miss your appointment you could find yourself back at the end of the queue. Another advantage of private medicine to companies is that they know that their senior executives can have medical care immediately they need it for conditions that may impair efficiency, even if they are not life-threatening.

Yet a further plus in private medical treatment is privacy. This can be extremely important to some people—just as important and perhaps even more so than the matter of timing. A private hospital or the private section of an NHS hospital guarantees that the patient will have a private room, or perhaps a bed in a very small ward. Visitors are allowed at any time and patients usually have constant access to a telephone.

We hear a great deal about costs in the NHS; they are even higher when it comes to private medical treatment, and it is as well to remember that we all contribute to the NHS through taxes and National Insurance contributions. Although publicity often suggests that there are queues for all NHS treatments, this is not so: queues vary depending on the condition we have and the area in which we live. There is no doubt that, for unusual and expensive operations, it is better to live in London, close to the major teaching hospitals.

Because of these differences, if you want cover for private medical treatment and have to pay for it yourself, but want to keep down the cost, you should shop around before deciding on what policy suits you best. Some companies provide fully comprehensive cover, and the cost rises according to (a) the number of people covered, (b) their ages, and (c) where you live. A family of four with the parents in their thirties could well pay over £800 a year for full medical cover. This is a lot of money, so it would probably be better to limit the cover to the parents. Children are rarely concerned about privacy, and it is only in those families where both parents are working in senior positions that the timing of their children's hospital treatment is important.

Debatably, far too much of this type of cover is taken out for rather dubious benefits. There is a sort of caché attached to private medical treatment which really does not mean very much at all. Snobbism is not absent when people decide to take out this cover, and particularly the young should ask themselves a series of questions before embarking on medical-expenses cover.

If you decide to go ahead with a policy, there are certain things you must look out for. For instance, there may be a limit on the amount of money available to treat your illness. The sum guaranteed may not be enough to cover your costs if you need a great deal of treatment. Again, you will be unlikely to get cover for a problem which already exists when you join, although this may not be true if you are part of a group scheme taken out by your employer.

If you decide that you cannot afford comprehensive medical-expenses cover, there are policies available which are cheaper and guarantee, for example, that if you cannot get treatment quickly on the NHS you can have what you need done privately at any price. It is extremely important to read what is available on these policies: it is no use paying premiums for years and then finding that you are not covered.

By far the biggest company offering medical-expenses cover in the United Kingdom is the British United Provident Association (BUPA), which has about 75 per cent of the market. The other two big ones are Private Patients Plan (PPP) and the Western Provident Association. There are many other small companies, but with these three taking up 98 per cent of the market you are likely to end up with one of them. Their addresses are:

- BUPA, Provident House, 122 High Street, Bromley, BR1 1TB
- PPP, Eynsham House, Crescent Road, Tunbridge Wells, Kent TN1 2PL
- WPA, Culver House, Culver Street, Bristol BS1 5JE

Accident insurance

To round off the insurance one needs to protect one's spouse and children, it is worthwhile considering some kind of accident insurance. You will probably be covered by accident insurance at work, but outside it you will need separate cover if your family is to be truly protected. First of all, there is simple insurance against death or disablement, and policies can often be extended to cover other members of your family. The cost is about £30 for £25,000's worth of cover should you be killed or disabled or lose a limb or an eye. Some policies allow a payment of £50 a week if you are temporarily away from work following an accident, so, if you cannot afford PHI, it may be worth considering accident insurance, so that you and your family have some temporary protection at least.

It is important to read any policy document carefully to look for the 'exclusions'. These set out what kind of accident is *not* covered by the policy. You will usually find that injuries incurred in a number of sporting activities and other pursuits are not covered. This list can be a long one, and may include not just such activities as hang-gliding and motor-racing but also hockey, football, rugby and squash. Insurance companies do not like the idea of you going mountaineering, sailing, potholing, or even riding—and they look even more askance at boxing or wrestling. Check to see if the policy carries an option to extend, for an extra premium, the cover to accidents following these activities.

You will also have to die or be disabled fairly soon after any accident for the benefit to be claimed. If you die more than one year later, the cover claim will usually not be met (although some companies do allow a two-year period). Weekly payments normally last for up to two years, and cover ceases on retirement at age 65 (although this consideration is of little interest to the newly married). If your policy does not carry a dangerous-sports option and you are, say, a regular squash player, it is a good idea to take out extra cover, particularly if your earning capacity would be damaged following an accident. It is impossible to give any estimate of costs. You may find that you have to go to a specialist broker and that your only means of getting insurance is through Lloyds, although there are companies which offer cover for particular pursuits to people who are not actually professional sportsmen or women. Among the larger companies, General Accident has a family sports policy. You will probably have very little choice about the kind of cover you can get, and you will have to pay whatever premium is demanded. You may also find that there are *still* some exclusions in such policies—if they sound alarming, it is perhaps better to give up the sport!

Twins

There is one further risk which a young married couple should consider: the possibility of producing two or more children at once. You may well be quite happy in a general sense about having twins, but two babies cost more than one and the extra money devolving to you from an insurance policy can come in handy. Such a policy is particularly sensible if there is a history of twins in the family—although of course then the premium will be more expensive. Where there is no family history of twins, the policy should cost between £2 and £2.50 for each £100 cover for a woman under 25. The maximum allowed is usually £1,500, which would cost between £30 and £37.50. There may be a minimum premium of £25, which would give a payment of £1,250 in the event of twins being born.

In cases of frequent recurrence of twins, the premium could be much higher and insurance may be refused where a woman has been taking fertility drugs (because these are quite likely to produce multiple births). If, however, triplets or even more children arrive, under the terms of a normal policy the payment may be doubled. This is, however, such a small risk that insurance companies are prepared to take a chance on it. One or two companies will cover you if you are on fertility drugs, but they will make you pay more for the privilege. Sometimes there is a condition that no payment will be made for twin babies who are born very prematurely and fail to survive.

It is worth noting that you must take out this form of cover very early in your pregnancy—at least six months before delivery, and well before it is confirmed by your doctor that you are expecting twins; the doctor must also confirm the delivery date. Then, if twins arrive, it's 'cash on delivery'!

Making a claim

Most of us make a claim on one or other of our insurances at some time in our lives, whether it is on the contents of our house, our car or someone else's life. When we make our claim we can sometimes have quite a shock: claims are not automatically met. We may think we are covered and our claim may be quite genuine, but the insurance company will not always pay out—often with justification. This can even happen with life policies. A company might not be prepared to meet a claim, or perhaps not meet it fully, if, say, someone had insured themselves at a stage in their lives when they knew they had terminal cancer or severe heart disease. It is important, therefore, to reveal all relevant details when taking out a policy—whether these might be a health condition, a particular risk of flood or subsidence in your home, a bad driving record, or whatever.

It is also important, particularly when it comes to contents insurance, to insure your contents for their full value (see page 79). If you do not, and later make a claim, it is highly likely that the insurance company will meet not the full value of the loss but only a proportion, based upon the actual cover you have taken out. For example, if your contents are worth £10,000 but you have insured them for only £5,000, and someone comes along and steals your TV, video and record player worth in total £2,000, you will probably get only £1,000 from your insurance company.

If you think that you have had a bad deal from the insurance company, and despite all your arguments it fails to meet your claim, you may be able to take your case to the Insurance Ombudsman Bureau. This is an independent body financed by the larger insurance companies which arbitrates in cases of dispute. Going to the ombudsman does not necessarily mean that your complaint will be met, but if the bureau finds in your favour it can award you up to £100,000 against the company. Before considering your complaint, the ombudsman will want to be satisfied that you have already taken all reasonable steps to work out an agreement with the insurance company. It is no use simply running off to him immediately the company refuses to pay your claim: you will have to have made several attempts to reach a settlement. Also, the ombudsman will not arbitrate if you have already started proceedings in a court of law. A further proviso is that you must make your complaint within six months of the company refusing to meet your claim or refusing to meet it in full. The ombudsman finds in the complainant's favour in less than 10 per cent of cases, because complaints arise most often because a policy does not cover what the policy-holder thinks it does. In other words, the policy-holder has not read the document carefully, so make sure that you do this. A threat to apply to the ombudsman can often get your claim settled immediately, but do not overuse this ploy. (See page 243 for address and telephone number.)

Spotcheck

When you marry

● make a new will immediately and discuss its contents with your spouse; if you both wish, make joint wills

In all matters concerning life assurance

● decide clearly at the start what kind of risk you want covered and to what extent
● work out precisely how much you can afford over the longer term
● be certain that you have chosen the correct policy for your needs
● get the salesperson/agent/broker/company to explain the policy and its benefits to you before signing the contract
● make sure that you provide the company with the fullest possible information
● after signing, think the whole matter through again and take advantage of the cooling-off period if necessary
● consider joint life policies for husband and wife
● remember that the with-profits element—'bonuses'—of life-assurance policies cannot be guaranteed, and beware of forecasts of very high bonuses; always calculate on seven per cent, no matter what the company may suggest
● if you are in temporary financial difficulties, inform the company immediately: do not simply stop paying the premiums
● surrender a policy only as a last resort: if you cannot go on paying, it is preferable to have it paid up.

To protect your family against the loss of income in case of long-term illness

● if you are a man, consider a Permanent Health Policy (PHI), but ask for several quotations, because premiums and benefits vary considerably
● if you are a woman, a PHI policy may be prohibitively expensive, but you should at least take out accident insurance
● think carefully before taking out cover for private medical expenses—policies vary, as does need; remember that it is rarely worthwhile to cover children
● accident cover is cheap, so consider it for all the family

Commonsense Borrowing

11

Credit

Very few homes are set up today without the couple involved living in a house with a great deal of furniture and domestic appliances which they do not really own. The house is not yours until the mortgage is totally repaid, and nor is the furniture if you are still buying it on HP. Until all these things are paid for, the 'owner' is (usually) technically the hirer. The volume of consumer credit to individuals in Britain is enormous: at the end of 1986 there was a massive £5,000 million of debt outstanding, or over £900 for every man, woman and child. Despite economic setbacks and large-scale unemployment, the amount rises steadily every year.

If we add together mortgage commitments and other household bills, some life insurance and further payments in credit sales, it becomes clear that the financial burden early in marriage can be a very heavy one. Unless care is taken, it is very easy for a young couple to overreach themselves. There are simple ways to avoid this, but they do require vigilance and planning, because today it is all too easy to borrow.

Let us be clear about this right at the start: there is nothing wrong with borrowing money to get the things we want in life—so long as we are not too greedy. It is important to remember, for instance, that using your credit card and not settling the total bill immediately it is presented to you is a form of taking credit, and must be counted as part of your outstanding debt.

Typical overborrowers

Before we look at ways of borrowing, here is a picture of the kind of family that lenders over the years have come to recognize as one which is likely to overborrow:

- The parents are young and have more than the average number of children.
- The family has a higher-than-average income. This may seem odd, but poorer wage earners have less chance of getting credit whereas the more affluent family may feel that it can run some hire purchase and all its credit cards to their limits.
- No one in the family takes responsibility for the family's total spending. Financial decisions are best taken jointly, with both husband and wife fully aware of the exact financial position at any one time. If the couple have a joint account to pay bills, it is better that only one of them signs the cheques, so that there is less danger of running into overdraft through one forgetting to tell the other that a cheque or cash has been drawn. If

possible—especially nowadays, when there are rarely bank charges if accounts are kept in credit—each partner should have an individual account for personal spending and contribute to a joint account to pay the household bills. The contribution should be regular and revised upwards as bills increase, and the partners should contribute according to their salary level.

- The newly married couple may not have been accustomed to personal budgeting, and buy without thinking rather than planning their spending. (The way out of this is simply to get into the habit of looking at spending and discussing what you can afford—and, indeed, what you are planning to buy and if you actually need it.)
- The family is constantly on the move from home to home.
- The couple has recently broken up, with the result that both adults are badly off in comparison with the time when they lived together.
- The couple has a predilection for keeping up with the Joneses—i.e., they try to live above their means.
- The couple may not read very much. They make financial decisions on the basis of what they see on television rather than reading and making enquiries about what they are doing and discussing the purchase thoroughly before going ahead.

Most of the people who come into these various categories are under 30 and not yet properly established in their careers or with their own homes. If you think you are in danger of carrying too much debt in relation to your total family income, take great care before involving yourself in further commitments.

It would be convenient if one could state fairly precisely how much HP or other borrowing one should have. But it is impossible to be exact. As a general rule of thumb you should not take on mortgage commitments of more than 20 per cent of your total disposable family income after tax. Except in very unusual circumstances, total insurances, including life assurance (although that may be part of your mortgage costs, as we have seen—page 63), should not be more than another 10 per cent, with a maximum of a further 15 per cent for any other borrowings. This gives a total of 45 per cent, leaving 55 per cent for all other expenses—some of which, like food, water rates, gas and electricity and phone bills, will be relatively fixed and unavoidable. Others, such as clothing and holidays, will be more flexible.

Have you borrowed too much?

You will very quickly become aware that you have borrowed too much if your total monthly outgoings are consistently more than your net monthly income. But there are warning signs which, if you heed them, mean that you can solve your problem before it becomes acute. For example, you will find you have a lot of debts you are finding hard to pay, each perhaps quite small, but to different lenders—a bank overdraft, credit cards and shopping account cards at their limit, and HP commitments, for instance. You may notice that, having previously been able to clear HP debts in a year, you are suddenly asking for longer-term credit, which will cost more in the end but offers a lower monthly payment. You may also become reluctant to pay an up-front deposit. The last straw is often thinking that, if you put all your debts in one place (by taking out a bank loan, for example), you might solve all your problems. But that in itself can produce another difficulty, in that some people have so little control over their spending that they start building up a whole new series of debts.

Let us assume for the moment that you are not going to get into too much debt, and look at the various sources of borrowing. Whatever means you use to get credit, borrowing for anything other than purchase or improvement of a home (to a limit of £30,000 per person or per married couple) carries no tax relief on the interest paid. The main sources of funds are:

- an overdraft or loan account at the bank on your current account,
- a personal loan from a bank or other lender,
- a credit or charge card, and
- a hire-purchase or credit-sale agreement.

Overdrafts and loan accounts

For most people, an overdraft is the cheapest form of borrowing. An overdraft means that you are using an account which is not in credit; in other words, the bank is allowing you to use money which you do not have. Overdrafts are unique to current accounts: it is only these which are allowed to go into the red.

Having a current account does not automatically mean that you can spend more money than you have: you will have to get the permission of your bank manager, who will set limits on the amount you will be allowed to overdraw and on the time for which you can have the overdraft facility. These limits will depend on your personal circumstances. You should not go lightly into an overdraft, because immediately you will (a) run into bank charges on every transaction in your account and (b) start to pay interest on the amount you have overdrawn.

Nevertheless, if you must borrow, an overdraft is usually the most efficient and cheapest way. The reason is that, while interest is charged every day, it is calculated only on the amount you are overdrawn on that day. This means that, if for example you have an overdraft facility of £500 and have a salary cheque coming in each month for £1,000, there will be some days when you will be in credit, so that no interest is charged on those days. Gradually, as pay day comes closer, your overdraft will rise as you use more money, and the interest costs will gradually rise.

Even if you are paying the same level of interest on an overdraft as you would be on a personal loan or HP agreement, because of the way interest is calculated the charge can be very much less. Interest can be expressed in two ways—the *flat rate* or the *true rate* (or annual percentage rate, APR, as it is today called). The latter can be much higher than the former. If you are paying interest daily, the flat and the true rate are the same, but if you are making repayments on a regular basis the true rate will be higher. This is because, if you are paying in, say, quarterly instalments the interest will be calculated at the beginning of the year, or when you take out the loan or sign the HP agreement for the full year, on the total amount of the loan. Although each quarter you will have reduced your debt, the calculation made at the beginning takes no account of that.

Today the law demands that retailers and providers of personal loans

119

tell customers what the true APR is so, whatever way you are borrowing, you should know exactly what you are paying for the privilege. Sometimes, however, the flat rate will be given in prominent print and the APR shown in only small type. Make no mistake, however. If the stated flat rate is 10 per cent and you are paying monthly, you will really be paying an APR of 19 per cent—i.e., almost double what you thought. To work out the true rate, you should multiply the flat rate by 1.8 if you are paying quarterly, by 1.9 if monthly, and by 2.0 if weekly.

If you have recently married, shop around for credit bargains, because rates can differ quite widely. You may even, if you can pay off the loan within a short period (say nine months or a year), get the loan interest-free. That is obviously better than an overdraft. In normal circumstances, however, the overdraft will be cheaper.

Even better than an overdraft is a loan account, if you can get one. It will run in tandem with your normal current account, which will always stay in credit, with money debited from the loan account rather than from the current account. That way, you get the advantage of overdraft terms of interest and pay no charges on your current account, as it always stays in credit. However, bank managers are often reluctant to offer loan accounts except to their more affluent customers.

The actual rate of interest paid on overdrafts is not fixed at any particular time for all customers. It will depend on how the bank manager views you as a borrower. The general level will be fixed by the bank's current *minimum lending rate*. The ordinary customer pays rather more than that: the rate may be only 2 or 3 per cent above the base rate if you are regarded as a prime customer, but, if you have a poor banking record or ask for your first overdraft, the rate could be 4 or 5 per cent higher than the base rate. If you have a really bad record, of course, the bank will not give you an overdraft. Although they are a cheap way to borrow, banks generally regard overdrafts as only a short-term form of borrowing, to plug a gap: if you want money long-term, you will have to turn to other forms of borrowing.

Personal loans

Personal loans differ from overdrafts in that they are not related to current accounts and are not necessarily made by the high-street banks—many financial institutions offer them. Personal loans also very often carry a higher rate of interest than overdrafts, and the way the interest is charged differs (as we have just seen) because of the way the debt is repaid in fixed regular instalments: the flat rate of interest will be much lower than the annual percentage rate which is actually paid. Personal loans, however, can have their uses and the discipline of the regular repayments is useful for many people. They can also—although this is very rare—be cheaper than overdrafts: the interest rate is fixed when the loan is taken out, and it is conceivable that, over the period, interest rates generally (and therefore those charged on overdrafts) might rise sufficiently to offset the APR on a personal loan.

If you run an overdraft beyond the time given to you by your bank manager, you may find that he or she insists you turn it into a personal loan and run your account in credit. That is less likely today than it used to be, because bank charges become quite punitive once you slip into the red and there is more profit for the bank that way.

Finance companies, which are the organizations financing a hire-purchase loan or credit sale you may have with a shop or store, are also prepared to make personal loans. They are less likely than the bank to ask what you want the money for, but they are more likely to charge you higher interest. Also, they prefer medium-sized loans to very small or very large ones, and some will put a minimum limit (perhaps £200) on what they are prepared to lend. The maximum allowed will depend on the personal circumstances of the applicant.

Credit and charge cards

Another source of credit which is being increasingly used, and which carries a whole host of dangers of overborrowing, is the credit card. The interest rate on credit cards is expressed as so much per cent a month, and it always looks low. But it is as well to remember that, if you pay off as slowly as possible, you can be paying quite a lot of interest: 1–2 per cent per month is 12.7–26.8 per cent per year.

For most of us, however, a credit card is a very useful financial tool as long as we do not let our use of it get out of hand. A newly married couple, in particular, should take care that both are not borrowing to the limit. They should be particularly careful if they have a joint card which they both use, and should note down the cost every time they use it.

As far as a woman is concerned, it is a good idea for her to get a card before marriage, if at all possible. Credit-card companies insist that they do not discriminate against women, but the way that they work out people's credit ratings can mean that married women in particular, are less likely than men to get cards.

CREDIT CARDS IN THE UK

Credit cards from banks*	Number
Access	8.3m
Barclaycard	7.9m
Trustcard	2.4m
Other Visa	0.8m

Charge cards	
American Express*	0.6m
Diners Club	0.3m
Company cards	0.15m

Credit and charge cards are big business today in the UK, with credit cards far outnumbering charge cards as these figures for 1986 show. The market is probably close to saturation point now, unless the charge companies bring down their criteria for accepting cardholders, a move which seems unlikely.

*Excluding gold and company cards.

121

CREDIT RATINGS

The companies which extend credit are increasingly using credit-rating systems to assess an individual's eligibility for loans. It has the benefit of being impersonal, but there is some evidence that the nature of the questions and the weight given to the answers discriminate against women. The reason for this is that women who might be perfectly sound borrowers may score lower points on questions to do with length of service, salary, and professional status than men.

Applicants for credit must fill in a questionnaire which has loaded questions about salary, age, type of job, length of service, other loans, and so on. Every scoring system differs, depending on the lender, but it is difficult to beat the system.

The various answers given to the questions merit different scores. All the scores are added up, and anyone who gets more than a certain total gets the loan. Below it, they do not.

There may be no right of appeal. The only lenders who are prepared to look again are usually the banks.

If you apply for a card, be very certain that you know what you will be getting. There are two forms of cards, the credit card and the charge card. The former—the true credit card—allows you to pay off the bill in full immediately you receive it or by the end of the month in which it arrives, or to pay in instalments. If you pay in full on the due date, there is no interest to pay and in the mean time you will have up to six weeks' credit for nothing. That can be very useful. If you pay in instalments you will be whacked for the full APR. You will be given a spending limit on your card which will be based on estimates of your ability to repay. But credit-card accounts are flexible things, and you can tailor your repayments to suit yourself, staggering them if you are in temporary difficulties or have a lot of calls on your funds for a month or two.

The two main credit cards in Britain are those attached to the international Visa system (including Barclays, the Yorkshire Bank, the TSB, the Co-operative Bank and the Bank of Scotland) and Access (including the Midland, National Westminster and Lloyds), which is linked with the worldwide Mastercharge network.

The charge card, by contrast, is not strictly speaking a credit card, because after presentation to the card-holder the bill must be settled in full by a certain date. If it is not settled, the card company quickly slaps on a hefty interest charge of 3 per cent a month, or 39 per cent a year, and, if you are still recalcitrant, it will withdraw your card so that, the next time you try to use it, the retailer will tell you that you have been 'blacked'. You will not be given a spending limit on your card but, if you wanted to buy something costing thousands of pounds, the retailer might check back with the card company on your ability to settle. Again, it does take time for the bill to come in and in the mean time you will have free credit. As with credit cards, the maximum period of free credit is usually about six weeks, although it can be longer—much longer—if you have made purchase abroad (although the system is becoming increasingly efficient, and foreign bills are being presented rather more quickly than before).

For new families, it can be a good idea to have a joint rather than two individual cards to avoid one partner overspending unknown to the other.

Store cards

There are a wide variety of account cards offered by stores. These may be charge cards, credit cards, or possibly revolving-credit cards. This last type is convenient for many young couples and highly profitable for the stores, because it keeps customers loyal to them. What happens is that the borrower agrees to pay a certain amount each month, and the amount he or she is able to spend in any one year will be between 20 and 30 times that amount. As each payment goes in, the credit facility is extended by the same amount. These accounts are often called 'budget accounts', and the interest on them is often called a 'service charge', but interest is what it is, and, while often it may be around the same level as the interest charged at any one time on a general credit card, in some cases it may be rather more.

Store cards may be confined to one store or may cover a whole chain, regardless of whether they are credit cards, charge cards or revolving-credit cards. You may find that your bank is prepared to offer you a similar revolving-credit account, which of course leaves you free to shop where you like and does not tie you to a particular store or chain.

If your card is lost

If your card is lost or stolen, you will be liable for the first £50 of anything spent on it before you have reported the loss; after that you have no liability. So always keep the telephone number of the card company handy, and do not carry your cards around when you know that you will not use them. It is a bad idea to use your card to buy goods over the phone and give the number, because there is not even a check on your signature. As an added protection, join a credit-card registration company. These do not cost much and can give you peace of mind. If you lose one or indeed all of your cards, a single transfer-charge call will deal with the matter. Card Protection Plan, for instance, costs £9 a year for an individual card and £12 for a joint one. (The telephone number is 01–938 1017.)

Hire-purchase

Although banks and other financial institutions are falling over themselves to give us loans today, a great deal of consumer credit still comes through hire-purchase agreements or credit sales. Borrowing money or running a credit card is usually simply a matter of an agreement between the lender and the borrower; hire-purchase and credit sales are rather more complicated, and are ringed with rules and regulations designed to protect both sides. These rules are incorporated in the Consumer Credit Act, which was passed in 1974 but which was gradually brought into force over the following decade. All agreements for £15,000 or less are covered by the Act, and only people or organizations with a licence to grant credit can advance anything more than £30. Under the Act, when you borrow you are entitled to be told in writing the annual percentage rate of interest

123

(APR) being charged as well as the flat rate. You must also have in writing details of the amount borrowed and of the frequency and number of payments. The deposit you have paid must be stated, as must the cash price and the total price (including interest) which you will eventually pay. These rules are designed to ensure that the purchaser is aware of exactly what they must pay and how the full price has been arrived at.

There are other safeguards, too. Sometimes people are induced to buy things which they do not really want or need. For a period after signing, would-be purchasers have the right to cancel any credit agreement. Until May 1984, this cooling-off period applied only to agreements signed away from the supplier's premises; it did not apply if a purchase had been made on the premises. The reason for the difference was that, in the latter case, the purchaser had actively been seeking to buy the goods, whereas anyone who was approached in the home might sign anything—if only to get rid of the salesman! Now, however, all customers have a right to second thoughts.

The cooling-off period is rather like the one allowed on life-assurance policies. Like that, it does not last forever. In HP or credit sales it lasts until five days after the second copy of the signed agreement has been received in the post. Cooling-off does not apply to purchases made on credit-card sales, although it does on mail order if you have dealt with the agent in your home. If you buy on mail order through the post, you have 14 days in which to change your mind.

The Act also allows the debtor to pay off the loan early without penalty, and usually to receive a rebate of the interest calculated for the full period of the loan. This is a change from the old practice, whereby sometimes there was a penalty for settling early—if it was allowed at all.

All borrowers must now receive a signed copy of the credit agreement, which must contain far more detailed information than previously. There must not, however, be any small print which could mislead the customer, or alter his or her rights. The agreement must contain a box setting out the customer's rights and where he or she can go for assistance.

These rules apply when goods are perfect; there are different criteria when goods are faulty. Before looking at those we will look first at the differences between cash purchases, hire-purchase sales and credit sales.

Cash purchases

Anyone purchasing by cash immediately becomes the owner of the goods in question. These goods cannot in law be returned if they meet three criteria laid down in law in the Fair Trading Act (1973). These criteria are:

● The goods must be of *merchantable quality*. This broadly means that the purchaser must know what condition the goods are in when they are bought. It does not mean that they must be perfect; they can be seconds, but, if they are, they must be known by the purchaser to be so.
● The goods must be *fit for the purpose* for which they are bought. In other words, they must work. If you bought a washing machine that proved not to function, it would obviously not be fit for the purpose for which it was bought—i.e., to wash clothes and get them clean. In such a case, you could demand your money back. You have to have a strong case to force the retailer to take goods back, though. And it is the retailer who must take

them: he or she cannot fob you off by saying that you should return the goods to the manufacturer. It is the retailer's responsibility to recompense you and then seek his or her own redress with the manufacturer.

● The goods must be exactly as they are described on a package, a display or an advertisement. Clearly a silk dress must be made of silk, a pound of biscuits exactly that, and so on.

These rules apply whether you buy for cash, use any form of credit, or buy by mail order.

| Mail order

Buying by mail order is a form of hire purchase, although it is rather more informal. If you are offered payment through an instalment plan, take it, because the mail-order price will include an interest element which is not deductable if you pay the full amount immediately (i.e., you save nothing by paying cash). Mail-order goods can be as cheap as those bought from a shop, because the mail-order companies do not have large overheads in the form of shops (rates) and sales staff (wages), so the interest charged is not apparent. All the normal rules about quality apply to mail-order sales.

| Hire-purchase or credit sale

There is a fundamental difference between a hire-purchase agreement and a credit sale. This difference rarely affects the purchaser, but it is as well to be aware of it. If you buy on hire purchase, you do not become the owner of the goods when you sign the agreement: in law, they do not belong to you until the final instalment is paid (hence the term 'hire purchase'). You are a hirer, just as you would be if, say, instead of buying a car you rented one permanently. This means that the lender has the right to take the goods back if the borrower defaults on payments.

This is not the case, however, if the goods have been purchased by means of a credit-sale agreement: in such agreements, the purchaser becomes the owner at the moment he or she signs up. Of course, someone purchasing on a credit sale may default, and in such cases the lender will demand that all outstanding debt is paid immediately.

There is one thing which follows from the difference. If you have bought something on HP you cannot legally sell it until you have paid for it. This does not apply with credit sales: you are the owner and can do what you like with the goods. You may of course have bought a car on HP and not have finished paying for it when you sell, but the legal process is that you settle the outstanding debt on one car before taking out a new loan on the other.

But the law does not allow the creditor—that is, the lender—to take back goods in all cases of defaulting payments. If you have paid off more than one third of the debt, you can keep the goods unless the lender gets a court order against you. In many cases, the lender will prefer to come to some agreement with you, if you happen to be in some financial difficulty and have defaulted simply because you have not got enough money to pay. Lenders want to get their money back, and they do not like the expensive process of going to law if they can avoid it. They are often willing to extend the repayment period, or allow you to pay only interest for a period and then recommence repaying the loan plus interest. Of course, such arrangements will cost you more money, but they can ease the situation temporarily.

In contrast to the rights of the lender, the rights of the borrower are that he or she can insist the goods be taken back at any time until the final payment has been made. However, the borrower cannot insist on getting his or her money back unless the goods do not meet the criteria laid down in the Fair Trading Act (see page 124).

If you do not want to find yourself involved in a legal action because you cannot pay your instalments, get in touch with the lender immediately you find yourself in difficulty. If you do this, you will almost always be able to work out some new agreement.

Credit ratings

If you want to borrow anything other than a small amount of money when you are purchasing goods on credit, you are almost certain to have your financial standing investigated. This process is known as a credit rating. Lenders, whether they are building societies or finance houses (who pay the money to the retailer on your behalf when you are buying on HP or by a credit sale), may not simply take your word for it that you are financially sound: they may check on you with one of the credit registers. In particular, they will want to know whether you have previously defaulted on a debt—and every year around 500,000 people in Britain do so.

If there has been an order against you for debt and it was for more than £10 (less than that is not officially registered, but some credit registers note that small amount, or even less), the Lord Chancellor's Department will supply details to credit organizations for a fee. Do not think that you will escape notice. If the debt is not repaid within a month, there is a permanent record against the debtor's name, although you can apply to have it removed if you eventually settle your debt. If you have been refused credit because your rating is bad and you think that you have been unfairly treated, you can get a copy of your file for 25p. If the information about you is wrong, and you can prove that it is wrong, the record must be amended within 28 days.

Credit rating—and, it follows, the amount of credit which will be made available to any particular person—will depend upon the past record (if any), present capital (although that is not especially relevant), wages or salary, and other commitments. It is on the basis of these considerations that the lender will assess how much he or she is prepared to lend. It will not be more than the lender thinks the borrower can easily repay.

Too much debt?

Let us assume that you are careful and have worked out your commitments properly, but, even so, you suddenly find you are having difficulty in financing all your debts. This can happen in the most ordered lives. So, what should you do?

● Resolve not to take out any more commitments, however tempting any offers might be.

● Work out your total debts and the repayments involved. If it is clear that, for the time being at least, you cannot meet them, see if the repayment periods of any could be extended, and contact the lender and try to work out a new deal with him or her. It may be that increasing your mortgage is the only way out of the problem, but you have to be careful here because mortgages are for home purchase and improvement only—and you will have to prove that this is the case if the extra borrowed is to qualify for tax relief.

Next, see if you can economize. Perhaps you could solve the problem by swapping your car for a smaller one, which would be cheaper to buy and to run? Or could you cancel your holiday, or stop smoking or drinking?

If you don't drive, don't have a mortgage, smoke or drink, or spend on entertainment and holidays, you are going to find it difficult to economize, but anyone leading such an abstemious life is unlikely to find themselves with debt problems unless they have lost their job (and in that case, lenders are almost invariably sympathetic). If you think that the situation would be helped if you consolidated your debts, by all means take out an overdraft or personal loan, but do not start borrowing all over again or you will eventually reach the stage all sensible people want to avoid: bankruptcy.

Bankruptcy

In Britain very few individuals are declared bankrupt—and, when they are, it is generally not because they have failed to pay their ordinary debts. If mortgage repayments are not made, for instance, a lender will eventually repossess the property. Defaulting on hire-purchase commitments leads ultimately to repossession of the goods. When individuals become bankrupt, it is almost always because they have failed to pay the taxes which are due on their income. Taxes take precedence over any other debt we have. Another cause of bankruptcy, particularly among men, is a failure to make alimony payments as directed by a court.

In simple terms, people become bankrupt when they can no longer pay outstanding debts and when they or any one of their creditors asks for them to be declared a bankrupt. This can happen only after what is called on 'act of bankruptcy'. Proceedings cannot be started until after this, which usually occurs when the person involved has failed to comply with a bankruptcy notice. The creditor must go to court to get an order that the debt must be paid before the notice can be served. The debtor then has seven days in which to pay and, if he or she does not do so, the bankruptcy notice can then be served.

There are other means of having people declared bankrupt, however. The creditor may not be able to find the debtor in order to serve the bankruptcy notice. He or she may have disappeared, or simply have said he or she will not pay, or have disposed of assets which could otherwise be sold to pay the debt. If a person asks to be declared bankrupt, there is a preliminary hearing in court. A receiving order may be made by the court registrar or, less frequently, the registrar may decide that there is no point in going ahead. The same procedure is followed if the bankruptcy petition comes from a creditor, although in that case a copy of the petition must be sent to the potential bankrupt, who then has to present himself at court for the hearing.

Once the receiving order has gone out, all the debtor's assets come under the control of the Official Receiver. This means that the debtor no longer has any control over his or her assets, including his or her money. In a sense, the debtor reverts to the status he or she had before reaching majority. (Incidentally, minors cannot be made bankrupt, as in law they cannot be held responsible for their debts.)

The debtor will have to make a statement of his or her assets and liabilities and, if he or she has any plan for paying off the debts, he or she should put that forward at the same time. Sometimes that is the end of the matter, but if agreement cannot be reached, there is a public examination in court. Every detail of the debtor's financial affairs will now be revealed: this will include an analysis of how the person involved managed to get into the debt. If he or she is declared bankrupt at this point, all his or her assets are removed and transferred to the person appointed by the Court as his or her 'trustee in bankruptcy'.

For practical purposes, what happens then is that the bankrupt is allowed to keep only his or her clothing, bedding and any 'tools of his trade'. He or she is not allowed to have a bank account, or to take out any other form of credit. It follows, too, that all credit and charge cards will have to be surrendered. Even all the bankrupt's wages and salary no longer belong to him or her. He or she will be allowed to keep enough as is 'reasonable' for him or her to live on. This can vary: someone with a rather expensive lifestyle may be allowed rather more than a person who, apart from the debt, lives modestly. Anything left over goes to the trustees, who will start paying off the creditors. It will include not only your wages and salary but any profits from a business. Any assets which can be sold or liquidated, such as the home, stocks and shares or money in a bank account, will also be used to reduce the debt.

It all sounds very embarrassing, to say the least, but to many people being declared bankrupt comes as something of a relief: the worst is known, responsibility for paying the debt has been transferred to someone else, and the bankrupt can get on with day-to-day survival.

A bankrupt can be discharged at any time, either on his or her own application or that of the trustees, if they have settled the debts. Not all bankruptcies are caused by mismanagement by the debtor of his or her funds, and where it has occurred because of factors outside the bankrupt's control—he or she might have been defrauded by someone, for instance—a 'certificate of misfortune' may be given and the bankrupt granted an absolute discharge from the bankruptcy.

Since October 1977, anyone who has been bankrupt for more than ten years receives an automatic discharge. If all the debts have not been paid, the discharge may be 'conditional'. This means that, until all the creditors have been satisfied, the former bankrupt will be required to pay them from any assets he or she may have.

Bankrupts are sometimes tempted to get rid of their assets in an effort to stop the trustees getting their hands on them and handing the proceeds over to the creditors. A common ploy is to sign an interest in a home over to a spouse. This does not work, however, as the trustees can reclaim any property which the bankrupt may have given away within two years of the bankruptcy being declared—this can be anyone, not just a member of the family. The trustee can go even further than that, and take any property back which has been given away within ten years, unless the bankrupt can prove he or she was solvent at the time. Further still, there is no time limit at all on reclaiming any property if it can be proved that you have been attempting to avoid paying creditors.

Similarly, a potential bankrupt cannot choose to pay some creditors rather than others. Creditors must take their place in line after the Inland Revenue, which has priority, followed by local authorities who levy rates and any employees the bankrupt might have; these are known as the preferred creditors. Any money given away to any creditors six months before the bankruptcy is declared can be reclaimed to pay preferred creditors before anyone else gets any money.

If you think that you may have to go bankrupt, take legal advice immediately. It is never too late to try to find ways of solving your problems.

Debts and the law

You must pay any legally incurred debts, but there are limits to how much pressure can be put on you. Basically, the law protects you from any harassment which is physically or mentally threatening. It is illegal to put pressure on you

- by sending letters threatening to take action which look as if they are legal documents because they are printed on special forms: if someone sends one to you, give it to the police
- by coming to your home and threatening you or demanding money
- by threatening you with a debt-collecting agency: debt-collecting agencies face prosecution if they threaten to tell your employer about your debt
- by blackmail: this is a crime.

Spotcheck

Before even thinking about borrowing, have you

- worked out your total outgoings and income each month to make sure that you can afford to repay?
- shopped around for the cheapest form of credit or checked to see if you can get it interest-free?
- tried first of all to get an overdraft from your bank if the annual percentage rate you must pay on HP is much higher?

Before signing the agreement, have you

- understood whether you are buying on a credit-sale or hire-purchase agreement and know the difference?
- checked that you know exactly what interest you are paying?
- read the small print of the contract?

Afterwards, if you have signed the agreement in your home, have you

- reflected whether you really need the goods and, if you do not, taken advantage of the 'cooling-off' period?

If you have problems in paying, have you

- told all the lenders immediately?
- checked to see if you can moderate your spending in any way to enable you to meet your commitments?
- asked your bank manager for help as a last resort?

If you recognize that you are a bad borrower, have you

- consolidated your debts and worked out a realistic time-scale for repayment?
- thrown away your credit cards and resolved never to use them again?

The Taxation of Married People

12

The way in which we are taxed changes fundamentally on marriage. For those on lower incomes, there is a tax advantage in being married: those on higher ones are penalized unless they take action. It is worth looking at the history of taxation to find out why this is so. The law on how married people are taxed goes back to the beginnings of formalized taxation in Britain. At first, married women had no property of their own—anything they had before marriage became the property of their husband on marriage—and so married women did not exist as taxable beings, because they had no income to tax. It was not until the Married Women's Property Act of 1882 that they were allowed to retain their own personal wealth on marriage. Extraordinarily, however, women still automatically cease to exist on marriage as far as the tax inspector is concerned.

One reason is that, when taxes were first imposed, there were very few married women in employment (let alone taxable employment), so it made administrative sense to tax married people together. All single people and married men receive as of right a personal allowance, but married women get an earned-income allowance, which is at the same level as the single person's allowance but, unlike the latter, cannot be set against income from investment and savings. The employer allows for earned-income allowance when assessing what tax he or she should take away from a married woman and remit to the Inland Revenue, but only the husband fills in a tax return. The husband completes this on his own account and on that of his wife, including all their incomes whether from employment or from savings and investment. The taxman totals up the incomes and decides the couple's tax liability. This immediately has several effects:

- As the married man gets an allowance for his wife simply by being married and a working wife gets hers, their joint income is liable for less tax to a certain level (but, and it is a big but, only to a certain level) than the same income of two single people would be. We have what is called a progressive tax system in Britain, which means that the rate of tax rises with income. The total incomes of a married couple reach the higher tax thresholds sooner than do those of two single people, eventually offsetting their gain from the two allowances. With no other tax allowances at all, a couple begins to be penalized for being married when their joint income reaches at least £26,870, of which the wife earns at least £6,545. Below that level they gain.
- A couple where the husband is unemployed and the wife working gets better tax treatment than a couple where the husband is working and the wife unemployed. The rule about the income being that of the man for tax purposes still applies, but the couple get his married man's allowance, plus

131

TABLE FOR TAX AND MARRIED COUPLES

The point at which it becomes profitable for a couple to opt for separate taxation of their earnings is different in every case, depending on the level of the two incomes and what proportion is earned or investment income. Here are four examples of how the system works: the first shows how those on the lower levels of income benefit from being taxed together; the others how couples on the same joint total income can face a quite different tax bill.

Income all earned

taxed together		separately taxed		
Husband £	Wife £	Husband £	Wife £	
10,000 = 20,000	10,000	10,000	10,000	salary
3,795		2,425		personal allowance
	2,425		2,425	wife's earned income allowance
	13,780	7,575	7,575	taxable pay
	3,720.60	2,045.25	2,045.25	tax at 27 per cent
	3,720.60		4,090.50	total tax

Tax saving by being taxed together: £369.90.

Income all earned

taxed together		taxed separately		
Husband £	Wife £	Husband £	Wife £	
15,000 = 30,000	15,000	15,000	15,000	salary
3,795				married man's allowance
		2,425		single person's allowance
	2,425		2,425	wife's earned income allowance
	23,780	12,575	12,575	taxable pay
17,900 at 27% 2,500 at 40% 3,380 at 45%		all at 27%		
	7,354	3,395.25 = 6,790.50	3,395.25	total tax

Tax saving by being separately taxed: £563.50.

but

Income partly earned, partly investment

Husband earning £15,000, wife £9,000, plus £3,000 investment income each.

taxed together		*taxed separately*		
Husband	*Wife*	*Husband*	*Wife*	
£	£	£	£	
12,000	12,000	15,000	9,000	earned income
3,000	3,000	6,000*		investment income
15,000	15,000	21,000	9,000	
= 30,000				
3,795				married man's allowance
		2,425		single person's allowance
	2,425		2,425	wife's earned income allowance
	23,780	18,575	6,575	taxable pay
	17,900 at 27%	17,900	all at 27%	
	2,500 at 40%	675 at 40%		
	3,380 at 45%			
		5,103	1,775.25	
	7,354	= 6,678.25		

*All investment income is taxed as if it belonged to the husband.

Tax saving by being taxed separately: £675.75.

Taking the same total income, but assuming, say, that the wife works only part-time and the disparity between the two incomes is large, particularly taking into account the rules about investment income can mean that even at £30,000 it is more financially advantageous to be taxed together. As in the last two examples, being taxed together would mean a total tax bill of £7,354. Now assume that the husband earns £16,500, his wife £7,500 and that each have £3,000 investment income:

Husband	*Wife*	
£	£	
16,500	7,500	earned income
6,000*		investment income
22,500	7,500	total income
2,425		single person's allowance
	2,425	wife's earned income allowance
20,075	5,075	taxable pay
17,900 at 27%	all at 27%	
2,175 at 40%		
5,703	1,370.25	individual tax paid
7,010.25		total tax paid

*All investment income is taxed as if it belonged to the husband.

Tax saving by being taxed separately: £343.75.

133

her earned-income allowance, set against her income. This compares with the married man with the nonworking wife who gets only the married man's allowance, because she has no earnings against which to set her tax.

- A husband gets secrecy in his financial affairs, if he wants it. Only he signs the tax return. He need not tell his wife what he earns, but she must tell him (if she doesn't the tax inspector can find out from her employer, if she is working, and has been known to tell the husband, who anyway can work it out from the total tax bill). In happy families there are no financial secrets, but problems can occur when, say, a wife quite innocently saves and earns interest and, understandably, thinks that as these are her savings she need not reveal details, only to find that some years later the tax inspector goes to her husband for the tax due.

- As wives do not exist as taxable beings, they do not of course normally get tax bills; these are the responsibility of the husband. Where a couple has underpaid tax, he will get the bill; where they have overpaid, he will get the rebate. This is the case whether or not it is on the wife's income that the tax has been under- or overpaid. That, too, can cause problems, even in the most harmonious households. If a wife has, after all, paid tax on her earnings and she is well within the standard rate of tax, she might feel aggrieved if lumping her earnings in with those of her husband put a 40 per cent rate on some of her earnings. He, too, might be within standard rate. Neither might feel any responsibility for paying the higher-rate tax. It is, however, the responsibility of the husband. Similarly, a wife who had overpaid tax could feel strongly about the rebate going to her husband. There was no way around this situation until the 1970s. It has to be said that there was not much pressure from either men or women for change, even after marrried women began after World War II to move into the workforce in large numbers: at the start they were usually in the lower-paid jobs, which attracted low levels of tax (if any), and it probably made little difference to them how they were taxed. The majority were probably unaware of the law.

After 1945, however, women began to enter further education in larger and larger numbers, and to compete with men for the higher-paid jobs in the professions. It quickly became clear that professional married people on higher incomes were being penalized simply for being married. Two single people living together in the same circumstances would pay far less tax. One did not have to be a financial genius to realize that, if you add two incomes together and tax them as one, you reach the higher levels of tax more quickly than if you tax them separately. In many cases, it was simply not financially worthwhile for a married woman to work.

It was the most highly qualified women who were hardest hit; also they, and their husbands, resented the lack of privacy in their financial affairs. There was—and still is—no tax relief for women who have to employ someone to look after their children in their absence. By the late 1960s, many groups were campaigning against the system, and the Finance Act of 1971 gave some relief (from 1973) to high-earning couples, although the basic principle of the husband being the sole tax unit was unchanged. A complete overhaul of the way in which married people are to be taxed has now been announced, but it will be some years before it comes into force.

The present situation

When they marry, a couple has various options:

- They can do nothing except inform the tax inspector that they are married, in which case the husband's personal allowance will rise from that of a single person to that of a married man. The wife's personal allowance will be replaced by an earned-income allowance at the same level.
- They can decide to take advantage of the 'wife's earned income election', which was introduced in the 1971 Finance Act. This means that a wife is entitled to be taxed quite separately from her husband (but only on her *earned* income: her income from savings and investments continues to be taxed as if it were that of her husband). To make this election, both partners must agree—a husband or wife cannot make the request singly. The couple must 'elect' not earlier than 12 months before the start of the financial year in which they want separate taxation and not less than 12 months after it. This margin of time means that a couple can look at each financial year and decide what is the best way to be taxed. There is a special Inland Revenue leaflet (No. 13, 'Taxation of Wife's Earnings') which describes the whole process and tells you each year the level of income at which you start to be better off being taxed separately. If an 'election' is made, the couple then have their own tax returns, but the wife must still give details of her income from savings, investments, rents, etc., to her husband, as he is always liable for the tax on these.
- The couple can opt for separate assessment. This cannot lower the tax bill in the same way as separate taxation of earnings, but it does mean that a wife will pay that proportion of the tax which applies to her investments, etc., and the husband that which applies to his. If their income from these sources is substantial, the tax payable may be higher than it would be for two single people with the same joint income.
- They can combine separate taxation of earnings with separate assessment.
- When people get married, the last thing they may be thinking about is the way in which they are taxed, although they are normally aware that the husband's personal allowance immediately increases. Later on, however, as incomes rise, this matter can become an important consideration. To show how much can be lost or saved, there are four examples of what can happen in different circumstances on pages 132–3. They are necessarily simple and I have assumed that in the first two cases the husband and wife earn the same, something which is rarely the case. Even if you do not have an accountant, try to work out the figures for your own case, or seek the advice of the Tax Inspector.

The new proposals

There is now general agreement that the present system of taxing married people is unsatisfactory—but there is not, unfortunately, agreement about what should be done about it. After a lot of discussion, the government has come up with various proposals, some of which are being bitterly fought. The basic disagreement is over whether the allowances husband and wife would be entitled to under the new proposals should be able to be transferred by one partner to the other should they not be fully used up. For the moment, the government is opting for full transferability of allowances between husband and wife. This means that, if a woman were not working, the personal allowance she had of right could be set against her husband's income, or the other way around. Here are the proposals:

● The married man's tax allowance is to be abolished and replaced by an allowance for everyone, regardless of whether or not they are in paid employment. This new allowance will be higher than the present single person's allowance.

● A married woman's investment income (that which comes from savings and investments, etc.) is to be regarded as her own, and taxed accordingly. She will no longer have to reveal details to her husband, and her personal allowance could be set against this income, unlike the case at present.

● Where allowances are not used at all, or only partly used, they can be transferred and set against the income of the spouse. This transfer will not be compulsory—if it was, there would be no possibility of privacy in financial affairs for either party—but the couple will lose out if they do not ask for the allowance to be transferred. In most cases it will be the wife who is transferring part or all of her allowance to her husband.

● The age allowance will go (see page 216). The reason for this change is that both pensioners will have a personal allowance, whereas at present the vast majority simply get the married man's age allowance.

● Single parents, who at present get what is called the 'additional personal allowance', which brings their allowances up to the level of the married man, will have no one from whom they can acquire a transferred allowance. To ensure that they do not suffer as a result, they will either have a special single-parent allowance or retain the additional allowance as at present.

● Homes, rather than people, will be eligible for tax relief on mortgages. At present, a nonmarried couple living together can get tax relief on mortgages of up to £60,000 (£30,000 each), whereas a married couple, being taxed as a single unit, are entitled to only £30,000 together. At the time of writing it is not clear whether or not this would mean that a married couple could buy two homes, each meriting a £30,000 limit.

There is quite a lot to be said for the new proposals. They recognize the reality that women are an important part of the workforce and entitled in the same way as men to equal tax treatment. The proposals would do away with the 'morality tax' on marriage, so that people cohabiting without marriage would not be better off than those who married. Tax allowances would be maintained for the time, however long, that a woman remained at home to look after children. Unemployment for one partner would not bring a fall in tax allowances, and single people and married women would earn more than they do at present before becoming liable for tax.

However, not everyone likes the proposals and in March 1987, the government announced that they will be reconsidered. This means that they will not be introduced for some years. The plans had already been deferred to 1990: now, the mid-1990s seem more likely before there is any change. Some people feel that taxation should be completely personal and independent, and that allowances should not be transferable. They believe that a transferable allowance might, for instance, discourage women from seeking work. This might affect as many as 250,000 women, but they would certainly be women whose jobs were in the lower earnings range. Say that the new allowance was set at £3,000 and the standard rate of tax was 25 per cent. A woman earning £3,000 would pay no tax, but if she did not work her husband would pay £750 less tax by taking on her allowance. This is not a lot, but it might perhaps be decisive for a couple with small children, after they had thought about the extra costs of having someone in to look after the children, the inevitably higher food bill (couples who both work will want to use foods they can cook quickly, and these almost always cost more), travelling costs, and so on.

There are objections, too, that the system would be very complicated, with people switching and transferring allowances all the time. This would of course also increase the administrative costs of the system. Whatever is finally decided, it will be impossible to please everyone.

The tax advantages in employing a wife

Under the present system of taxation for married people, there are considerable tax advantages in suitable circumstances if a husband employs his wife. It is an option not open to a man who is simply an employee: he must be in business as a sole trader or as a partner or director of a company. By syphoning some income away from himself (and possibly saving tax at the higher rates), he can pay his wife an effectively tax-free income by using up her earned-income allowance and providing her with a pension which will benefit from tax relief all of her life.

You cannot simply tell the Inland Revenue that you are employing your wife: there must be a real job for her to do. The inspectors look very closely to make sure that a couple are not just transferring money from one to the other to save tax. You will have to be able to prove that the wife does some work in the business—keeping the books, typing, answering the 'phone, or whatever. Many wives in small businesses do this anyway and do not get paid for it. Not only is that unfair, it is also financially foolish because of the tax which can be saved.

However, it must be accepted that a husband cannot pay his wife a very large income. It must be kept below the level of the wife's earned-income allowance in order not to become liable for tax nor incur any National Insurance contributions. The tax saved may not seem a lot, but the system does provide a wife with some financial independence, too. Let us assume that a husband starts to pay his wife £2,000 (well below the earned-income allowance), and that before that he was paying tax at a marginal rate of 40 per cent: the couple immediately saves £800 in tax because the wife is not liable for any tax and the husband's tax bill is reduced by £800. At the same time, a pension for long-term benefit can often be bought for the wife. Contributions to a pension fund are fully allowed for tax, so that the £2,000 could continue to be paid without the couple becoming liable for any tax on her income. Eventually, in retirement, the earned-income allowance can be set against the pension. As the tax system stands at the moment, any tax allowance a woman has is worthless if she has only an income on her husband's pension or National Insurance contributions, because the pension does not arise from her own earnings. All this is complicated, and it is worth consulting an accountant to see what scope you have.

Under the present system, the benefits do not work the other way round. There is no point in a working wife employing her otherwise unemployed husband, except possibly to buy him a pension. If she is the only one working, his married man's allowance is automatically set against her earnings, unlike the case with the wife's earned-income allowance, which can only go against her earnings.

13 Coping with Unemployment

As we have seen in the past few years, almost no one in Britain can rely on complete job security: even the best laid plans and highest qualifications do not guarantee lifetime employment. Redundancies and job losses can hit the newly married just as much as those nearing retirement.

Unemployment can have a devastating effect on a family's lifestyle, and it is important that the possibility is faced and the financial losses minimized. One advantage that the married have over the single is that there are two people with working potential, so that in many cases one can support the other through a difficult time. Also, the state is more generous in the social-security payments which it makes available to the married. But it has to be remembered that most family benefits are geared to the principle that the man is the wage-earner, and it is when *he* becomes unemployed that the family as a whole gets social-security benefits. When a woman is unemployed, she will get unemployment benefit on her own behalf as long as she meets the National Insurance contribution requirements, but she will get nothing as of right for her husband or children.

What to do

Long before the questions of redundancy and unemployment loom, make sure that you have some savings to fall back on should the family income for any reason suddenly fall. This may of course be due not to unemployment but to sickness.

The first step in dealing with unemployment is to talk about it. This may sound very obvious, but it is not unknown for people who lose their jobs not to discuss the matter with their family. Every member of a family is affected by the loss of earnings, and a couple needs to plan together how they will best cope with the situation.

If you are made redundant through no fault of your own and you have not been dismissed for misconduct or dishonesty, you may be entitled to some redundancy payment. This will be so in the following cases:

- An employer may have simply declared an employee redundant.

- An employee may be able to claim that his or her employer has *in effect* made him or her redundant. This could happen if someone is demoted for no apparent reason, or (although this is very rare) that salary or wages have not been paid—such a thing could happen if a company were on the verge of liquidation.
- Redundancy has occurred when there has been a lay-off or short-time working for four consecutive weeks, or for any six weeks out of thirteen. A redundancy payment must then be paid to eligible employees unless the

employer can prove that full-time working will be operating within four weeks.

Redundancy monies are not automatically payable when one of the above conditions is fulfilled. Most importantly, no redundancy payment need be made to anyone who has been employed by a company for less than two years; there may be instances when a company is prepared to make some payment in such a case, but it is strictly voluntary.

If an employer offers alternative employment, the employee will not be held to be redundant unless he or she is offered a position which is obviously inferior to the one previously held, or one for which the qualifications of the employee are clearly unsuitable. When employees cannot reach agreement with an employer about redundancy or redeployment, they have the right to go to an industrial tribunal, which will decide on the merits of the case. Such cases can be taken to appeal, if necessary.

Going to an industrial tribunal costs the complainant nothing, but it is a step which should be taken only when all else has failed. Companies can afford to be represented by skilful lawyers who are likely to be able to present the company's case far better than former employees are able to present theirs. Moreover, the tribunal offers only its time free to the complainant: he or she would have to pay for any outside legal help and, if the case were lost, the tribunal would be unlikely to award costs against the company.

If you are married and made redundant, it is important, if you are thinking of going to a tribunal, to discuss all the implications with your spouse.

Assuming that you and your employer agree that you are being made redundant, there are levels of payment laid down for the amount of redundancy money to which you are entitled. These are minimum levels, and many companies have house agreements which offer rather more to employees who are made redundant; one month's pay for every year worked is common in many house agreements. However, if you are offered only what is required in law, the following scale of payments applies at present (1987), depending on how long you have worked for the company.

for each year of employment between the ages of	employees' minimum payment
18 and 21	half a week's pay
21 and 40	1 week's pay
40 and 65 (men)	$1\frac{1}{2}$ weeks' pay
40 and 60 (women)	$1\frac{1}{2}$ weeks' pay

Even within these payment levels, which are not especially generous, there are maxima. No more than 20 years' employment is counted, and the maximum pay you are assumed to be earning is £158 a week. So, if your company does not have a special redundancy scheme, the highest redundancy payment you can get is £4,740—i.e., 20 times (the maximum number of years) £237 ($1\frac{1}{2}$ weeks' pay). The payment is tax-free, but even so such a sum is not going to tide a young couple over a long period—especially since the actual redundancy payment will obviously be a lot less than this example.

If you cannot agree with your employer that you have been made redundant, you must generally make your claim for redundancy in writing to him or her within six months of your employment ceasing, or refer your claim to an industrial tribunal by then. Exceptions to this rule can be made, but they are not common. Your claim for redundancy is not affected should you have found new work in the meantime.

Unfair or wrongful dismissal

Redundancy is not the same as unfair dismissal or wrongful dismissal. Unfair dismissal is subject to maximum levels of payment which are raised from time to time, and vary depending on whether or not reinstatement is refused. You might claim unfair dismissal if, for instance, your employer terminated your employment without compensation, or if your employer wanted to move you to another area and you were unwilling or unable to move.

The onus in cases of unfair dismissal is on the employer to prove that his or her action was justified. If the employer then claims that the employee was in fact redundant, he or she will have to pay a redundancy payment. The employer may claim that the employee's conduct was such that it justified dismissal, but this will have to be on grounds of dishonesty, gross incompetence, or because the employee's qualifications and capabilities were inadequate for the job.

In unfair-dismissal cases, the so-called 'basic award' is calculated in a similar manner to redundancy payments. But there are additional payments, which are influenced by how much or how little the conduct of the employee led to the dismissal, the loss of earnings which followed the loss of the job, and sometimes for 'hurt feelings'.

Wrongful dismissal is different again. It can occur when the contract-of-employment conditions are not carried out when someone is dismissed. The correct period of notice may not be given or, in the case of a fixed-term contract, the employer may dismiss the employee before it expires.

If you are dismissed for any reason

● Discuss the situation with your spouse.
● If there is any danger that you will be unable to keep up mortgage payments or hire-purchase commitments, do not delay in informing the lender. If you do this in time you will usually be able to come to some sort of agreement to defer capital repayments and for a period pay only interest. If you delay, the process of repossessing your home or the goods may start, and you will be involved in legal expenses.
● If you think you have grounds for claiming that your dismissal was unfair or wrongful, or that your redundancy payment is too low, or you have received nothing at all when you believe you have an entitlement, think carefully before taking legal action. Be certain that you are not going to get anything from your former employer unless you resort to the tribunal. Even if you win at the tribunal, the award may not be more than whatever payment the employer may have offered, however inadequate, and if you lose you will get nothing.
● Even if your former company does not have an in-house redundancy agreement, it is worthwhile negotiating with the employer for an additional payment. You have nothing to lose.
● Register yourself as unemployed. Go to your local unemployment office

on the first day you become unemployed. This is most important—if you don't do this you will lose benefit. Unemployment pay continues for 312 days: after that, you will no longer be eligible for unemployment benefit until you have worked again for at least 13 weeks and for at least 21 hours in each of those weeks. This does not mean that you and your family will starve, but the kind of benefit changes.

- Go to your local Job Centre and register yourself as available for work. Your unemployment benefit will be affected if you unreasonably refuse any work you are offered, but you will not be expected to take a job for which your qualifications are totally unsuitable.
- Think carefully as a couple how you can best maximize your resources; for instance, in some areas and industries it is easier for women to get jobs than men. In such cases it makes sense at least for a time for the wife to work if her husband is having great difficulty in finding a job. Sharing family responsibilities for a time need not damage male pride or destroy the security of children—in fact, cooperation between husband and wife in these circumstances can help a family weather the financial crisis and make it stronger.
- If you have been in a job where the opportunities are shrinking, do consider changing your profession or work altogether. Consider retraining.

Unemployment pay

Not everyone is eligible for unemployment benefit. There is a basic requirement that you must have paid 26 class-one National Insurance contributions to qualify for any payment at all. To get the standard rate of benefit you must have paid or been credited with class-one contributions of at least 50 times the lower earnings limit for the relevant tax year. The lower earnings limit moves up each year, more or less in line with inflation.

There is a level of benefit which covers all eligible persons, then an additional payment for wives and dependent children. Women may get the additional benefit if their husbands are getting invalidity or retirement pensions, or any unemployment allowance. If there are any adult dependants who are incapable of self-support, for any reason, or if they are women who are on very low incomes, there are further allowances. The main benefits (from April 1987) are:

Single person	£31.45
Adult dependency	£19.40
Married man	£50.85

These benefits are paid only to people who have no work at all. If you work part-time you may be eligible for supplementary benefit (income support from April 1988) because you are on a very low income, but you will not get unemployment benefit. Additionally, you must declare that you are able and willing to work.

You should bear in mind, too, that generally speaking unemployment benefit goes only to those who lose their jobs through no fault of their own. If you simply leave your job without 'just cause', you will be denied benefit for 13 weeks. Redundancy of any kind, either compulsory or voluntary, does not affect your right to benefit. If you have been justifiably dismissed for any kind of misconduct, or lay down conditions about the sort of work you will accept, you may be refused benefit altogether.

Benefit for a married man will not be affected if his wife is working. Unemployment pay, unlike some other benefits, is not means-tested. If you are still unemployed after 312 days, however, unemployment pay ceases and any benefits you then apply for will be means-tested.

Payment is usually by a fortnightly Giro cheque, which comes through the post. For benefit to continue for the full 312 days, you will have to continue to visit the unemployment office to re-register that you still have no work.

Other benefits

Once you are eligible for unemployment pay, you may also become entitled to other benefits. The main one is Family Credit, which from April 1988 will replace the old Family Income Supplement and is for those whose total income is low. This allowance is means-tested, so all sources of family income and savings are taken into account by the DHSS before the level of payment is decided upon.

Eligibility for these benefits leads to the right to others, such as free National Health prescriptions and free school meals for your children. Make sure that you get everything to which you are entitled. These benefits are yours of right, because of the National Insurance contributions you have made: they are not charity.

WHEN THE CHILDREN ARRIVE

There are financial implications for every married couple when the first child arrives. Children cost money, and their birth may result in a sharp drop in family income, at least for a time, because the mother gives up paid employment. A couple need to look at all aspects of their financial life. A check should be made on what state benefits, if any, the mother can claim. Written application should have been made during the pregnancy for her job to be left open for her, if she has been with the same employer for at least two years; this should be done even if the mother is undecided about whether to return to work, or the right is forfeited. Life-assurance needs must be reassessed, and adjustments made accordingly. If private education has been decided upon, how to fund school fees should not be delayed. Parents' wills may need changing.

14 | The Financial Impact of Children

The arrival of children, particularly of the first child, usually totally changes the basis of the family's finances. Children cost money. How much they cost is debatable, and quite exaggerated claims are made. Estimates usually take into account not only the actual costs involved in rearing a child but also the loss of the mother's earnings, at least for some years, and some notional price is put on the hours she spends taking care of the child, which would of course cost money if a professional child-minder were employed. These calculations are all rather far-fetched, but a glance at the estimates made towards the end of 1986 do show how much children can cost if all these figures are taken into account.

The Family Policy Studies Centre suggested in 1986 that the raising of two children costs a mother £135,000 in actual outgoings, lost earnings and unpaid work in the home. Pregnancy and the first year of the child's life are reckoned to cost about £1,500 just for the maternity clothes and equipment and clothes for the baby. The child's food, clothing and shoes work out at about £30,000 from birth until the 16th birthday. On average, the loss of a mother's earnings is put at £54,000, if a mother of two takes seven years out of the labour force altogether. Many return after that not to full-time but to part-time work, so a further £48,000 is added on to allow for this. Then there is an estimate of a further £32,000 because part-time work tends to be lower paid per hour than full-time work. One third of mothers go to a lower-paid job when they return to work than they had when they gave up. Finally, assuming a mother looks after her children for seven hours a day, it is reckoned that she is saving the family £10,000.

In November 1986, the *Sunday Times* produced a detailed costing of the upbringing of children. These were actual costs, and did not include the hypothetical loss of earnings. The report recognized that different income groups have differing priorities in child rearing: the poorer the family, the less discretionary income it has, and private education is not even an option for around 90 per cent of families, for example. All children bring increased bills into the family, however, quite apart from their simple equipment, clothing and food needs. Children can require the family to move to a larger home; this in turn means higher mortgage and fuel costs, and perhaps higher travelling expenses for the wage-earners if a family has moved further from the town centre to acquire a bigger house at reasonable cost. A second car may eventually become necessary.

The *Sunday Times* costing included not only items like holidays and school trips, which we would automatically think of, but such items as the cost of a christening, baby-sitting, the money the tooth fairy leaves, music and sports lessons, and an 18th-birthday party. Then the paper applied these varying costs to three families in differing income groups, assuming that both parents worked and that there were two children, a boy and a girl. The lower-income group, the paper calculated, would spend £76,000 on the two children by the time they reached 18. For middle-income groups, the cost soared to £146,000, and it was more than doubled up again for the higher-income group to £356,000, mainly because of private education, more expensive leisure activities, holidays and eating out. Even before they were born, the two children of a lower-income family were reckoned to cost £565, assuming National Health Service facilities were used. A middle-income mother might use National Health combined with a private consultant, bringing the cost to £1,000. All-private medical care would cost a higher-earning family £4,800, including the costs of the consultant and a private hospital. These are formidable figures. A layette (which can of course be used for more than one child) may not leave much change out of £1,000 unless one can benefit from equipment being passed on by relatives or friends or rely on presents.

Fortunately, most parents do not look at family life in such stark financial terms, whatever set of figures one chooses to accept. Marriage, after all, is all about families, and living costs money whether one is married or single. Parents are aware that the family income is likely to drop for a time after the children's birth, and few mothers would dream of costing their work in the home at £10,000 a year. But the figures do serve to show how a family's financial circumstances can change when children are born. It makes sense to have some savings to cope with the initial costs and also to recognize that, even when a woman plans to return to full-time work soon after having children, this may not always be possible. The best laid plans 'gang aft a-gley', even if only for a time. Where a woman does not plan to return to work after the birth, she may hope to work as long as possible during her pregnancy; but even pregnancy is not always exactly predictable, and some women find that they have to give up work before they want to because it becomes too tiring. For all these reasons, getting a 'float' together to cover pregnancy and the early months of a child's life can be useful.

The state and maternity

To some extent—although in general to a lessening degree—the state recognizes that there are special costs involved in pregnancy and child-birth. Several benefits were introduced some years ago, but the number of women who qualify for them has been cut by between 75,000 and 85,000 a year, making it even more important to have an adequate 'float'. These benefits are:

- The Maternity Grant. This is £75, but does not go to every pregnant woman. It comes from the Social Fund, and is paid only to women of limited means. It is available only for those getting Income Support (the new name for supplementary benefit) or Family Credit (which will replace family-income supplement). This payment replaces the £25 which was paid for many years to all new mothers. Single payments previously made to pregnant women in exceptional need have also been abolished.
- State Maternity Pay (SMP). To get paid maternity leave a woman must have worked for her present employer for at least six months up to and including the 15th week before the week of expected confinement. The money is paid by the employer (as opposed to the old scheme whereby the

145

state paid), and is pitched at the lowest rate of statutory sick pay. It is normally paid for a maximum of 18 weeks starting six weeks before the baby is born, but there is flexibility in the timing chosen (see below). If a woman has been with her employer for two years or more, the SMP is equivalent to current rates of maternity pay which are 90 per cent of her earnings for the first six weeks of maternity leave: thereafter it falls to the lowest rate of statutory sick pay. Women who do not qualify for the pay, but who have paid National Insurance contributions for 16 of the past 52 weeks, can claim state maternity allowance from the DHSS, which is paid at the same level as sickness benefit.

Women can choose when to take their maternity leave. There is a 'core' 13-week period, which starts six weeks before the baby is due, but the woman can choose when to take the remaining five weeks' entitlement. This can be important. Many women feel unable to work right through until six weeks before the birth, and so will have to accept that they must do without any pay for a period after the birth, until they eventually return to work. Many prefer to work to the last possible minute and have as much paid time as possible at home with the baby. Such women lose their paid maternity leave for the period they go on working after six weeks before the birth, but of course they are getting their normal pay during these weeks.

Many companies have maternity benefits included in their house agreements with employees. Where they do, these offer better maternity-pay terms and often longer periods away from work than statutorily required. They may also offer better job protection. In law, maternity rights related to redundancy, unfair dismissal and reinstatement after the birth are based upon the employment record. A woman must have worked for her employer for either 16 hours a week for two years or eight hours a week for five years. There are suggestions at present that these requirements should be changed to 20 hours for two years, or 12 hours for five years. This would reduce both eligibility and, more importantly, job security for many women. It is important to check the current position as soon as you know you are pregnant.

Inform your employer in writing as soon as possible that you intend to return to work. You can always change your mind, if for any reason it becomes difficult or even impossible to return to work or if you simply decide you do not want to. If you have said you are leaving, your employer need not hold your job open for you if you then change your mind. Check your rights and what action you should take as soon as you know you are pregnant. Remember that these are *rights*, and not simply gifts from generous employers.

The state and children

So much for pregnancy. The state becomes involved the moment the child arrives.

Child benefit is the most important payment made to anyone looking after a child. It is not (at the moment, although this could change) earnings-related, and it is paid to anyone who is responsible for a child under the age of 16 (extended to under 19 for children who are still in full-time school education, although not university or college education: as we shall see later, adult student children and their parents can take advantage of the tax system to supplement their grants). Child benefit is the one social-security benefit which tends to be paid directly to the mother rather than to the father. Benefit is paid four weeks in arrears.

There are a series of other benefits for the children of families on low incomes. They normally do not arise until a child goes to school, but can include: free school meals and milk (not in all local authorities, and only then for those aged up to seven), fares to get to and from school, educational maintenance allowances, and school-uniform and clothing grants. Families who qualify for the above will probably also qualify for free National Health Service prescriptions and dental treatment. Expectant and nursing mothers and children under school age in families which are getting Family Credit or housing-benefit supplement may get free milk and vitamins automatically, or be able to claim them.

Planning for the family

The rundown we looked at (page 144) on what children cost gives frighteningly high figures, at least for the first child. Subsequent children can have equipment and clothes passed on to them, but even so every new member of the family increases the family budget to some degree. Wage and salary increases do not automatically come along as the children do, and in every family, even where the mother continues to work, there may come a point when she feels she has to give up working for some reason.

Plans should be made to cope with these higher costs before the baby or babies arrive and, unless you have religious objections to family planning, it obviously makes sense to have your children at a time when the family income can take the strain.

You will leave yourself with more options if, for instance:

You have built up your savings float to help you cover the weeks, months or even years when the family is surviving on only one income. You will probably have to reduce your savings sharply, and perhaps eliminate them altogether for a time, but try to restart some form of regular saving, however small, as soon as you can, to avoid sudden big calls on current income—e.g., for holidays.
You manage to buy in the first place a home which is large enough to accommodate the children you plan to have.
Assuming you are concerned about education but do not have the means nor want to educate your children privately, you choose a home in an area where there are good state schools and move to it while there are still two incomes and the family budget is not strained.
You try to time the birth to ensure that, if the mother wants to continue working after the baby's birth, she has fulfilled the two-years' continuous employment requirement with a single employer. She should inform her employer in writing as soon as possible, and not later than three weeks before intending to take the leave. If that is not done, the right is lost. Work must also continue until eleven weeks before the birth. If these conditions are fulfilled, a woman cannot be dismissed from employment because of pregnancy. Remember that the employer must be told in writing: word of mouth will not do.

New mothers can return to their jobs at any time up to 29 weeks after the birth, and in special circumstances this period may be extended for another four weeks. Of course, very few women are likely to get maternity pay for this length of time, even if the company has a special house agreement, but many mothers who do not want to leave their babies after a few weeks often feel more relaxed about going out to work again after six months or so.

One reason for informing the employer as soon as possible is to maintain good relations with him. Where a woman is in a position of responsibility, her prolonged absence can sometimes pose special problems for employers in finding a stopgap. People who have stepped into a job for several months are often unwilling to face demotion when the job-owner returns. Not only is a pregnant woman guaranteed that she will not be sacked, she is guaranteed the same job back.

The longer you can give your employer to plan for your absence, the less disruptive it will be.

Anyone who is uncertain about whether they will want to return to work should make a claim in writing anyway. Many women who start off determined to return to work change their mind for one reason or another and decide to stay out of the job market for some years, but it is only sensible for them to protect their rights. If you do decide not to return, do not keep your employer in suspense: tell him or her immediately. You never know when you may want to work for that employer again or need a reference from him or her at some later date when you are once again looking for work.

● If you are in a position where the wife can be employed by her husband (see page 137), you will be able to take advantage of the wife's earned-income allowance. Her wages should be kept below the level of the allowance to avoid paying tax or National Insurance contributions. Remember, too, that a woman can stay out of the labour force for up to 20 years without losing her right to a pension.

When the baby is born

As soon as the child is born and registered, apply to the Department of Health and Social Security for child benefit. At present, this goes to the person responsible for the day-to-day care of the child, which is usually the mother. All children are eligible and the benefit is not means-tested, so all children (except the first child in single-parent families) get the same amount. The idea behind child benefit is to ensure that the person immediately caring for the child has some money as of right. If child benefits eventually are means-tested, total family income will probably be taken into account, not just that of the mother.

If you can afford to live without the benefit, try to save it: you can collect it at the post office and immediately redeposit the money in an account. That way you will be able to build up a fund to cope with expenses incurred when your child goes to school.

Life assurance

As soon as a child is born, particularly the first, you need to reassess your life-assurance needs. If you own your home you will probably have either endowment life assurance or mortgage protection attached to it. If that is all you have, it is no longer enough.

There is now a member of the family who will be totally dependent on the parents for many years to come. Should either of those parents die, the child will suffer financially. The mother, too, may stop working for a period, so she too is financially vulnerable: should her husband die, she may well not be able to get a job comparable to the one she had before, and she will certainly lose out in the salary stakes if she stays out of paid employment for a period of years—i.e., she will earn less than those of her contemporaries who remained in the workforce.

Term life assurance is ideal for the new family. It is cheap and can provide cover for up to 20 years while the family is growing. (For details of this and other life policies, see pages 98–107.) Both husband and wife should take out cover. Later on, when there is more disposable family income, many term policies can be converted into whole-of-life policies, so that the benefit of the early premiums is not thrown away.

Do not insure the life of the child. Life cover of this kind is intended for financial protection. The death of a child will bring family grief, but it will not cause financial problems. It is the child which should be protected in the event of the untimely death of one of its parents. It is sometimes argued that children need endowment life cover to mature at a point when the money might come in handy, such as at entrance to university. But even then cover on the parent's life, written for the benefit of the child, is preferable, because the parent is more likely to die than the child during the life of the policy.

While it is true that the premiums paid on life assurance are based on risk—the lower the risk, the lower the premium—young adults do not have a higher risk of premature death than children, so in terms of cost, too, there is little if any benefit in insuring the child rather than the parent.

If, nevertheless, you are thinking of any insurance cover for a child, personal accident insurance is cheap and can provide a sum to help in the extra costs involved in caring for a child who is either temporarily or permanently disabled.

Every individual has his or her own particular life-assurance needs. The Life Offices' Association and the Scottish Life Offices have worked out what they think is a typically sensible plan for family protection. Copies of a booklet explaining it are available from: LOA/ASLO, Information Centre, Cheapside, London EC2V 6AX. The only quarrel with this programme is that it does not take full cognizance of the very vital contribution made by many women today to the total family income. If you opt for anything like this plan, the woman should take out a similar policy, or the policy should be a joint one, on the lives of both husband and wife.

First step: age 25
Newly married, starting to buy a first home on mortgage, intending to start a family shortly, husband in company's pension scheme.

Take out	Monthly premium	Cover provided
(a) Mortgage-protection policy to cover £30,000 building-society loan repayable over 25 years	£4.00	£30,000 initially

(b) Family income benefit policy on husband's life for £3,000 a year for remainder of 25 years	£3.00	£75,000 initially (£3,000 a year for 25 years)
(c) Family income benefit policy on wife's life for £3,000 a year for remainder of 25 years	£2.80	£75,000 initially (£3,000 a year for 25 years)
(d) Whole-of-life policy, with profits or unit-linked policy; Premiums to cease at age 65	£6.00	£3,000
(e) Permanent health insurance (PHI) policy, to provide £120 a week if husband is unable to work through illness for 26 weeks or more	£7.00	—
Total monthly premium		£22.80, providing initial cover of £183,000

Second step: age 35

Budget allows more savings.

Take out	*Monthly premium*	*Cover provided at age 35*
Endowment policy with profits or unit-linked policy payable when husband retires at 65	£14.00	£4,000
Previous policies:		
Mortgage protection	£4.00	£27,150
Family income (husband)	£3.00	£45,000
Family income (wife)	£2.80	£45,000
Whole life	£6.00	£4,770
PHI	£7.00	—
Total monthly premiums		£36.80, providing cover of £125,920

Third step: age 43

Eldest son leaves school

Take out	*Monthly premium*	*Cover provided at age 43*
Further endowment policies with profits or unit-linked policy payable when husband retires at 65	£17.00	£3,500
Previous policies:		
Mortgage protection	£4.00	£19,320

Family income (husband)	£3.00	£21,000
Family income (wife)	£2.80	£21,000
Whole life	£6.00	£6,915
With-profits endowment	£13.80	£5,800
PHI	£7.00	—

Total monthly premiums: £53.60, providing cover of £77,535

Retirement (husband aged 65)

Mortgage protection policy: this stopped when the mortgage was fully repaid.

Family income policies: these both stopped after the 25-year period.

Now, the *endowment* or *unit-linked policies* mature, providing a lump sum to supplement the pension. The first policy matures with benefits of £19,900; the second policy matures with benefits of £11,580; and the whole-of-life policy still goes on providing cover of £18,330, including bonuses, and can go on increasing the total sum although no more premiums are to be paid.

Education

The education of children cannot be considered too soon. Make your mind up the moment the child is born whether you want him or her to be educated privately or to go through the state system. While you can always change your mind and switch from private to state education, it is often difficult to make the decision the other way round. School fees are high and will continue to rise. Finding them can be crippling for a family. There are not a few families where the mother's decision to return to work has been prompted by the need to find school fees, and all her earnings may very well be swallowed up by the fees.

The best way to cope with school fees is in a sense to assume that you are paying them from the moment the child is born. If you do this you can, by using life assurance or one of the school-fees schemes set out on pages 11–13, take a great deal of the pain out of it all. You can also make the amount of money involved more manageable by deciding to put your children into private education only at the secondary level, using the years before then to build up your funds. If you want them to be in the private sector throughout, try if at all possible to pay the fees at the junior level from your current income. They are lower then and you can meanwhile be building up funds via insurance or a school-fees scheme for the later stages. The earlier you make these arrangements, the cheaper they will be.

If you are determined on a particular school, put the child's name down immediately he or she is born. That way, you may be able to guarantee your child a place and you will also learn of any school-fees schemes particular to that school.

Discuss with grandparents, godparents and any other interested relatives and friends how they might help you bear the burden. As we saw on page 14, there are highly tax-efficient covenant schemes which people other than the parents can set up for the benefit of children.

151

Utilizing your savings

It may be that, for a period at least, you will have to use up some of the savings you have amassed before your children were born. As you are likely to be standard-rate taxpayers at this stage in your life, all your savings, wherever they have been in the past, should now go into tax-paid savings and preferably savings which pay a regular income, so that you can come to regard it as part of normal family income. Building societies are probably best. Choose the highest interest rate possible. And try to keep the amount of capital intact. (See pages 237–9 for the options available to you.)

Your will

If you have been planning properly, you will have made a will on marriage. It is time, once you have a child, to look at it again and decide what changes, if any, should be made. You may decide that you do not want to make any changes at this stage. On the other hand, you may feel that you should leave some of your assets to your children. They will have to receive this in trust (see pages 88 and 157) until they reach majority, so you may need professional help in drawing up your plan. Remember that anything you leave to your spouse is not subject to Inheritance Tax rules, and also that anything you give away seven years before you die is not taxable. If you do die within the seven years, there is a sliding scale of tax— see page 199. You can cover the liability for any tax by taking out a term assurance policy for the amount of money concerned. The cost will be well below the level of any tax to which your estate might be liable.

Spotcheck

Before you decide when and how many children you will have, have you

- thought of all the costs involved?
- worked out that you can afford the size of family you want?
- checked on your maternity rights and made sure you will get your entitlement?
- made a written statement to your employer, if you are pregnant and know you will or might wish to return to your job?

Once you have become parents, have you

- applied for child benefit as soon as the child is born?
- checked the family life-assurance cover to see that it is adequate?
- taken steps immediately to start funding school fees, if you have definitely decided on private education?
- adjusted your savings plan if necessary?
- altered your will to take account of the existence of your children?

AS THE CHILDREN GROW

As the children grow, financial priorities change once again. Mothers who have stayed at home for some years often return to work, and the family budget becomes easier to manage. The parents can begin looking towards the day when the children will have left home and become self-supporting. They can start to look ahead to their retirement years, and put an increasing amount on one side for their eventual pension. They may even be able to begin to think about taking a risk and putting money into investments which may bring capital growth, rather than absolute security. Some of their life assurance plans will begin to mature, and the lump sums from these can also be put aside to help boost income when earnings cease. These are the years when sensible financial planning begins to pay off.

15 | Providing for Children

Further education

If you have made proper plans or are using the state system, you will not have to think very much about financing your children's education until they reach 16, which is the minimum school-leaving age. Thereafter, education becomes voluntary. Although it is unusual, a child may qualify for an education grant to help maintain him or her while still at school. Grants are normally for further education at college or university, and it is only if the family is very poor that the child receives a grant while still at school.

The amount of grant paid to a school, college or university student is based on parental income, and today it is rarely enough for a student to live on, especially if the student has to live away from home. There seems little doubt that grant levels will in real terms be further reduced in years to come, so some thought ought to be given to how a student is to be maintained.

Grants are available only to people who have been normally resident in the United Kingdom for the three years prior to the commencement of the course. Anyone living abroad with parents who are in the armed services is counted as if they were living in the UK, and sometimes the same applies to children of parents working abroad.

Grants can be mandatory or discretionary. The former go to students who are taking a degree course or its equivalent; discretionary grants are for courses of lower than degree standard. Education authorities have a great deal of control over how they award these grants, and the attitude can vary depending on where you live. If you are refused a grant you can appeal, but you cannot *force* a change of mind. There is of course nothing to stop you trying again next year if you have been refused a grant this year.

The maximum level of grant at the time of writing is £2,330 for students studying in London and living away from home. Grants for students outside London and/or living at home are lower and post-graduate students get rather more than undergraduates. For students getting the maximum grant, the parent is expected to contribute at least £40 a year to their child's upkeep. If the parent refuses to give details of his or her income, the student will get nothing. Where both parents work, each will be expected to provide income details. Where parents are divorced, the child can be held to be dependent on the parent whom he or she lives with, and this can affect the level of the grant.

The grant is based on residual income, which is not the same as total income. Gross income before tax is taken as a starting point, but then deductions are allowed. These are: mortgage interest or rent; any company or private pension contributions, but not National Insurance contributions; and an allowance for other dependent children. Where a family has more than one student child at any time, the maximum contribution that the parents are expected to make each year to all the children together is £4,600.

Some students qualify for so-called 'independent status', but not on immediately leaving school. The minimum qualifying age is 25 and the student must have been earning for at least three years before starting the course. Six months' unemployment is allowed in this period, and for married students any time spent at home looking after children does not affect the right to a grant. Anyone over 26 may get an extra payment related to age.

Students can sometimes contribute to their living expenses at college or university by working during the vacations. To do this, the level of grant they receive is not taken as part of their income in assessing any liability they may have to tax. It is rare, however, for a student to be able to be completely self-supporting, especially if he or she is getting only the minimum grant. It has to be said, too, that, although there is an assumption that parents on higher incomes will contribute to a student's maintenance, there is no legal requirement for them to do so.

Banks are looking with increasing sympathy on the needs of students who cannot get support from their parents, but anyone borrowing during their degree or other course must be mindful that the debt will eventually have to be repaid out of taxed income when employment starts, and the bank may require a guarantor before it will lend you the money.

The best solution for many families is to use the tax system to benefit students. Once a child reaches the age of 18, the parent can use covenants to pay the child in a tax-efficient way rather than simply give the child money.

Covenants for student children

As the income of dependent children under the age of 18 is normally regarded as part of their parents' income, there is no tax saving if parents make covenant payments to such dependent children. When the offspring reach the age of 18, however, everything changes, and while the child remains in full-time education parents who want to contribute to the child's upkeep at college or university can use this tax-efficient method of paying them—in the same way as people other than the parents can do before the child reaches 18 (see page 14).

The reason for this is that, when a covenant is written to a child over 18 by the parent, the latter deducts the standard rate of tax from the gross payment. The student then applies to the tax inspector, who pays the amount of deducted tax to the student. There are limits to this happy arrangement, however. The gross amount of the covenant should be kept below the single person's tax allowance, because above that level the tax relief begins to be lost and is eventually eliminated altogether. This could be an important consideration when the student in question has other income from, say, savings or investments. However, the amount of any grant from an education authority is not taken into account by the tax authorities in assessing a student's total income.

Tax relief will not be allowed if the Inland Revenue thinks that the

DEED OF COVENANT FROM A PARENT TO A STUDENT CHILD OVER THE AGE OF 18

I, ..., of ...., covenant to pay my son/daughter, ... of ...., an amount which after deduction of tax at the standard rate amounts to £...... on the first day of each month January/April/July/October, for the period of seven years or for the period of our joint lives, or until he/she ceases to be receiving full-time education at any university, school or other educational establishment (whichever is the shortest period), the first payment to be made on ....

Signature ....

Signed, sealed and delivered ....

Witnessed by ....

Witness's address ....

covenant is simply a dodge whereby the family gets tax relief without the money being handed over. If the income of the covenantor, after taking into account the deduction of personal allowances and essential payments like mortgages and rates, were to be lower than the amount of the gross annual payment, it is highly unlikely that the inspectors would accept that a genuine covenant had been signed!

There are a few points to bear in mind because, although you need not take professional advice when drawing up a covenant, it will only be valid if it is done correctly. First, the covenant must be properly witnessed and then sealed with a small red paper disc or a wax or water seal. Payments under the covenant cannot start until it is signed; any payments made before that date will not receive any tax relief. As a general rule, the level of payments cannot be varied once the covenant has started, although it may be possible to write in an annual increase in line with the expected increase in the level of personal allowance. On the whole, however, it is best to avoid complications by giving as much as possible right at the start.

Payments must be made directly to the student child. The covenantor must fill in an Inland Revenue form, R185 (AP), each time a payment is made. Similarly, to get the tax relief, the student must apply to the inspector on Tax Claim Form R40. The student should keep the original of the covenant and the parent (or whoever is covenanting the money) should have a copy of it to show to the Inland Revenue on demand.

Covenants can be abandoned at any time by agreement between the parties, but this should not be written into the document. It is a general requirement that covenants should be written for a period exceeding six years, so, if there is an agreement right at the start that it will continue only for the three- or four-year period of the average degree course, technically no tax relief will apply.

The Inland Revenue has produced a form, IR47, called 'Deed of Covenant by Parent to Adult Student', which is very helpful.

The addition of each child to the family may require some adjustments to be made to your will. When the children are small you may feel the need to protect them directly by writing some of your eventual estate into trust for them. You will need the professional assistance of a solicitor to do this. The changes needed may not require a completely new will to be made: if the modifications are small, you can add them as a codicil to the existing will. Remember, however, that any codicils must be witnessed in the same way as a full will or they will be invalid. This means two witnesses to your signature who are people who do not benefit under your will.

When your children reach their majority at 18, however, or begin working and become self-supporting, you may then want to revert to leaving your entire estate to your spouse, so that there is no question of Inheritance Tax when the first one of you dies. This is likely to require a completely fresh will.

If your estate is beginning to look large and will attract substantial Inheritance Tax when the surviving spouse dies, consider a joint whole-of-life assurance policy which will pay out on the second death. There will of course be monthly premiums to be paid for the rest of your lives (or at least until a certain age, which may be as high as 80), but the total cost is likely to be far less than the tax to which your estate will eventually become liable. Try to estimate what the tax might be, leave a margin in case you are wrong and it is ultimately higher than you expect, and take out a non-profits whole-of-life policy for that amount. As an example, cover for a man aged 40 for an eventual payment of £150,000 would cost about £2,300 a year, well within the annual gifts limit. If he died at, say, 70, the total premiums he had paid would be only about £70,000.

If you run a business, it is even more important to consider whole-of-life assurance to cover your eventual Inheritance Tax liability. There is relief on business assets which cuts the liability in half in comparison with anyone leaving other assets, but even so it is not unknown for family businesses to have to be split up and sold off to pay the tax when the proprietor dies. If you are in partnership or running a company with someone else, you should consider insuring the lives of all the owners of the business.

16 | Looking to Retirement

One of the most important aspects of financial planning is to begin and continue to make provision throughout our working lives for those years when our income from employment ceases. We should start to do this as soon as possible after we reach our 20s, and certainly it is essential that we do so as soon as possible after marriage, not only to protect ourselves against poverty in old age but also to provide our family with an income should we die at a time when they are most financially vulnerable.

Succeeding governments in this century have recognized that, with many calls on their financial resources when they are young, there is a temptation for individuals to fail to make adequate provision for their later years. So, since 1911, there has been a state-provided pension. This pension has never been at more than a basic level, and, because many people have failed to plan to supplement their state pension, they spend their final years in poverty. Also, the pensions situation in Britain is in a mess, and always has been. All governments have treated this very important area as a means of vote-catching. New schemes have been introduced by one government only to be stifled by another before they have had any real chance to prove themselves.

If state pension levels have formerly been inadequate, they are going to be even more so in future. With the prospect, too, of other social-security benefits to help the poor also likely to be reduced in real (if not actual) terms, people are going to be forced into pension planning far more than they have been in the past.

What makes the state scheme inadequate for most retired people is the fact that it generally remains at effectively the same level once we have retired until our death: increases are announced every year in the Budget, but these are only in line with inflation over the past year, so the pension will buy only the same amount. Occasionally there is an above-average increase, but it is rarely very generous. The situation can become critical for couples after the death of one of the partners. Two may be able to live as cheaply as one, but the government, like most people, does not think so: it cuts the married man's (i.e., the couple's) pension back after the first death to the level of that for a single person (for current rates see page 214). The same, alas, is true of some private schemes. For this reason, many people need to supplement their income by higher-interest-rate savings during retirement (see pages 216–17). Since January 1986 there has been some improvement in this situation. Each year there must be an increase in private pensions by the amount of inflation or by 5 per cent, whichever is the greater, but that applies only to pensions earned since that date, so will not be significant for people retiring in the next few years.

State pensions are a right which we pay for through our National Insurance contributions. As we have seen (page 25), from the very day we are in employment we begin to contribute towards the basic pension and, in some cases, the additional earnings-related pension. Here, though, we shall concentrate on the provision of private pensions, obtained either through a scheme run by our employer or as a result of a personal plan.

First, a few general points:

- There are tax advantages in making contributions to a private pension fund but there is no allowance for National Insurance contributions.
- People who are contracted into the SERPS scheme pay rather more in National Insurance contributions than those contracted out.
- Contributions to certain limits to a company pension scheme are fully allowed for tax. What happens is that the total paid is sliced off gross income before the liability for tax is calculated.
- The present retirement ages for men and women differ, and this has implications for their pensions. Women are entitled to retire at 60, five years before men, but their basic state pension is the same. In private schemes and the additional state pension, technically known as SERPS (the State Earnings-related Pension Scheme), however, what you get out as an income depends on what you have put in, so women often retire on less than a man because inevitably they have paid lower total contributions during their shorter working life.
- Private schemes for men almost always include a widow's and dependent children's element. Today, there are also some widowers' pensions.
- Although it is highly unlikely that the right to a basic pension will ever be abolished, the same cannot be said of SERPS, which is to be modified and have its benefits reduced.

To compensate for the loss through these changes to the SERPS calculations, the government is extending the rights to invest in personal pensions to people who at present are not eligible. From January 1988 new tax reliefs for personal pensions for both employees and the self-employed will replace the present retirement annuity provisions, although existing contracts will continue to qualify. The basic aim is to get more people out of SERPS and into contracted-out personal schemes. This will of course eventually reduce the government's spending on pensions.

Pensions in future

Radical changes are being made to the way in which we build up our pensions. The changes come in from two dates: January 1988 and 6 April 1988. Although further modifications may be made, the new rules, which apply to both the self-employed and employees, can be summarized as follows:

1. From 4 January 1988 any employee will have the right to contract out of SERPS and buy a personal pension. As previously, the self-employed will not be able to join SERPS. Any new personal pension contracts starting from 1988 to 5 April 1993, will get a 2 per cent bonus from the Government towards their schemes. Anyone with an existing contract will not get this.
2. If the employee contracts out of SERPS, he will still pay the full National Insurance contributions and the DHSS will pay the difference between the full rate and the lower basic contracted-out rate towards the personal pension. This means that in future everyone will have a minimum personal pension or SERPS and not just the basic State pension.

No interest will be paid on the contracted-out rebates paid by the DHSS to the chosen fund, even though the department will have been holding the sum deducted from the employee's salary for about six months from the end of the tax year.

3. Employees can have only one personal pension at a time. Those in company plans cannot buy a personal plan as well, except under the Additional Voluntary Contribution scheme. The self-employed, however, may buy any number, as long as they keep within the tax-relief limits (see below). It is not clear how often employees will be able to switch to another plan if they are not satisfied with the performance of the one they have chosen—once a year seems likely, as the holder can nominate a financial institution at the beginning or the end of a tax year.

4. Those now in company schemes will be able to opt out of them or choose not to join when they take up new employment. They can make their own arrangements. For most employees (anyone under 50), the maximum they will be able to put into a pension fund with full tax relief will be $17\frac{1}{2}$ per cent of their annual earnings.

5. At present, members of private company schemes can withdraw their funds up to five years after joining if they leave the firm. From 1988, this period is reduced to two years.

Anyone who chooses to leave his company's private pension plan will probably find himself paying more for the same level of benefits, facing a greater risk of a bad investment decision and poor annuity rates in the future. Membership of a company scheme offers pension levels related to service and/or salary, which cannot be guaranteed for the individual. For this reason, a decision to leave a company scheme should be taken only after considerable thought and taking professional advice.

6. Employers can contribute to an employee's personal pension plan, if he decides not to join or to leave the company fund, or where one is not available, but there is no legal requirement for them to so do. Where they do, the total contributions of employer and employee must not be more than $17\frac{1}{2}$ per cent of total earnings.

7. From 6 April 1988 the additional SERPS pension will be reduced and based on lifetime earnings instead of the average of the best 20 years' earnings used until now. The new formula will take in lower-earning years as well as higher ones and so will produce a lower average. The maximum pension on the equivalent of these earnings is also being reduced—from 25 to 20 per cent.

8. From the same date, the maximum pension which can be inherited by either spouse in the State scheme will be halved to 50 per cent from the 100 per cent which at present goes to widows, but not widowers. Now that most women earn some pension in their own right, this change will bring some benefits to widowed men but the cut to 50 per cent will affect far more women as they usually outlive men.

9. Employees will be able to make Additional Voluntary Contributions (AVCs) up to the $17\frac{1}{2}$ per cent of earnings above the minimum into a personal pension plan. These will work in more or less the same way as present retirement annuities for the self-employed, the so-called Section 226 policies which still qualify for tax relief at all levels of earnings. The options for employees are limited as they can have only one pension plan, so their AVCs must be made with the same financial institution.

10. The tax relief will be given to employees rather like the MIRAS

arrangement for mortgages. They will pay contributions net of the standard rate. The self-employed, in contrast, will continue to pay gross as in the past and reclaim the relief.

The new rules about the basic benefits which a personal pension plan must provide differ and are less than the old ones for recognized schemes.

Firstly, new personal schemes will not have to provide a guaranteed minimum pension—which is the basic requirement at present. There will have to be a minimum level of contribution and whatever level is decided upon—between 5.25 and 5.5 per cent of earnings seems likely—will be deducted from the National Insurance contribution for those who decide to contract out. So that people do not simply contract out and then use the money for another purpose, the government proposes to pay the rebated money through the DHSS into a scheme chosen by the employee.

Secondly, employers whose schemes have not before been eligible for contracting-out, as they have not met the minimum requirements, will be able to do so if the minimum contribution is made to the state scheme.

Thirdly, if this minimum is not paid, the only requirement for a scheme to be contracted out will be that it provides a minimum level of benefits; i.e., guaranteed minimum pension for the employee and his/her widow/widower. This means that those schemes into which only the employer contributes, which are rarely recognized schemes under the present rules and therefore require that the employees are contracted in to SERPS, will in future generally be allowed to contract out.

What should the employee do in the new circumstances? On balance:
- People with limited means who feel they simply cannot cope with running their own scheme should stay in SERPS but remember that the benefits are being reduced. They should try to save regularly over the long-term to help supplement their income in retirement in one of the savings schemes set out on pages 237–9 or in unit trusts (pages 47–51).
- People in private company schemes should stay in them. If many people do decide to leave to set up their own personal funds the long-term benefits from company funds could diminish. For this reason, anyone who can afford to pay into AVCs should do so to top up their company pension.
- Those who are setting up their own pension plans should seek professional advice from an insurance broker and look at several proposals.

Anyone who possibly can should start thinking and acting to supplement what they get from the state as soon as possible in their working career. In all investment—and buying a pension is as much an investment as saving, buying stocks and shares or life assurance—you benefit, unless you have made a bad mistake, according to what you have put in. The sooner you embark on a maximum pension plan the more it will yield when you retire.

Pensions today

Every time you start a new job, ask about the pension arrangements available to you. The most common situations are:
- Contracted out of SERPS (you could be contracted in, but this usually happens only when a company's private fund is optional) with a private scheme run by the company.
- As above but with an additional option of 'Advance Voluntary Contributions' (AVCs).
- As above, but with a 'Salary Sacrifice' scheme.

161

- Contracted into SERPS and with no private pension available.
- Self-employed.

The total pension finally available when you retire will be different in every case and, even if the sum of money is actually the same, the component parts that go to make it up will differ.

Contracted out of SERPS with private pension

If you are contracted out of SERPS, you will pay lower National Insurance contributions than if you are not. The difference is, however, more than likely to be made up by the contribution you make to the company scheme, or after January 1988 your own personal plan. About one third of employees are in what are commonly called 'top hat' schemes, which give them a pension without their having to make any contributions. The benefits in these tend to be minimal, however, and other arrangements should be made under the AVC scheme or some other personal plan.

It is highly unlikely that you personally and alone could make any changes in a scheme (although alterations are occasionally made if pressure from employees is strong). Before making your decision to join a company pension scheme, ask about the total benefits package:

- Does it offer a pension only at 60 or 65?
- Does it offer a reduced pension with the option of taking part of the benefit as a tax-free lump sum?
- Will the pension be a proportion of final salary or of an average taken over a number of years?
- Does it offer other benefits, such as a widow's or widower's pension, continuing private health care, or guaranteed increases in line with inflation?

Finally, ask what it will cost. Contributions vary between 5 per cent and 15 per cent of salary, although the higher level is unusual: 7.5 per cent is common. The employer will put in a matching or even a higher amount, so the total salary you are offered is better than stated—by the amount of the employer's contribution. All contributions are fully allowable for tax up to $17\frac{1}{2}$ per cent of earnings.

The answers to all these questions will affect your final pension and therefore your standard of living in retirement. By simply asking if the scheme was recognized (under the rules applying until the end of 1987) you will know that

- you will get a minimum of one-eightieth of your earnings for each year you are contracted out of SERPS,
- you will get a private pension which is at least equal to any SERPS pension you would have got,
- there will be a widow's element in the pension should you die while you are still employed, and your widow will get at least half of your pension entitlement until she dies,
- you have an absolute right to retire at 60 (women) and 65 (men),
- the value of your benefits cannot be lost if you change your job (what happens is that a deferred pension is calculated and then revalued as time goes on; this revaluation can sometimes be substantial, but it is wise not to rely upon it), and
- men and women must be treated in the same way—previously common practices like excluding women from some schemes or insisting on higher age-entry requirements for them are no longer permitted.

Within these rules, pension schemes have varied a great deal in the level of benefits offered and the cost to the employer and employee. There is one major broad difference between schemes: the matter of whether or not part of the pension can be commuted into a tax-free lump sum. Tax-free at present, that is: the concession could be removed at any time, as indeed could any of the tax advantages of investing in private pensions—contributions allowable for tax, no tax paid on the profits on investments in a fund, and the lump sum. At the moment the law is that only when the money invested in the fund starts to come back as a regular income is it taxed as income. All of these concessions should remove any doubts anyone might have about the financial sense of buying a private pension of some kind or other. In some cases, although not many, all the pension must be taken as a lump sum; also, in certain cases including public-sector pensions, part must be taken as a lump sum. In the 1987 Budget, the Chancellor of the Exchequer limited the lump sum to a maximum of £150,000.

The majority of private schemes, however, leave the final decision to the member of the fund. Although the lump sum comes tax-free, the choice is not always an easy one, especially since you cannot change your mind. You cannot, for example, decided to have all your benefits as pension and then later ask for part to be commuted. Similarly, once accepted, the lump sum cannot be given back.

The lump sum obviously has immediate attractions, but remember that you will be losing out on any annual increases which may come along: these apply only to that part of your personal fund taken as pension.

Your decision will be influenced by how useful you would find a cash sum and by the rules of the particular fund. Increases—index-linked or not—may be guaranteed, or they may be at the discretion of the trustees of the fund. You may also feel that the people managing your investments have not done particularly well and that you can do better yourself by choosing your own investments.

A married man should remember that, should he pre-decease his wife, she will probably receive only half the pension. Should the wife die first, however, the husband will continue to receive his full pension.

Additional Voluntary Contributions

One sweetener in some—not all—private company pension schemes in the past has been that they offer the possibility for members to make contributions, with tax relief, to the fund over and above the normal percentage. This can be very useful, particularly as we get older. Paying 5 or 7.5 per cent of our earnings may be all that we can afford in the early years of our working life, but later on, as we come to realize that inflation is eating into the value of the pension we can expect, the facility to make additional payments can greatly enhance our ultimate pension.

Not everyone can make AVCs.

- To qualify for the tax relief, the total of contributions to the ordinary pension fund plus AVCs cannot be more than $17\frac{1}{2}$ per cent of earnings.
- Once you start making AVCs, you have to continue them as long as you remain in the same job. The Inland Revenue may permit you to stop if you can prove you are suffering severe financial hardship, but it is unlikely.
- AVCs can be for only certain approved benefits with certain limits: (a) the

maximum personal pension allowed is two-thirds of final pay (this includes all private pensions from previous jobs, but not state pensions); (b) the whole pension can be continued by dependants, as long as no single dependant gets more than two-thirds of it; (c) pension increases are limited to increases in inflation, as measured by the Index of Retail Prices; and (d) any cash lump sum taken instead of pension is limited to 1.5 times final pay.

To get the full benefit from AVCs, you need ten years' contributions; otherwise the amount of pension is restricted. If you do not have 20 years' contributions, so is the amount of cash. Nevertheless, it is well worth considering making AVCs at any stage in your career, however late, even though the full benefits come only with long-term investment. You can continue them in retirement, if you wish to get the best return.

Salary sacrifice

For most people, a reduction in income on retirement is inevitable, because of the limits set by the government on what can be paid in pension. But there is one way around the two-thirds limit, and that is by agreeing with your employer to sacrifice some of your salary while you are working. As with AVCs, there are tax benefits, as you pay tax only on what you receive—i.e., not on the part you are giving up. The employer buys an endowment life-assurance policy for the employee, due to mature on retirement. The lump sum assured goes tax-free to the employee at that point. Most people under the age of 40 probably would not wish to give up part of their earnings in this way—indeed, probably could not—but it is well worth considering when you reach this age.

Self-employed

The self-employed often complain that, when it comes to pensions and other social-security benefits, they are badly off compared with employees. While it is true that they qualify only for the basic pension from their National Insurance contributions and cannot join SERPS, the weekly contribution rate is low compared with that for employees, and the government has been generous in its treatment of the self-employed when it comes to providing pensions for themselves. From now on, they will be treated more or less in the same way as employees, except that they will pay their contributions gross into their pension plan and reclaim tax relief and they can have more than one plan, as long as they keep within the limits for tax relief. These are $17\frac{1}{2}$ per cent for anyone born before 1934. After that, the percentage is even better, rising on a sliding scale to 27.5 per cent for those over 75.

It is very important for the self-employed to consider such schemes, because the basic state pension is woefully inadequate and will become increasingly so as time goes on. The sooner you enter such a scheme the better, because it will be cheaper and the benefits will be greater, and there is no other way of combining pensions and life assurance with such generous tax treatment.

In future, employees will have to have at least the basic State pension plus SERPS but there is no requirement for the self-employed to make any pension arrangements at all. Anyone in business on their own account is foolish not to make maximum use of the concessions available.

The schemes offered by insurance companies vary to some extent, so it is worth getting two or three quotes to see what benefits you will be offered for a given sum of money. The scheme must be flexible enough to cope with fluctuations in your income and, if you are unable to contribute to the limit allowed in law at the outset, you should be able to increase the payments to that limit should you so wish. Similarly, should you face financial difficulties, you should be able to cut your payments or eliminate them altogether for a while. In law, you are allowed to pick any retirement age between 50 and 75 for your annuity.

You cannot get at any of the funds used to purchase a pension until the date of your retirement, nor can you use the plan as security for any loan in the way that a life-assurance policy can be used. Nevertheless, some insurance companies have recently developed loan-back schemes, so that you can use the funds for the development of your business.

Remember that, in a family business where both husband and wife work, both can buy personal pensions, so that a wife, too, can build up a pension in her own right. (See also the general discussion of tax and married people on pages 131–7.)

If you have previously made pension arrangements under the old retirement annuity schemes, these will continue to qualify for tax relief. There is no need to abandon them and it would be unwise to do so, especially if you have already built up considerable benefits.

Women and pensions

Despite the fact that today the majority of women work, married or not, it is surprising how few of them think seriously about pensions. They assume that they are covered by their husband's schemes and, even when he may have only the basic state pension and some SERPS, they do not always take advantage of the opportunities offered to them by the tax rules. SERPS benefits which have only been earned since 1978 are not likely to be substantial for anyone retiring now or in the next few years and, as we have seen (pages 159–60), those benefits are to be eroded.

In the past, apart from the fact that women get the same basic pension as men—if they have the appropriate number of National Insurance contributions—at age 60 rather than 65, women have usually been badly treated as far as pensions go. Even if they are in SERPS, the fact that women's wages are still on average much lower than those of men means that they inevitably get a lower pension from this source. Thanks to the 1975 Sex Discrimination Act, women can no longer be excluded from pension funds nor have different entry rules applied to them, but again it will be many years before the full benefits are seen.

It is just as important for a woman to have a pension in her own right as for a man, and this is true whether or not she is married. Until 1978, married women had the choice of opting in or out of contributions towards the basic pension. This is no longer true and, apart from a few women who opted out before then, all married women, if in employment, are contributing at least to the basic pension and SERPS. There is generous treatment of them, too, if they leave employment for a period to bring up their children: they are allowed to be out of the workforce for up to 20 years for this purpose (so are men, but that applies far less often) without losing any of their rights to a basic state pension.

165

17 | Moving from Savings to Investment

It is a general rule that moving from the safety of savings schemes into risk investment in the stock market happens during one's 30s or 40s. It could well occur earlier, but nevertheless the 30s are generally a busy financial period. Many people can start filling in the spaces in their financial planning. By this time, several questions about our lives will either have been answered or may at least be in the process of being answered. We have often been married for several years. Our family is often complete, with the children growing up and at school. Wives have often returned to work. We know the financial commitment on our homes. We have a good idea of where we are going in our career. If we have planned properly, we generally have some secure savings to help us cope with any sudden financial problem. We should also by this time have basic life assurance.

All these things mean that, for the first time, many of us can ask ourselves whether we can afford to take a risk and thereby hope to increase the value of our capital. For most people, this means stock-market investment, although today opportunities have widened to allow investment in currencies and in financial futures, even for those who do not have many thousands of pounds to invest. The latter options are very much in their infancy and should be undertaken only by the very knowledgeable, so we shall concentrate on stock-market investment, but look back to unit trusts (see page 47), as these should be your first step in risk investment.

First of all, we should recognize the difference between saving and investment. In the former, the value of the original amount of money (the capital) you save is or should be guaranteed; the value of the total funds you have rises as interest is credited to the account. In the latter, a new element is introduced—that of risk. You will probably get interest—in this case called a dividend—but on the other hand you may not. But there is also the possibility that the amount of the original capital invested will rise, if you have chosen your investment well, giving you what is known as a capital profit.

The risk element is implicit in all kinds of investment. For example, property, where the value of the property may rise while at the same time you are receiving dividends in the form of rent. Your own home is certainly a form of investment, and the fact that you live there rent-free constitutes a type of dividend. You may buy antiques, paintings, stamps or coins. There is a wide range of this type of investment. You may buy currencies or 'futures' in currencies or commodities. You may make a profit from any of these activities: on the other hand, you may make a loss.

The most common form of investment for the average person is in the stock market. This is where we are able to invest in companies, both at home and overseas. If they are profitable and these profits rise, the companies will increase dividends to their shareholders, and the price of the shares in the companies will rise. Shares are exactly what they sound like: investors buy parcels of shares in the company, thereby becoming part-owners of the particular company whose shares they purchase.

Naturally, the price of the shares may fall if the company does badly and is forced to cut or eliminate its dividends. There are other reasons, too, for a fall in share prices. The economy of a country may turn down, and this can adversely affect the prices of even the most profitable companies. Interest rates generally may rise, which means that the return people get on their savings increases: then investors expect a bigger return on their shares as well. This brings in another concept—the return on an investment, commonly called the yield. This differs from interest on savings. For instance, if you are told by a savings institution that you will get 7.5 per cent on your savings, that is what you will get at that particular time. The interest rate may change, if the banks change their minimum lending rate, but the announced rate is guaranteed for the time being and means that for every £100 you have invested you will get £7.50 in interest each year. (See discussion on pages 44 and 119 on how the same interest rate charged or paid can differ.) As the price of shares varies, you cannot calculate the real return you will get from dividends simply by stating it. The calculation is as follows. Say a company announces a 15 per cent dividend on its shares, which will have a nominal (or par) value. Let's take this as 25p, a very common par value. It is most unlikely that the market price will also be 25p. Assume that it is 50p. This means that, although you will be getting 15 per cent (i.e., 3.25p) on each 25p share, you will have to pay twice the par value for one share, and so you need to divide the dividend by two to calculate your true return on every £100 invested. In this case, it would be 7.5 per cent. The formula for working out yields is:

$$\frac{\text{par value} \times \text{dividend}}{\text{market price}}$$

Yields on every share at any one time are not the same. General interest rates are a guide to yields overall, but people are willing to accept a lower return on some shares and expect a higher one on others. They will pay more for shares in companies which are expected to increase their profits—and therefore their dividends—at a rate higher than the average, and so they will accept a lower-than-average return to begin with. If, on the other hand, they expect a disappointing profits trend with little growth or even with a decline and lower dividends, they will want a higher-than-average true return when they buy, in case the share price falls. General industrial conditions and those of individual companies vary all the time, and of course investors may make the wrong decisions. An industry may be doing badly, so that people sell the shares and the price falls, but one company could be doing well despite the general trend. When this is the case, the share price will eventually rise to reflect its better-than-average performance.

This is the whole concept of risk, and choosing correctly is the key to success in investing, giving a gradually rising income and an improvement in the actual capital value of an investment.

Before looking at how you can minimize the risk and maximize your chances of becoming a successful investor, we need to look at the kinds of shares available and how you go about buying and selling them. Stocks and shares make up what is called the capital of the company. There will be an authorized amount, all of which may not actually have been issued for sale to the public, or some of which may have been used, say, to buy other companies.

Debentures and loans

Strictly speaking, debentures are not part of the capital of the company: they are more a debt which would have to be repaid, should the company be wound up, before any money could be distributed to the holders of the risk capital.

Debentures are usually quoted in £100 amounts, and are called stock rather than shares. They carry a fixed rate of dividend and do not therefore benefit shareholders when a company is doing well: holders simply get their dividend each year. This means that the prices of debentures will usually move up and down with interest rates. When rates rise prices fall, and vice versa. If a company is doing very badly and it is thought that even this stock could not be repaid in the event of a liquidation, the price may fall. Governments issue a similar kind of stock (see later, page 170).

Sometimes the debenture may be 'secured' on a certain piece of company's property, in the same way a home-loan company knows that it will get back the money it has lent on a mortgage, because the mortgage is 'secured' on the home itself. This means that the piece of property can always be sold to pay off the debenture holder. Where there is no security, the term 'loan' is often used rather than 'debenture'. As they come first in any share-out of the company's assets, they are the least risky of stock-market investments.

Debentures and loans may have a redemption date attached to them. This is the date by which the company guarantees to repay the original capital to the holders. Investors may get an option of a repayment of the loan or a switch into the equity (the risk capital) of the company at an earlier date than redemption. Where this option is available, the investor will over a period of years get several chances at switching. In this case, the price will move with that of the ordinary shares. Such a debenture is called a convertible debenture, and is useful for someone who needs a regular income now but would like the chance of switching to the true risk capital of the company at a later date. As a rule, the number of shares for which the debenture may be swapped falls each year. It might look like this:

1988—20 ordinary shares for each £100 debenture
1989—17 ordinary shares for each £100 debenture
1990—15 ordinary shares for each £100 debenture
1991—option lapses

Now say that the 1988 share price is £5, the 1989 share price £8 and the 1990 share price £6.50. If loans and debentures on average are offering a yield of about 6 per cent through all these years and, for simplicity, that the company's debenture carries a dividend (sometimes called a coupon) of 6 per cent, the debenture would normally be quoted at £100 throughout the period. So in 1988 the debenture and the cost of 20 shares would both be worth £100. However, in 1989 the debenture would be worth £100 but the

17 equities at £8 each would be worth £136, so it would be worthwhile switching. During this time, the price of the debenture will move up to match the price of the equity.

In 1990 the picture looks quite different. The debenture on the interest paid would be quoted at £100, but the 15 shares would be worth only £97.50, so the switch would not be worthwhile.

After the option lapses, of course, the stock becomes like any debenture—i.e., it has no conversion rights attached to it. Buying convertible debentures and loans can be an important part of investment planning, giving a good income to begin with and capital growth as time goes on, if a company does well.

Preference shares

Preference shares are part of the true share capital of the company, but carry less risk than the equity (see below). Preference shares also carry a fixed dividend, and repayment comes after debentures and loan stock if a company is liquidated. Dividends do not fluctuate with company profits, although a dividend may not be paid out if a company does very badly indeed.

A preference share may be 'cumulative'. If the dividend is not paid in one or more years, when profits recover the arrears are paid before anything is paid out on the risk capital.

Once again, prices tend to vary only with interest rates, and high capital profits are unlikely on preference shares. An exception to this could happen when interest rates, having risen, fall very sharply indeed. The price of preference shares will also improve, so timing is important for anyone buying this stock.

Equities

Equities are the risk capital of a company, and it is in this field that the big losses and profits are made. They are also called ordinary shares, or stock units, or, in the United States, common stocks. They carry all the risk of investing in the company. Each year, after the debts and the fixed-interest stock dividends have been paid, holders of equities are entitled to all the remaining company profits after company tax has been paid. These are called earnings. When a company is doing well, the directors of the company will raise the dividend on the equity. When a company does badly, the investor is the first to suffer, for his or her dividend can be cut or eliminated altogether. In a liquidation, the ordinary shareholders get everything which is left—if anything—after all the other debts have been paid. The market price may fluctuate quite sharply, not only on what is actually happening in the individual company but on the general domestic economy and, indeed, the world economy. There are two prices quoted—bid and offer. The first is the price at which the dealer is prepared to buy stock, and the latter the price at which the dealer will sell. The latter will be higher, and the difference between the two is part of the profit made by the stockbroker who does the buying and selling of shares.

It can be difficult, looking at all the prices, to decide what has been happening on the stock market and whether prices generally are rising or falling. To help investors various indices have been produced, primarily by

169

THE DIFFERENT KINDS OF GILT-EDGED STOCKS

Short-dated: stocks due to be redeemed within five years.

Medium-dated: stocks due for redemption within a five-to-fifteen-year period.

Long-dated: stocks with a remaining life of more than fifteen years.

Irredeemable: stock which is never likely to be redeemed.

Index-linked: stock in which both the capital value and interest rise with inflation; they carry a redemption date.

the *Financial Times* and by the Stock Exchange itself. Every day, the price changes in a number of leading active stocks on each market are calculated and averaged. The resulting figure can be compared with earlier figures over the short or long term, so it is an indicator not only of how daily dealings move but also (over a period) of the general mood in the market.

Government stock

It is necessary to mention one more type of investment before moving onto the planning of an individual or family portfolio (the total of the various shares anyone holds). This is government stock, commonly called gilt-edged securities because the original stock documents had a gold border around them.

All governments need money to run a country. They get it through taxes and through the money we lend them when we invest in National Savings schemes. This is not enough, however, for their needs, so from time to time they issue their own stock, which is rather like the secured debenture. The 'security' in this case is the guarantee that the government gives to repay the stock eventually. In Britain, historically, the stock has been issued in £100 units and carries a 'coupon', or fixed rate of interest.

Today, all the new stock issued has a finite life and a redemption date: otherwise investors would not purchase it. In the past, there have been a few so-called undated stocks on which people have lost money because they have never been, and are most unlikely ever to be, redeemed. (These stocks today simply move with interest rates, so the prices fluctuate and they have their uses in an overall portfolio.) Even dated stocks move with interest rates, although their prices will gradually move towards the issue price, or the price at which redemption is promised, as the redemption date draws nearer. For this reason, government securities have two yields, a normal one based on every £100 invested, and a redemption yield which takes the repayment date into account. Depending on interest rates, the redemption yield can be higher or lower than the straight yield. At any one time, different stocks have differing maturity periods and their yields will vary in relation to how investors are expecting interest to move in the future. Make sure that you understand the terminology. (The box above describes the different types.)

Gilt-edged securities are often bought for income by those with limited means, but, if they are bought at a time when interest rates are high, on the basis that a fall is coming, capital gain is just as possible as in shares. In addition to buying gilt-edged securities through the stock market, it is also possible to buy them—at the current market price, of course—through what is called the National Savings Stock Register. The list is changed from time to time, if for no other reason than that some stocks are redeemed and others introduced. Write to the Director, Bonds and Stock Office, Lytham St Annes, Lancashire FY0 1YN. You do not escape dealing charges through using the stock register, but they are low: £1 for every £250 nominal amount of stock, then 50p for every £125 of nominal stock.

Index-linked gilts

Index-linking was extended beyond National Savings into gilt-edged stock in 1982. Both the principal (the actual amount of capital invested) and the interest are linked to movements in the Retail Prices Index. Anyone who bought the first issue, Treasury 2 per cent, due for redemption in 1988, and continues to hold it throughout its life, will get back the original capital invested, but this will have been increased according to the rate of inflation over the six-year period. (The 2 per cent interest will have been increased each year by the level of inflation in the preceding year.)

That first stock was relatively short-dated, but today there are index-linked stocks running past the year 2000. Anyone buying and selling on the open market has no price guarantee, of course, and the case for buying such stock varies with the level of inflation. When that is running high, an index-linked stock can guarantee that the value of the original capital is maintained and that interest rates keep up. When inflation is low, however, the safety net is still there but there are probably better avenues for income and capital growth than index-linked gilts. Because of the index-linking element, the initial income of these gilts tends to be on the low side.

The Stock Exchange

Investing in stocks and shares takes place in three markets. The most important of these by far is the Stock Exchange, based in London and with branches around the country. Investors are not confined to the British market—the whole investment scene is becoming more international as communications speed up—but for the beginner, at least until a reasonably sized portfolio has been built up, investments in Britain should be the focus of attention.

To get a quotation—that is, to have its share prices quoted daily on the Stock Exchange—a company has to fulfil certain listing requirements, which change from time to time. New companies seeking a market quote will have to provide (including a profits record for some years) a dividend forecast and details of the directors, a description of the business, and so on. A minimum 25 per cent of the company's total equity must be brought to the market.

The many thousands of companies which have been brought to the stock market during the two centuries for which it has been operating all have two prices quoted on the market every day, a buying price and a selling price, unless for any reason their market quotation has been suspended.

Shares have to be bought through market traders, who make a charge, known as commission, for dealing for you. (For current rates see pages 174–5.) Only people licensed to deal in securities are permitted to trade on the exchange, which, since the so-called Big Bang in October 1986, has operated not so much as a physical market, where traders—the stockbrokers—go to set prices and deal, but electronically between brokers' offices.

It is too soon to say yet whether the new system is of benefit to investors or not. Certainly it has helped the larger institutional investor, who may be buying on behalf of a pension fund, an insurance company or an investment or unit trust, but smaller investors may have found their dealing costs increased.

The Unlisted Securities Market

The Stock Exchange does not like to take any risks, apart from the normal commercial ones, in the companies it allows to be quoted. This means that many smaller concerns, which could benefit and grow from outside investor involvement, have been unable to get a market quotation because they do not meet the listing requirements.

Their problem in raising finance for development was partly solved in 1981 with the setting up of the Unlisted Securities Market (USM). This has listing requirements not nearly as strict as the Stock Exchange's, and the cost of getting a listing is much lower. Companies need issue only 10 per cent of their stock, rather than 25 per cent, and they do not have to be of a minimum size. The details of business activity can be much briefer and, although an issue will go better if there is a business record revealed (three years is likely), it is not required at all, and the listing need not show profits.

It will be obvious that companies listed on the USM can carry far more risk than those on the main exchange. However, by the end of 1986, when it had been running for five years, the USM was quoting over 500 stocks and there had been very few failures. The market has to be considered a success, and some companies have moved to the main stock market.

If you recognize and can live with the higher risk, USM stocks are well worth considering because their profit potential can be high. You may well need to keep a closer eye on price movements, however, than when you invest in major companies.

The third market

Following the success of the Unlisted Securities Market, the London Stock Exchange on 26 January 1987 launched a third market. This new market is for companies too small or too young to qualify for the main listing or even the USM. The third market is in direct competition with the over-the-counter market (see below), which many stockbrokers felt was just too uncontrolled.

There is no minimum size or age for companies coming to the third market. To qualify, companies should have at least one full year's audited figures, but even that requirement can be waived in special circumstances—for example, if a company can show that they have fully costed and researched a project, even if work has not actually started on it. This means that so-called 'greenfield' enterprises may be allowed onto the market.

There are two limited safeguards. Certain highly speculative operations are banned—companies dealing in properties, investments or commodities. Further, a company must be 'sponsored' by an existing member of the market; sponsors are usually stockbroking firms.

Companies requiring as little as £10,000 may qualify for the market, and it is clear that some enterprises will be highly risky. Anyone not prepared to accept such a risk should steer clear of this market: it is not for those who are concerned primarily with safety.

Having said that, small companies, on average, grow faster than large ones, and anyone with a gambling instinct who can spread the risk over three or four such companies could do very well indeed.

The over-the-counter markets

Over-the-counter markets (OTCs) go one step further than the USM. They are not supervised and regulated in the same way as the other two markets, and are therefore highly risky. Dealings in the market are made in one of two ways. Firstly, there are agents who match buyers and sellers, and charge both a commission for getting them together. Other dealers act as principals, buying and selling on their own account, rather like stockbrokers. They set bid and offer prices, and their profit is the gap between the two.

This is not a market for the small inexperienced investor, but it could become more important as time goes on, so it is worthwhile being aware of it. Be very conscious of the risk: it is high. If you want to invest directly in British business away from the stock market, try the Business Expansion Scheme, which offers tax relief at the highest marginal rates on up to £40,000 investment a year.

173

PAYING FOR YOUR SHARES

You do not have to pay for shares as soon as you buy them. Similarly, if you sell, you do not get the money immediately. The Stock Exchange year is divided into a series of 'accounts', each generally of two weeks' duration, although there are a few which last three weeks during periods of public holidays.

Accounts run from Monday to the Friday of the following week. All deals done during that period are then itemized and balanced out if necessary. Statements go out and any bills must be settled on the second Tuesday of the following account—the so-called Account Day. Any cheques due are sent at the same time.

You can buy in one account for settlement on the Account Day of the next account. You must pay extra, however, for 'new time' dealings, which can be done the Thursday before the start of the new account.

If you buy and sell within one account, there is only one lot of commission to pay, so dealing within the account is popular with speculators.

Building up an investment portfolio

Here we shall not go into all the technicalities of the stock market: there are many excellent books which do that. All we need to look at here is how to begin and develop an investment portfolio which will fulfil our financial aims. Not everyone has the same purpose when investing. Some are looking for income now, while others have sufficient income and prefer to go for those investments which offer good prospects of capital growth. Still others want a combination of growth and income. Moreover, for each person, there are times when investment needs change.

Dealing costs

It costs money to deal, in addition to the purchase price of the shares. You will need to be aware of these costs before you start. The general rule is that, the more you invest, the lower the unit cost of purchase will be. You can buy either through a stockbroker directly, or use your bank. There are also in the major cities today a number of share shops to which you can go directly to buy.

Whatever avenue you choose, there will be a basic minimum cost of at least £10, no matter how small the cost of the parcel of shares ('the bargain') you buy. Since the Big Bang in the City of London in October 1986, which revolutionized the way in which share dealings take place, there has been no fixed level of commission. By shopping around you may save a little, but that is unlikely on a small deal. It is surprising what uniformity there is among different dealers. Before the Big Bang, for instance, after the £10 minimum, most charged 1.65 per cent on the first £7,000, after which the rate fell sharply until it was 0.5 per cent. Then, if you had a very large sum to invest in a single share deal, the rate would fall again, to 0.2 per cent. Even within these broad figures, however, there were variations. For example, the minimum charge might be as high as £15.

These rates, which have changed little since the Big Bang, are the so-called 'advisory' rates for when you want to consult the broker rather than simply put in a dealing request. Dealing-only rates are lower and you can save anything between 20 and 30 per cent on dealing-only, but be very sure that you want dealing-only. It may mean just that: you may not even be able to enquire about the current price of the share you are buying or selling. Not everyone has two rates, either, so there is a lot more thinking for the investor to do when considering commission rates than there was when the old fixed rates prevailed.

Remember that dealing costs are applied to both purchases and sales, unless bought within the same 'account' (accounts are the two-week periods into which the Stock Exchange dealing year is divided—see box), and it is important to note that there are further costs. You will have to pay Value Added Tax (VAT) on the commission. Next, there is a 0.5 per cent stamp duty to pay on purchases, although not on sales. Finally, you must not forget that there are two prices. The price at which the broker will buy from you is always lower than his offer price to you. It is impossible to state what this gap will be at any particular time. The more active a share—that is, the more often it is traded—the narrower will be the gap: in very active shares, it might be only a penny or two, but for a share which is traded only a few times a week or month it could be 50p or even more. Check on all this before you buy but, whatever share you choose, you must reckon that there will have to be an increase of at least 10 per cent in the price of the share before you can be sure of making a profit on a sale.

Before investing in the stock market

- make sure you have your 'rainy day' money safely and securely invested
- if you have only small amounts of capital, consider instead unit trusts (see page 47)—you can always turn to individual shares later when you have built up more funds
- decide against going into the stock market if you cannot afford to take a risk, however much you would like to
- remember that stocks and shares are not for the nervous so that, even if you have sufficient capital, there is no point in investing if you are going to worry the whole time about the possibility of losing money

First questions to ask

We will all have different answers to the questions considered here. Only you yourself can decide if the answers in your own particular case mean that you should or should not invest.

First, how old are you? Anyone over the age of 18 can invest but, unless we have absolutely no financial responsibilities to others, investing is best left until we have made provision for all emergencies. The younger the investor, the more likely he or she is to go for growth in capital rather than for income now. A balance between income and growth comes with our mature years, when our families are established and our commitments are

INVESTMENT AND MARRIED PEOPLE

Any income from investments for a married couple is treated in the same way as interest on savings accounts. In law, this means that the income of both is amalgamated and taxed as if it all accrued to the husband. As with savings, the Inland Revenue will want to know from the husband details of all his wife's investments as well as his own. It implies careful planning, even if the couple are each investing independently. As their joint incomes will attract higher levels of tax before the same joint income of two unmarried people would, they may feel, for example, that they prefer to sacrifice high income now for the possibility of capital growth for their mutual benefit in the future. Even if they run into the Capital Gains Tax net later, the maximum rate is 30 per cent. Now that the CGT exemption is index-linked, it is relatively easy to minimize any CGT liability you may have by timing when you make sales and take profits.

known. Towards the end of our lives, income begins to take precedence, but there is no reason completely to give up prospects of capital gain.

Second, are you single or married? There is a distinct difference in investment policies for the unmarried and the married. Generally, the unmarried can take more risk. The married must balance the needs of others in the family and, in particular, have to be aware of the implications of the impact of their joint taxation on their dividends. (See box.)

Third, what are your sources of income? Work out exactly what your income is (your joint income if you are married), and then set your tax allowances against it. Remember that you will have to pay tax on your dividends at the highest rate of tax you pay (this is called the marginal rate). You can work it out by calculating your net income and then setting the various tax bands against it as shown in the table on page 27. Remember, too, that married people reach the higher marginal rates of tax sooner than two single people. Investment income under the current tax system cannot be separated in the same way as earnings for married couples.

Fourth, what is your life-assurance cover? Do not begin investing if you do not have sufficient life cover. Remember that life assurance is just as much a part of long-term financial planning as investment in stocks and shares. Even if you do not eventually get the money, your heirs can use it to minimize any Inheritance Tax there may be to pay.

Fifth, do you have a hobby which could be turned to profit and which could play a part in your overall investment portfolio?

Sixth, and last, it can pay to look at the total value of all your assets, because this will affect the amount and extent of the risk you are able to take.

Next you must consider your investment requirements—i.e., whether you want income now, capital growth, or a combination of the two.

An income portfolio will include any savings you already have and probably some government securities or fixed-interest stocks. Together these should make up about 50 per cent of your portfolio.

A capital-growth portfolio might include some government securities, although perhaps only if you are buying on hopes of a fall in interest rates. Most of your investments will be in equities, probably today in companies with an international content; these will protect you from the uncertainties of the ups and downs of the British economy. As a general rule, try to avoid having more than 5 per cent in any one stock (or at most 7.5 per cent), except in very special situations. If one investment does particularly well, its value in your portfolio may of course rise to more than this ideal amount. Even if you think that the investment will continue to do well, though, it is worth considering whether to sell at least some of the shares to protect your profits and to diversify into a wider range of investment. The prices of shares in even the best companies can fall when market conditions are unfavourable. Timing, particularly knowing when to take a profit or cut a loss, is a vital element in successful investment. Two investors might go into the same share but, because they buy and sell at slightly different times, one could make a big profit and the other a loss.

It is important not to confine yourself to one or two shares. If you cannot afford to buy, say, five different shares to begin with, stay with unit trusts.

Do not think that you can simply buy shares and then sit back and forget about them while the profits come rolling in. No matter how good the companies you have chosen, there will be times when it is important to sell. Read the financial press, but remember that the stock market can be very nervous and respond quickly to any comments in the press: it is not unusual for this to be an over-reaction and have only a very temporary effect, so do not allow yourself to be panicked because of an unfavourable comment—the price may well be restored after only a day or two. This is more true of market prices as a whole than of one particular share after favourable or adverse comment. The market as a whole can fall steeply on bad international news, a forecast of slower growth or of an economic setback, or a fall in stock markets abroad (especially New York), but a week later the level may be back to where it was before the news. This is not always true, of course, so assess the importance of any announcement carefully and read what the investment analysts have to say about it.

Investment strategy

Whether you are choosing to invest at home or in international companies, the criteria for selecting a market are the same.

The political situation must be stable. Often, even if a country is basically completely stable, there may be times of political instability; when an election approaches, for instance, or when the result of an election suggests that the particular government may have to call another general election before very long. Change, even if it is ultimately beneficial, may make a market move erratically for a time.

Exchange rates must be stable. The value of one currency when set against another can have a marked effect on a company's profits. For instance, if a company has to import a large proportion of its raw materials, a fall in the value of the importing country's currency will put import prices up, thereby depressing profits. The converse is true if the company is an exporter: as the value of its country's currency declines its products become cheaper to foreign buyers and so again profits will generally decline. Rises in the value of a currency have precisely the opposite effects. Today, companies hedge against movements in the values of currencies by buying what are called 'futures'. This means that they buy and sell currencies for delivery at a fixed date ahead, in an attempt to overcome any fluctuations in value and so be able to keep their profitability under control. It is not always possible to do this, so the currency factor must always be considered. (Individuals can also today invest in currencies, but this is not for the average family.)

There must be a genuine stock market, wherever you decide to invest. Modern technology is gradually transforming the stock exchanges of the world into one vast stock market. If you are investing at home there is no problem, but clearly, where a market is very small, there are much greater risks. You should not venture into any except the biggest markets or the major foreign companies until you have become something of an expert. You will find that some of the very largest foreign companies in which you want to invest are quoted on the British market. At the beginning of your investment programme, you would probably be advised to stick to British stocks and get into the international scene via one of the unit trusts specializing in foreign stocks. There are a great number of these, covering particular areas of the world.

Choosing the sector

Having decided where you want to invest, do not simply pick a share at random, or just go for one which has been recommended to you. You must look first of all at what sector of the economy will make the best investment at the particular time you are investing. An economy may be generally doing well, but not all sectors will benefit to the same degree. Likewise, even though an economy is generally doing badly, some sectors may be doing well. After reading all you can about your chosen market, and perhaps consulting your broker, make your decision about which industry or business activity you want to invest in.

Choosing the company

Having chosen your sector, you must go through the whole process again in order to choose a company within that sector. Just as sector performance varies, so does the profitability of companies within a particular sector. At the beginning you will probably be guided by your stockbroker, by more knowledgeable friends, or by the advice given in the financial pages of newspapers and investment magazines. But all of these are no substitute for doing some research on your own.

Use your experience when narrowing down the choice of investment. Many investors have done well by backing their hunches and by bearing in mind that industries have their own spending patterns. Keep your eyes and ears open, but remember that just because, to choose retailing as an example, a shop or store appears to be doing a roaring trade, this does not automatically mean that the company is making good profits.

You may not understand a great deal when you first start to invest, although that will come with time. This means that you must take great care with your early investments. There are certain measurements against which you can check your selection of stocks. Choose the one which best meets the criteria you have set yourself.

First, yield. Look at the yield on the stock. Yield, as we know (see page 167), is the true return you get on every £100 you have invested: it is not the dividend declared on the shares. You will notice that there is an average for shares in the sector. If the yield on the share you are analysing is lower, ask yourself why. It may be that investors are expecting that the company's profits will rise more quickly than the average, so that dividends will also be raised and the yield at the present price accordingly rise quickly. The low return may be quite justified but, conversely, investors may be being too optimistic. If they are, and the company results are eventually disappointing, the share price will slip back so that the yield is nearer the average for the industry. Similarly, the yield may be higher than average because the company is not expected to show much growth— perhaps in the past its performance has been rather dull. Is the higher yield then justified by the poorer prospects of growth? Maybe, but company conditions do change—so watch out for these changes. Is the company facing a big currency risk? Has it lost a major order, or gained one? Has there been some technological breakthrough? Is a company which has had a large share of the total business in its field now facing increased competition? Circumstances like these are reported in the news, quite apart from any comments about shares. If you want to maximize your profits, you will have to spot these things as quickly as anyone else.

Second, what about dividend cover? This tells you how easy the company has found it to pay the dividend. Equity shareholders, as we have seen (page 169), are entitled to all the profits left after the debentures, loans and preference shareholders (if any) have been paid. Normally, however, directors of a company do not pay out the whole of profits. They put part ('retained profits') on one side to provide a cushion against profits falling and also to finance further expansion. The figure for dividend cover tells you how safe the dividend is and also gives you an idea whether it could easily be increased or, in a profits setback, maintained.

This is how it works. Say the cost of a dividend to the company is £750,000 and profits are £1.8 million. Dividend cover is therefore 2.4 times $(1,800,000 \div 750,000)$; in other words, the directors of the company could, if they wished, pay a dividend 2.4 times bigger without having to dip into the company's reserves. Similarly, profits could drop by over £1 million before any consideration would have to be given to a dividend cut. Just as there are average yields for sectors, there are averages for dividend cover. But these are a less important guide for investors, because boards of directors have very individual approaches to dividend policy.

Third, there is the price/earning ratio. This tells you how many years of profits at their present level are reflected in the share price, and is worked out by calculating the amount of profit which is due to each share and then dividing that into the price. Say profits are, once again, £1.8 million and there are one million shares in issue. Each share will have £1.80 profit due to it. Let's suppose, then, that the share price is 580p. Divide £1.80 into the 580p and you get the result 3.2. This means that, at the present level of profits, the current price will be earned in 3.2 years; this is a rather low level. Price/earning ratios vary enormously. Generally, the higher the figure, the more favoured the share is, and investors are believing that profits will rise very sharply very quickly, so that the present price will soon be covered by profits—i.e., it is worth paying what looks like a very high price for a stock. When price/earning ratios are low, on the other hand, investors may be pessimistic about the profits trend, believing that it may not be maintained and that it will take rather longer for profits to cover the price of the shares.

By applying these three indicators, you can often whittle down the list of shares you might want to buy in a particular sector. You must now look at the individual companies.

What to look for

There are four things to look at here: the basic financial health of the company, the quality of the management, the company's past record and, finally, its prospects. While you are looking at all these factors you must also be working out the length of time for which the investment might be suitable. Think of short-term as a month or so, medium-term as three to six months, and long-term as anything beyond that.

You can assess the company's financial health by looking at its annual accounts. If you are using a stockbroking firm, check to see if it has done any research on the company in which you are interested and find out what view, if any, it is taking on the shares. It is relatively easy to get hold of a copy of the company's accounts from a company itself—indeed, a company may well be prepared to give you the accounts for a few years back, so that you can get a continuing picture.

Company accounts contain a lot of information, but what you will be looking for are trends over several years. Many companies today give a five-year record, so it is relatively easy to see what has happened over a reasonable period. You will want to see a rising trend in all the following:

- Sales (also referred to as turnover).
- Profits (or decreasing losses).
- Profit margins—i.e., the amounts of profits made on sales. Say a company made £500,000 profits from 10 million sales in one year but that in the next year sales stayed the same while profits rose to £700,000 because the company made economies or brought in new equipment which lowered the cost of production. The margin of profit made on each sale would therefore have increased by 40 per cent.
- Return on capital employed. This is a very interesting figure and is taken by many investors to be the best indicator of efficiency in a company. It measures how much profit is made on every £100 of capital invested in the business. The higher it is, the argument goes, the better the company. But again the value of this measurement varies in different sectors of industry. Nothing in investment is an exact science, and return on capital employed is like any other indicator. Some capital-intensive industries never have a very large return on capital employed; these include sectors like electrical, shipbuilding, oil refining and heavy engineering. These sectors, you will note, all need to invest very large amounts of money in plant before they can manufacture a single item. Other industries need very few assets. These are mainly the service industries, which can make large profits from relatively small premises and few staff. So, once again, it is important to look and see how return on capital employed averages out for a sector, and to check that of your chosen company against it.
- Dividends paid. How generous is the company in its dividend policy? Is it cautious, or generous? Have dividends been rising steadily?

● Earnings. These are the amounts of profits after all charges have been paid, including taxation and interest on all stock except the equity. The earnings are what are left for equity holders, and these, too, should ideally show a rising trend. However, although we are looking for a rising trend, one year's setback may not be significant: the company could merely have run into a temporary bad patch. Other companies are in businesses where the normal pattern of trading is cyclical: there are definite troughs and heights in performance. The trick here is to buy when the company is in trough but when recovery is about to begin, although it may not yet have shown up in the published figures. The shares are likely to be depressed, and recovery later can bring a good profit to shareholders.

Before leaving the company accounts, turn to the balance sheet, which gives you the financial state of the company on one particular day. Look on the assets side to see how much cash the company has; then turn to the debit side and look for loans and overdrafts. Balance these out with cash and bank deposits, and you will be able to see whether the company has plenty of cash to get on with its business. If it is short of cash, or has very large short-term debt, the company may soon be coming to the share-holders for extra money to ease its liquidity position. Such approaches are known as rights issues (see page 185), and they can sometimes depress the price of an otherwise good investment.

If all the financial measurements suggest that the company is a sound investment, the implication is that the management is good. As a final check, however, turn to the annual statement made by the chairman or chairwoman in the annual report. He or she should give some indication about how trading is going in the current year. Very often several months of the year have gone before the previous year's accounts are made public, so if he or she is silent about the current year that could be a warning sign. Watch out, too, for any boardroom rows. Rapid changes in management make a company more speculative until the new team has settled down.

If you have looked carefully at the accounts, you will know how the company has performed over a number of years. But that is not enough. You must now compare its performance against those of other companies in the sector. Maybe profits have risen, but perhaps those of other companies have risen at a different rate. In contrast, profits may have fallen, but by rather more or less than those of other similar companies.

So far, what we have looked at is all in the past—'jobbing backwards', to use Stock Exchange parlance. This is quite useful, but of course what has gone before cannot always be regarded as a guide to the future. To get an idea of what is coming, you need to read the chairman's statement in the annual report as well as study anything he or she may have to add at the company's annual general meeting. In major companies, these remarks are usually reported in the press.

You need to look also at the potential of the sector and of the company in terms of the economy as a whole. Industries wax and wane and, if they are to continue to be successful, they have to adapt to changing conditions and demands. Look out for special situations which might favour a particular company. Read as much as you can, and keep alert as you go about your business for anything which might be an interesting investment situation. Remember always that the companies which were last year's stock-market stars may be this year's duds.

181

International considerations

Investing at home carries enough risks, but there are added ones if you move into international markets and buy in the local currency. When making your purchase, you will have to convert sterling into the local currency and then, when you sell, convert the money back. If the value of the currency has not moved against sterling you will be converting on the same basis, but currencies do move, and sometimes sharply. It is not uncommon for all the profits made on a share to be wiped out by a fall in the value of the currency on reconversion. In contrast, of course, an increase in the value of a currency can compensate for losses made on shares. Timing the sale to allow for currency changes can be an important part of investment strategy. So important have currencies become in international investment that many people with substantial funds to invest go straight into investing in the currencies themselves, rather than investing in companies.

Managing your portfolio

Let us assume that you have applied all the above criteria to a number of shares and have made the selection for your portfolio. This does not mean you can just sit back and wait for the profits. From the moment you purchase, things are in flux. Companies develop, levels of profitability change, economic conditions alter, and demand for a particular company's products may rise or fall. These factors mean that you must treat your investments as if they were a small business, with yourself as the manager—helped, of course, by stockbrokers, bank managers, knowledgeable friends and newspaper reports. Now you must go back to your initial reasons for investing:

● Are you prepared to take a fair amount of risk, or do you want to go for maximum safety?
● Do you want income, or growth, or both? It is important to set down your own rules and not to be deflected from them. If an investment does not meet your rules, do not buy it. If you have bought it and it is failing to achieve your aims, sell it.

When you are checking the price of shares in your portfolio, which you should do once a week:

● Look out for any changes in the economy or economies in which the company operates.
● Watch for anything unusual happening in the company. Is the price falling for apparently no reason, or rising beyond what you think it is worth? There can be many reasons for unusual activity, not all of them sinister—a takeover rumour, for instance—but the point may come when you ought to take a profit or cut a loss.
● Don't just buy and sell for the sake of dealing and excitement. Once you have bought a share, keep it until you have a good reason for selling. This might be simply that you need the money; if so, select from your portfolio the stock which you think currently offers the least prospect of growth. Sell if a company is doing badly and if there is no sign of an early recovery. It is

often better to take a loss and try to recoup the money elsewhere than to hang on: recovery situations can be long and painful. You can always limit your loss by deciding to sell a share if it shows a 10 per cent loss—and by sticking to the rule. Some people have a 10 per cent profit rule, too, and no one ever went broke using it. You may have a profitable but rather dull and steady investment. Switch if you see a better prospect for either growth or income. Finally, there comes a point when it might be a good idea to go 'liquid' for a period—for example, when the whole stock market looks set for a fall, or a particular sector is looking weak. You might go 100 per cent liquid, or simply weed out the vulnerable stocks, putting the money into savings until new opportunities occur. Do not worry if you miss an investment opportunity: another one will always come along. The market is always throwing them up. Do not chase after an investment when it is clear that most of the immediate profits have been made.

Keeping records

Do not lose your share certificates. Keep them all in one place—the bank, if you think they would be safer there (there will be a small charge to pay for this service). Keep a separate list of the denomination and serial number of the shares and of the number you have. If they are lost, stolen or destroyed, share certificates can be replaced only by completing an expensive indemnity.

Keep a note of all the interest and dividends you receive. You will need to know these when filling in your tax return. A married man must also provide details of his wife's investments. It goes almost without saying that, if a married couple are investing together, they should discuss investment strategy and choice of shares together. The day will come when one will die and the other—very often the woman—will have to manage financial affairs alone. It pays to know what you are doing if you are to avoid acting on bad advice in your later years.

Do not throw contract notes away. You need them when it comes to working out whether you are liable for capital gains tax (see pages 201–3). Remember that losses can be set against gains and that dealing costs are deductible.

Remember that your investment needs can change with your financial circumstances. So, in addition to your weekly check on prices, every six months carry out a more general review of your portfolio. Reassess your whole investment strategy at least once a year.

Buying new issues

There have been more new investors in Britain in the past few years than ever before, mainly because of the government's privatization programme. Privatized companies are companies which were previously owned by the government (i.e., by the people as a whole) and which have now been sold partly, or wholly, to private investors. When you are deciding whether to buy a new issue, you must carefully read the prospectus, which is published before the shares are quoted, and all the press comment before deciding. After the success of some privatization issues, it is tempting to think that they all offer the prospect of early capital gain within the gains-tax exemption. This is not so. Every issue is individual, and prices are pitched at different levels.

Many people buy new issues with the aim of selling them immediately; this is called 'stagging' the issue. Too much stagging can have a temporarily dampening effect on the price and, if you can afford to hold on, you may do better by waiting a few weeks.

Stock Exchange jargon contains two other animals: bulls, who expect prices to rise (bulls toss things upwards, though not as high as stags), and bears, who think they will fall (bears tug down their victims). You will see these terms used frequently in stock-market reports. You may also hear of 'bear covering'. This happens when investors who have sold stocks on the expectation that they will be able to buy back at lower levels very quickly and so make a profit have started buying to protect their investment. There are also 'stale bulls', who have overbought and are quite likely to sell.

The main types of new issues

Companies which are complete newcomers to the stock market will issue their share in one of the following ways:

- A public issue. Here the company produces a prospectus which outlines its record and prospects and invites the public to subscribe. This is much less common than an offer for sale.
- An offer for sale is similar to a public issue but has been underwritten by an issuing house. It is the most common means by which new companies come to the market. Underwriting means that the issuing house or houses (including banks, brokers and special issuing houses, both domestic and foreign) have already bought the shares at a lower price than that at which they are offered to the general investing public. If all the shares are sold, the issuing houses make a profit; if the public do not take up all the shares, the shares are left with the underwriters, who must keep them or sell them, probably at a loss, when the shares are quoted. Whatever happens, the company offering the shares gets its money.

  Investors subscribe for the shares and, when an issue is thought to be very good, it is often 'oversubscribed'. Then, following what amounts to a huge raffle, many investors do not get any allotment of shares or the amount they have asked for may be scaled down. In such cases, the opening market price of the shares is often much higher than the offer price.
- Introductions. These are less common than offers for sale, and are not often used for equities, although they can happen where a company already has enough investors to make a market but where such a market does not officially exist in the stock market. Shares are not offered in the same way as in an offer for sale, although some holders may state that they are prepared to sell their stock in the market at certain prices.
- An alternative is a placing. Shares are allocated to financial institutions or large investors. A quotation on the Stock Exchange will follow only if enough shares are available to make a reasonable market.
- Finally, tenders are becoming increasingly popular. These are similar to offers for sale, but the issuing company does not set an issue price apart from a minimum level below which it is not prepared to sell. Bids are made

184

by the public in writing. The bids are considered in order: those offering the highest price are counted first, next those at the next highest price, and so on until all the shares are accounted for. Everyone who eventually gets the shares pays the same price—i.e., that of the lowest successful bid.

Rights and scrip issues

Companies which already have a quote occasionally issue new shares, usually as 'rights' issues, when they want further working capital, or scrip issues, which they give away. In both types of issue the new shares are offered in a certain ratio to those already held: the more you already have, the more you are offered.

First, rights issues. A company needing new capital to develop its business, pay off debts or acquire new companies may come to its shareholders and ask them to put up the money. The company will declare a rights issue of, let us say, one new ordinary share for every six already held. The market price of the existing shares may be, say, £12 and the 'rights' may be put on offer to existing shareholders at only £2.50.

There is a temptation to say that this is a very generous offer, and, indeed, newspapers often say just that—as may your broker. But they may not be right. This is because, after the new shares have been issued, the price of all the shares adjusts to allow for the issue. Let us take the example above. Your six existing shares at £12 cost £72; add in the one 'rights' share at £2.50 and you get a total of £74.50 for the seven shares. After the shares go 'ex-rights', as it is called, the market will adjust the price of the shares and divide £74.50 by seven to give an ex-rights price of £10.64. The investor has put up new money for very little immediate benefit.

Investors, however, should in general accept rights shares when they are offered. A company which is on the verge of bankruptcy would not normally dare to come to its shareholders for more money. Generally, the new money eventually brings benefits to shareholders, and anyone who does not accept the offer is actually losing part of his or her interest in the company (this is called 'watering your equity'). In the case above, the investor would need seven shares to keep his or her proportionate interest in the company.

Added to this is the fact that the market adjustment in price is rarely complete. More often than not, there is an effective increase in the price of the shares, so that the investor benefits. Any investor can sell the rights in the market, if he or she does not wish to add to his or her holding, before the money to be paid on the new shares is due. If a shareholder completely ignores the offer, he or she may lose money because the value of the original holding will probably fall somewhat, even if there is not a total adjustment—although the company will often sell the rights to which the investor is entitled and send him or her the proceeds.

The other type of share issue by a company which already has a share quotation is the scrip issue, sometimes called a bonus. These shares are often described as 'free', but are nothing of the kind. A company may decide to issue bonus shares to its shareholders in the ratio of one-to-one. It simply tells shareholders, gets them to vote on the issue (they never refuse), then sends the new shares out. Anyone who had 1,000 shares before the issue will have 2,000 afterwards. But nothing has happened to the total *value* of the holding. If the shares were quoted at £2 before the

185

issue, and therefore the investor's shares were worth £2,000, they will be quoted at £1 after it, so that the investor's shares are still worth £2,000. Dividends, too, will be adjusted downwards.

So why do companies do it? Often it is to capitalize on a company's reserves. It may have been trading profitably for some years and gradually the existing issued capital loan—preference shares, equity, etc.—which is on the debit side of the balance sheet (the shareholders would have to be repaid if the company was wound up), is looking small in relation to the reserves the company has built up. It brings the capital more into line with reserves by issuing more shares; so a scrip issue is simply a book-keeping transaction.

A company, however, generally does not make a scrip issue if it is doing badly. A bonus issue may be an expression of confidence in the future, and the company may well not adjust the dividend down totally to allow for the new shares. This means that there is often an effective rise in the price of the shares. On the one-for-one ratio described above, the price, instead of being adjusted from £2 down to £1, might drop only as far as £1.20 or so. However, while this possibility exists, investors should not take it for granted unless a company forecasts effectively higher dividends.

New shares come to the market in other ways, but these are less common. A few shares may be issued as a result of takeover bids or when holders of convertible debentures exercise their options to switch into equities.

Shares are sometimes split into smaller units if the price becomes too high. These are not new issues, just a means of increasing the marketability of shares by bringing the price down.

Your stockbroker

You may buy your shares through a stockbroker, bank, or anyone licensed to deal in securities. If you are paying 'advisory' commission rates (see page 175) you are entitled to advice from your stockbroker, who is an expert. Stockbrokers will—if you insist—deal in whatever way you tell them to, but it is worth listening to them if they have words of warning for you against a particular investment, or, alternatively, advise you in favour of one. You can expect your stockbroker to get the best possible price and to give you all the background information you need to enable you to reach the correct decision—the bigger brokerage houses all have research departments which analyse the merits and otherwise of companies.

But, although an expert, your broker is not all-knowing. He or she cannot forecast absolutely how a share will move; that can depend as much on market sentiment as on the prospects for a particular company. The stockbroker cannot stop a share price from tumbling, even if it is a first-class investment, if all around share prices are falling.

The broker cannot legally give you any information he or she may have acquired from contacts inside a company about a particular share. If stockbrokers get such information, they cannot act on it themselves; that is called 'insider dealing', and is illegal. But there is nothing, however, to stop a stockbroker and you from working out what may or may not be a good investment.

Always be open with your broker. If you are making only a short-term purchase, tell him or her so. The stockbroker may be able to warn you off. Do not buy on any rumours you hear: check with your broker first.

INVESTMENT ANALYSIS

You can go through the process of deciding which shares to buy yourself, or you can take advantage of the very large research departments which stockbrokers run today.

When you are reading about shares, you may notice that some tipsters talk about fundamental analysis, which means that they have looked at past performance, prospects, dividend policy, yield and so on. They balance out all these factors in deciding whether a share is worth buying or holding, or should be sold.

Some investors, however, pay no attention whatsoever to fundamental analysis and base all their dealings on charts. A few are prepared to say that they do not need to know even the name of a company to tell from a chart whether it should be bought or sold.

This approach is very technical, and its details too complex to be discussed here, but broadly it is based on the premise that share prices behave according to patterns. If you plot the share price on graph paper over a period, chartists claim that you can assess the future trend of the share price according to what has gone before.

Various sets of lines are drawn on the graph and, if the share price breaks through these lines, chartists take the movement as a buying or selling signal, depending on the direction in which the share price breaks through the lines.

Charts may be applied to the movement of the stock market as a whole, as well as to individual shares.

Many investors have made a great deal of money by putting their faith in charts, but it is probably better for new or nonprofessional investors to look at all the forecasts before dealing. It takes some time and expertise to follow charts.

Rumours may well come true, but the chances are that other people have heard them, too, and have got into the share at a much lower price than you can get. There may be no profit left in the prevailing share price.

Speculation

Speculating is gambling, but a gamble in which you may well not run the risk of losing your original stake. It is exciting, but dangerous. You can just as easily lose as gain. Here are some general notes in summary.

Many speculators buy and sell in the same account (see page 174). This means that they do not actually have to put any money up: they just pay the difference if the price goes down and get a cheque if it goes up. Make sure you have sufficient funds to meet the bill if you lose, or are forced to take up the shares for the longer term.

Be careful before acting on 'inside' information. Insider dealing is against the law.

Speculate only in shares where the market is active. Profits can vanish quickly if you cannot find a buyer.

Do not be too greedy. A 10 per cent profit is reasonable.

Cut your losses fast if your speculation is going wrong.

18 | Divorce

Not all marriages last forever; about one third of them break up and, in the vast majority of cases, dependent children are involved. Even when a wife is working, her income is very often not as high as that of her former husband, and anyway the couple's total resources will now have to support two homes, rather than one, and possibly a new family as well. As a result, although anger and resentment may be uppermost in people's minds at the time of the break-up, everything in the end usually comes down to money. And coming down to money involves, as in so many things, taxation. The government recognizes that the end of a marriage can bring financial hardship to both parties, so it is fairly generous in the tax treatment of divorced people.

It is important for a divorcing or separating couple to try to sort out the whole matter as amicably as possible, preferably between themselves before consulting a solicitor. Legal time is expensive, so the less it is used the better. Where a couple can agree on who files the divorce petition (if it is not to be fought) and on what arrangements, if any, are to be made for maintenance, the divorce will go through at minimum cost. Start arguing, and the cost can quickly rise to thousands of pounds. Where there are no children involved, a couple can get a do-it-yourself divorce for a mere £40. Where there are children, the court must be satisfied that their interests are being fully taken into account in any final agreement, and so a court appearance is necessary.

Anyone who has no financial resources may be able to get legal aid to cover the costs of the divorce, but there are pitfalls in this. Legal aid is not a no-strings present, and many people have found that, sometimes years later—when, say, the family home is sold—they are expected to pay the legal costs of their divorce out of the proceeds of the sale. Women, particularly, often enthusiastically pursue ex-husbands and argue over very minor details, often unaware that eventually they are going to have to pay what may be a very substantial bill.

There are no circumstances when it is worthwhile dragging out negotiations, especially if the only real motive is vengeance.

Maintenance

For many years it was unheard-of for a woman to have to maintain a former husband or children. Women were usually awarded lifetime maintenance—although not, it must be admitted, at a very generous level—and children received a sum until they started working. The latter is still usually true, but the Matrimonial and Family Proceedings Act (1984) introduced the concept of the 'clean break' after a divorce as well as the idea that wives with financial assets could just as easily be sued for maintenance as husbands. So far the new act has not had a great effect on financial settlements in divorce cases: it is still usually the woman who asks for maintenance, and, in cases where a wife is getting older and may not be capable of working, she will usually still be awarded lifetime maintenance (although at any time a former husband can apply to have it reduced or eliminated altogether, just as a former wife can apply for an increase). Under the 'clean break' concept, however, a former spouse may receive maintenance only for a period—perhaps, in the case of a wife, for about five years, until all the children have gone to school and she has had time to train or retrain for a job and thereby become self-supporting. Every case is treated on its merits, and it is impossible to be categorical about what will happen.

Anyone who knows that they are in a 'clean break' situation and likely to lose maintenance after a few years might find the idea of a once-for-all lump sum now more attractive than temporary maintenance.

The 'clean break' concept also brought back an old idea when assessing maintenance: the conduct of the parties involved. This can affect not only the level of maintenance awarded to a former wife but also for how long. A frequent complaint of husbands in the past was that their wives had moved out of the home, started living with another man—and then still managed to get high levels of alimony as long as they did not marry. In future, courts will take into account that sort of behaviour, and may cut maintenance if they think that the other man is capable of contributing to the upkeep of the new establishment.

On the whole, however, as we have noted, the new act has so far had little impact. It is usually the husband who provides the main source of income for the former wife and children, if she is not working. The situation is the same whether the couple are seeking a divorce or have opted for a legal separation.

All rights to maintenance cease on remarriage. Anyone contemplating an early remarriage might be well advised to try to get a lump sum pay-off rather than seek maintenance. The paying ex-spouse, however, would be equally well advised to resist this. There is no doubt that the financial interests of a divorcing husband and wife can be diametrically opposed.

It is no use thinking that former living standards can be completely maintained when a marriage breaks up. Money has to go further and, although the rules about tax do help, they are not enough to compensate fully. What most commonly happens—although every case has its unique features—is that a former spouse will get up to one third of the joint income, plus something for children. An ex-husband's total income will be taken to include any income a second wife may have, an assessment many second wives feel is unfair. However, they do contribute to the upkeep of the man's new home, and it is likely that he will be able to afford more for a former wife and family than he could if there were only his own income to draw on. The court is concerned only about how much money the husband has potentially available and, if that includes the income of a second wife, they include it accordingly. There are arguments in both directions on this, but the court's view is probably the correct one, and it is just tough on the second wife.

The one third of income, however, may not actually represent one third in money terms. Today, unless the former wife has been very foolish, she will already be a joint owner of the home and, if the children are to stay with her, she will very often get full ownership in any financial settlement. In such cases, the courts will allow for that, if the couple have not themselves been able to reach an agreement to cut the maintenance by an amount to allow for the husband giving up his asset. This may be a simple cut or what is often described as a 'lost interest' allowance, because, had the man put his money into savings rather than into the home, he would have earned interest on the money.

When the amount of maintenance has been settled, it is then up to the couple to maximize their joint incomes. They can do this through the various tax reliefs available. As these tax reliefs apply only after a Court Order, it is in the interests of both parties to go to court as soon as possible after the separation. This should be done even if there is hope of a reconciliation, because the order can always be cancelled. The five reliefs concern:

● Tax relief on maintenance payments. Maintenance payments may be either voluntary (no one can make you pay them) or enforceable in law (you must pay them, and failure to so do can result in imprisonment). The former attract no tax relief, but the latter are allowable at all levels of tax. Enforceable payments must be set out in a Court Order, a separation deed or some other form of legal contract. What happens is that the payments are made net of the standard rate of tax and adjustments are then made to the paying ex-spouse's tax coding. Higher rate relief is allowed for in the coding.

The person receiving the payments may not be liable for the full tax which has been deducted, so he/she then has to negotiate a refund with the tax inspector. Tax can be reclaimed on Form R40 (or R232 if maintenance payments are made directly to a child). The person making the payments should supply details of tax deducted, and these go onto Form 185. Repayments can usually be made quarterly, so that the former spouse receiving the payments does not have to wait a whole year to get the tax back. A very high-earning wife is unlikely in today's climate to be awarded maintenance for herself, and she might anyway prefer a smaller voluntary payment on which she did not have to pay tax (and he would not get relief) to something which is whittled away by tax. Couples should try to reach an amicable agreement.

● Personal tax allowances. Once a couple divorces, the husband loses the married man's allowance, although he will of course get full tax relief on any maintenance payments he makes. In contrast, the wife then receives the single person's allowance rather than the earned-income allowance, but, if there are dependent children, she is usually able to claim the additional personal allowance as well. This brings her allowance up to the level of the married man's allowance. If a couple separates rather than divorces, the husband can continue to keep the married man's allowance if he is wholly maintaining the wife. There is special relief for the wife for the year of divorce. She will get an earned-income allowance if she is working and also the single person's allowance, so her tax bill may be very small indeed in the year of divorce.

● Children's tax allowances. The taxman remembers that children are people too, and as such entitled to the single person's allowance on any income they might have. Normally, their income is amalgamated with that of their parent (in this case it would be the parent they are living with), but the allowance can still be set against their own income. For this reason, it makes sense for part of the alimony payments to be directed specifically to the child under the Court Order. The Court Order must state that the payments are made *to* the child and not *for* it, otherwise no relief can be claimed. If you are not making payments in this way, you can go back to the court and have the order altered, so that the benefit of the tax relief can be achieved. This concession means that maintenance for children is effectively increased, which can be important in cases where children are being privately educated. Ex-wives should remember, however, that maintenance for children ceases when they finish full-time education. It is also unlikely that a person in their first job could contribute as much to the family budget as was previously received in child maintenance. The additional personal allowance, too, is lost and the child's personal allowance is set against any income from employment he or she might have. It will probably be necessary for an ex-wife to renegotiate her maintenance level if she is not to face a sudden sharp fall in her living standards when child maintenance ceases.

- Tax relief on mortgages. This can be a pitfall for divorcing couples. A married couple is entitled to relief on only one mortgage on a principal residence up to a maximum of £30,000. But a divorced couple is no longer treated as one unit, and so the relief rules for single people apply. There are cases where, say, a husband goes on making the mortgage payments on a property in which he no longer lives. Then it would be neither his home nor his principal residence, so the right to tax relief could lapse—although ex-husbands are allowed tax relief on two homes as long as the total borrowing does not go over £30,000. This has the effect of raising interest payments by the standard rate of tax. The main problems arise when a husband buys a new home, on a mortgage, for an ex-wife. To make sure that there are no problems, if two homes have to be maintained and if the amount borrowed comes to over £30,000, the divorcing couple should make sure that they totally separate their financial affairs. Rather than the paying spouse continuing to make the mortgage payments, maintenance should be increased so that the receiving spouse can make the payments him- or herself and claim the relief as a single person. This should be written into the Court Order.
- Capital Transfer Tax. There is no CTT in transfers between husband and wife, so, if you are planning to give a husband or wife any assets, do it before rather than after the divorce. Transfers made as part of a divorce settlement are tax-free, but after the divorce there can be problems—so sort all that out before the divorce goes through. The same applies to capital gains tax.

Pensions after divorce

Not enough people think about what is going to happen to them financially after their former spouses retire or die. Either former spouse can apply to have a maintenance order varied, if financial circumstances change. And they do change on retirement and death. For a long time, divorced women were badly treated from this point of view, and very few of them had any rights to maintenance after their husband's death. New rights have been written into the law, but widows' pensions, for instance, can normally be paid only to widows—not divorcees whose ex-husbands have died.

191

Trustees of pension funds usually can and often do make *ex gratia* payments to former wives, particularly if they are young and have dependent children, but it is important to remember that these are not paid as of right. Ex-husbands quite often tell the trustees of their pension fund that they do not want their ex-wife to get any money at all, and trustees are quite likely to take such wishes into consideration when deciding whether or not to make a payment.

Where a wife is divorced as she approaches retirement age, and has not worked and therefore has no right to a pension from her own contributions, she can find herself in difficulties if a former husband dies. One way out of the system is for a husband to agree that, on his death, an annuity will be purchased for a former wife, so that she has some guaranteed income for the rest of her life. Alternatively, he could take out a life-assurance policy during his lifetime, similarly designed to give her an income after his death. As far as his state pension is concerned, she will have some rights to part of his pension for the years of her marriage to him, although some will go to any present wife. An ex-wife is allowed to use her ex-husband's National Insurance contribution record to build up a full right to a basic pension. This rule recognizes that a woman may have spent a great deal of time at home because of family responsibilities and have been unable to work in paid employment. These rights are lost on remarriage, as are all financial claims on an ex-husband.

As private pension schemes almost always refer to widows rather than former wives, it is vitally important to discuss this matter when the financial settlement is being worked out.

Let us take a couple of examples to see how tax reliefs and tax allowances can be used to benefit both former spouses.

1. A nonworking ex-wife who has two dependent children and whose former husband earns £20,000 a year.

(a) A voluntary agreement to pay a total of £7,000 a year. This will cost the ex-husband the full £7,000 a year from his income, after tax and National Insurance contributions, of approximately £12,000, assuming he has only the personal allowance and is contracted into SERPS (see page 159). That would leave the ex-husband with around £6,825 net, and the ex-wife with the full £7,000.

(b) A Court Order to pay a total of £7,000 a year, divided £1,750 to each child and £3,500 to the mother. In this case, the husband would pay *not* the full £7,000 to the wife for herself and in respect of the children, but £5,110 (£7,000, less tax at the standard rate). The former wife would be entitled to set her personal allowance and the additional personal allowance (£3,795 together) against her £3,500, and therefore be liable to no tax. Further, she could set each child's personal allowance (£2,425) against their maintenance. Equally, they would not be liable for tax, so she could reclaim the £1,890 tax deducted by the husband. She would get the full £7,000, but the financial burden on her ex-husband would immediately be 27 per cent lower (the standard rate of tax for 1987–88). That would leave the ex-husband with around £8,718 net, and the ex-wife with the full £7,000.

2. A working wife with two dependent children, ex-husband earning £20,000 a year and ex-wife £10,000. This gives a total income of £30,000, of which the wife would probably be entitled to one-third. She already earns that, and anyway will have used up her tax allowances on her own earnings. In this case, the best financial agreement is for the Court Order to apply solely to the children. As long as the maintenance to each child is below the personal allowance of £2,335, their mother will be able to reclaim the tax paid.

In this example, an ex-wife might feel it would be better not to work and instead to try to survive on maintenance. It is true that it would be more costly to the ex-husband, but under the new 'clean break' law, a court would not look favourably on such a decision, particularly if the wife had already been working at the time of the separation. There is a nonfinancial consideration here, too. Working women tend to have more friends and a better social life than nonworking ones: that can be important in the period immediately after a separation.

Divorce is one situation in which the wisdom of financial planning and cooperation between the separating couple is immediately obvious. A full legal agreement should be sought as soon as possible after separation, and a periodic review should take into account the changing needs of both former partners.

Single parents and the state

Once a couple separates or divorces, the state recognizes that finances can be uncomfortably stretched. In addition to the extra tax allowance, there are also

- One-parent benefit. This is an automatic non-earnings-related addition which goes to all single parents for their first or only child in addition to the normal child benefit (£7.25). For 1987–88, it is £4.70.
- Child's special allowance. This is paid to a woman whose marriage has been dissolved or annulled if, at the time of death of her former husband, he was (or should have been) helping to support one or more of her children.

There are also special conditions which apply to single parents who apply for some social-security benefits. As far as family income supplement (to become Family Credit in April 1988) is concerned, a lone parent need work only 24 hours a week in order to satisfy the 'full-time work' conditions. On supplementary benefit (to become Income Support in April 1988) up to £15 of earnings is not counted as income when claims are made. No work expenses or child care costs can be deducted from the £15.

Spotcheck

As the children grow, have you

● thought about further education?
● tapped friends and relatives who might help you pay school fees using tax-efficient covenants?
● thought about covenanting student children yourself when they reach the age of 18?
● readjusted your will once your children become self-supporting?
● begun to think about the longer-term and retirement years when it comes to savings?
● made sure that your pension arrangements will provide an adequate pension for both spouses when the time comes?
● considered, if you have the funds, moving the absolute safety of savings into the risk and possibility of capital growth through investment?

If you are investing

● are you sure that you have the temperament for it and that you will be able to run a portfolio successfully?

If your marriage has broken or is breaking down, have you taken steps

● to see that the separation is done as amicably and efficiently as possible, so that both sides get the maximum benefit from the tax allowances available?

THE FINAL WORKING YEARS

After the children have grown and left home, a married couple often enter the most financially comfortable period of their lives. Both may be at their peak earnings level; the mortgage on the home will probably have been paid off; life-assurance policies are beginning to mature; savings are ample for everyday and even longer-term needs; and a sound investment plan for maximum capital growth is operating. The couple may feel that they can afford to move from a large family home into a smaller one, thereby not only making a substantial profit on the former one, and reinvesting it, but also cutting down on the home's running costs. It is time now to ensure that proper arrangements are made for the retirement years— by topping-up pensions wherever possible, by minimizing any Capital Gains Tax due on profits each year, by taking steps to reduce or eliminate any liability for Inheritance Tax, and by making any necessary adjustments to the couple's joint or individual wills.

19 | Tax Efficiency in our Later Years

| Minimizing our taxes

The final years of our working life are likely to be the highest-earning, whether we are single or part of a couple. It makes sense, therefore, to look at our financial arrangements to see if we can minimize the impact of these high earnings.

If you are a high earner, it is worth taking the advice of an accountant. You will not be able to charge against your income tax any fees you pay simply to have your tax return filled in, but fees for any advice beyond that are deductible. (Do not attempt to minimize the taxes you pay by breaking the law. To see how you might do this, look at the difference between tax evasion and tax avoidance as set out in the box on page 198.)

To begin with, look at all your savings and investments and, if you are paying tax at the highest levels, make sure that you have all the tax-free savings possible. Buy up to the limit on National Savings certificates and index-linked certificates. The increase in the value of these is not taxable. It is even worth having enough in the National Savings Ordinary Account to make sure that you get the £70 tax-free interest allowed every year. Once you reach the limit of tax-free savings, put your money into tax-paid rather than taxable savings. Go for growth and currently low yields on your investments. If you are a standard-rate taxpayer, keep your money in tax-paid savings. (Details of savings schemes currently available are shown in Appendix I.) Buy one of the new Personal Equity Plans each year (for details see page 51).

When it comes to minimizing your tax bill—once you have netted down your total income as much as possible—the next step (it may seem obvious but not everyone does it) is to check to see that you are getting all the allowances to which you are entitled. These will be shown in a statement of your tax coding, which has a number and which your employer uses to work out how much tax to take away from you before paying you a net wage or salary.

Next, make sure that you are claiming any permitted outgoings and allowable expenses. There are a great variety of these, and there is little doubt that many people who are entitled to claim do not do so. They include the cost of protective and functional clothing necessary to your job; the cost, maintenance and repair of tools essential to your trade; books and stationery which are necessary to your job; reasonable hotel and food expenses for yourself when you have to travel away from home on business, but not expenses involved in entertaining guests, unless they are business contacts based abroad, travelling expenses incurred wholly in the course of carrying out your job (but not travelling expenses between your home and your place of work), including the use of your own car;

some fees and subscriptions to professional bodies which may be a condition of your employment; interest on loans for equipment necessary in your job; sometimes part of the upkeep of your home, if you are self-employed or required to do some of your work from home; and the travelling costs for a husband or wife (only if they actually do some work) accompanying you on a business trip.

How much you will be allowed depends on your particular circumstances, and you will have to set out details of all your expenses and the purpose for which they have been incurred. The inspector will then adjust your tax coding accordingly.

In addition to expenses, there are a wide range of outgoings which can be set against tax. The main considerations which may affect you are:

● Interest on loans for a home or its improvement. These come within the £30,000 limit for each person or married couple for a principal residence. You will automatically get the relief on your home loan, but not on the interest on an improvement. The Inland Revenue is getting stricter about these loans, because it suspects that many have not been for genuine improvement, so you may have to provide proof along with the bills.

● If you pay alimony or child maintenance you will be entitled to full tax relief on the payments if they are made under a Court Order, although not if they are made voluntarily. You make the payments net of standard-rate tax, and the recipient reclaims the tax, if he or she is not liable for tax, or for the full amount you have deducted. (For more details see pages 190–1.)

● Annuity or covenant payments are made net of tax, so that if, for instance, you are supporting a student child at college or university, it makes sense to pay in this way rather than simply to make voluntary payments. You will save the standard rate of tax of £27 on every £100 you pay.

● You can minimize any Capital Gains Tax liability you may have by balancing out the losses and gains at the end of the tax year. Remember that, if you are married, you and your spouse are treated as one and get only one person's allowance of tax-free gains. It is important to keep receipts which will show any expenses involved in purchase and sale to offset against the gain. (For more details see pages 201–3.)

● You can minimize your potential Inheritance Tax by making use of the annual £3,000 exemption to make gifts to people to whom you would anyway be leaving your money. As you get older, you should consider transferring your assets under the seven-year Inheritance Tax rules. (For more details see page 199.)

● You should consider at the beginning of every tax year, if you are married, whether you would be better off being taxed separately, or, if you already are taxed separately, whether you would gain by being taxed together (this can happen if one of you stops working).

● If you are getting married, try to do it as near to the beginning of the tax year as possible, because a husband immediately gets the married man's allowance, but the couple also get an extra year taxed as single persons.

● If you are getting divorced, try to time that as near to the beginning of the tax year as possible, because there are generous tax allowances in the year of divorce, which are worth more at the begining of the year than at the end.

● If you have plenty of money and a high income, consider a Business Expansion Scheme. There is full tax relief up to a maximum investment of

EVASION AND AVOIDANCE

Organizing your financial affairs so that you pay less tax involves two definitions:

Tax Evasion
This is illegal and carries severe penalties. You may, for instance,

- Be fined £50 for filling in an incorrect Tax Return, although this may not happen if you have simply made a mistake. As well as the fine, you will have to pay any additional tax due in the case of a mistake, but if you have tried to cheat you will pay the fine and twice the additional tax.
- Be fined £500 if you help someone to prepare an incorrect return. This is a warning mainly to professional advisers, particularly accountants.
- Be fined £500 if you have deliberately given wrong information to the Inland Revenue and are later convicted for fraud, or £250 if you are not charged.
- Be fined £100 if you do not tell the Inland Revenue that you have taxable income.

Tax Avoidance
This is when you simply use the legal rules to your advantage. You could sensibly, for instance, balance out your losses and gains to reduce any Capital Gains Tax liability, or buy a self-employed deferred annuity which is completely allowable for tax. Avoidance used to be quite straightforward, but is less so now since the Inland Revenue has won important test cases in instances where a taxpayer and his or her advisers went through a series of steps which in themselves were quite legal, but when the end result, set against the first step, was illegal. This affects only a very small minority of taxpayers, but it is a warning to us all that the Inland Revenue is prepared to be tough.

£40,000 per person. At the top rate of 60 per cent, this is a very worthwhile saving.

Inheritance Tax

As we enter the last half of our lives, and certainly by the time we reach 50, it is time to think about what will happen to our assets—our so-called estate—when we die. The basic rule about this is that, with some exemptions, anything we leave is potentially liable to tax. Since the April 1986 Budget this overall tax on our estate has been called the Inheritance Tax.

Further, assets which we give away during our lifetime may be liable to tax, at different levels, unless we survive for at least seven years after making the gift. As the tax can be as much as 60 per cent, it makes sense to minimize it as far as possible. Do not think it will not affect you: Inheritance Tax begins at £91,000 (1987–88) and, if you compare that with the average price of a house (which today is over £40,000), it is clear that many people may be close to being ensnared by the tax.

Not all gifts and transfers of assets are exempt from tax, but 'Potentially Exempt Transfers' (PETs) come under the seven-year survival rule. These must be outright gifts from one individual to another (or certain payments into trusts, which do not affect the majority of us). First of all, let us look at the exemptions:

- There is a general annual exemption of £3,000 a year. This means that we can each give away up to £3,000 a year without attracting any tax.
- Second, any number of small gifts of up to £250 may be given away each tax year.
- Third, when people are getting married, cash gifts can be made in the following amounts: from a parent £5,000, from a grandparent £2,500, and from others £1,000.
- Fourth, all transfers to charities are tax-free, with no limit.
- Fifth, transfers between spouses are always totally free of tax. This means that the joint estate of a husband and wife attracts Inheritance Tax only on the second death. This is important in tax planning, and it makes sense for husbands and wives to leave everything, or at least the bulk of the estate, to one another. The situation should be reconsidered after the first death.
- Sixth, any normal maintenance for the family is free of tax.

Everything else may attract Inheritance Tax, even if given away during our lifetime, if we do not live for seven years after making the gift. There is a sliding scale of tax liability during the seven years as follows:

Years of survival after making gift	Reduction in tax
6–7	80 per cent
5–6	60 per cent
4–5	40 per cent
3–4	20 per cent
0–3	nil

Because of this sliding scale, anyone who has sufficient assets to attract Inheritance Tax should take out a term life-assurance policy to cover the seven-year period, so that the tax liability will be covered. As we saw on page 102, term assurance is relatively cheap, even as we get older (although there are age limits), and provides a tax-free lump sum in the event of our death which can be used to pay any tax liability. This is not needed where a husband and wife leave everything to one another, but the survivor should consider taking out a whole-of-life policy if they want the estate, whatever it is, to pass on intact to the next generation. The same agreement might apply to a brother and sister, two friends sharing a home, and certainly for an unmarried couple living together: only transfers between spouses are tax-free, not those between cohabitees.

When you look at the rates of tax, it becomes immediately clear why minimizing or eliminating it altogether makes sound financial sense. The rate starts at 30 per cent and very quickly reaches 60 per cent:

Taxable amount (1987/88) £	Rate
first 90,000	nil
91,000–140,000	30 per cent
140,000–220,000	40 per cent
220,000–330,000	50 per cent
Over 330,000	60 per cent

The value of the gift for tax purposes is its value at the time it is made: any increase in value of the gift between then and the date of death is entirely ignored for tax purposes. This means that if, say, you gave your son or daughter £100,000 during your lifetime and you survived for seven years, there would be no tax to pay, but if you died within three years and the money was liable for tax at, say, 40 per cent (assuming you had other assets), £40,000 would have to be found; however, if the £100,000 had earned £20,000 interest in that time the £20,000 would be taxed as the offspring's income and would not be liable for Inheritance Tax. When property passes on death the value for tax purposes is, of course, the value on the day of death. Any tax which is due on a PET must be paid six months after the end of the month in which the person making the gift dies.

So we have a situation where tax is payable on the estate of anyone not leaving all their assets to their spouses or to a charity, but this tax is avoidable or can be covered by using life assurance. It is avoidable by giving away our assets during our lifetime and protecting the gift with term assurance, or by using whole-of-life assurance policies to provide the lump sum which we reckon may be required on death.

'All very well,' you may say, 'but I don't want to give away my assets before I die!' You may feel you cannot trust your children to make sure that you are comfortable for the rest of your life if you give them all your assets. And the Inland Revenue will not regard a gift as outright, and therefore potentially free of Inheritance Tax, if you attach conditions to it—e.g., if you give your children all your money but the income from it goes to your own upkeep until you die. Such conditional gifts are known as 'Gifts with Reservation' (GWRs), and under the Inheritance Tax rules a gift is treated as having been made outright only when the donor ceases to get any benefit from it. For instance, you might decide to give your child your home but remain living in it until you die. In that case, the Inland Revenue would take the view that the gift was made at the point of death, not on whatever date you and your child established the contract. The gift would not, therefore, escape Inheritance Tax.

Each family needs to think through the question of Inheritance Tax. Some parents are very willing to give a large proportion of their assets to their children and keep just enough for themselves to live on. If they live the required seven years after that, the amount of Inheritance Tax to be paid may be relatively small and provide no problem for the heirs to pay. Where there is trust between members of a family, quite genuine gifts can be made without damage to anyone, but where this trust does not exist no gifts should be contemplated. If you do not want to make a lifetime gift coupled with term life assurance—a typical premium for £50,000 term life assurance for a man of 50 for 10 years would be £35 a month for level term (increasable term would start off cheaper around £28, but would rise by 30 per cent every three years or so)—consider seriously a whole-of-life policy. Here is one example of what a 40-year-old employed man might do:

He wishes to leave his entire estate to his children. On his death he reckons that he will have a house worth £250,000 and other assets totalling £150,000, making the whole estate worth £400,000. He can cut down the Inheritance Tax liability, or eliminate it altogether, using whole-of-life assurance.

All the surplus estate over the starting level of £90,000 or in this case £309,000 is liable for Inheritance Tax.

How tax is charged

band	rate	cumulative tax
£90,000–£140,000	30 per cent	£15,000
£140,001–£220,000	40 per cent	£47,000
£220,001–£309,000	50 per cent	£91,500

Total tax payable: £91,500

If this 40-year-old man were to take out a whole-of-life assurance policy without profits for a sum assured of £100,000 at death, it would cost him about £1,500 a year. Such a policy would more than pay the total estimated tax liability at death, leaving a margin to allow for some extra growth in the value of the estate. The annual premiums would be treated as a gift under the Inheritance Tax rules on lifetime transfers, and they are well within the £3,000 annual exemption for such transfers.

Assume the man dies at 70. He would then have been paying premiums for 30 years at a total cost of £45,000 for a guaranteed tax-free sum assured to his heirs of £100,000, or £9,000 more than the estimated tax liability.

Points to notice:

- premiums vary slightly from company to company
- whole-of-life with profits would be much dearer, but the proceeds correspondingly greater
- in some whole-of-life policies, premiums cease at a certain age
- the proceeds of whole-of-life policies are always tax-free to the named beneficiary

Capital Gains Tax

Capital Gains Tax (CGT) applies to any profits which we may make on the disposal of assets. It is a tax on capital, not on income, and applies to a wide range of gains we may make. CGT is levied at the rate of 30 per cent on any profits made, after allowing for a number of exemptions. Most of us first come across it when we fill in our annual tax return, and for the majority of us it does not have any relevance until we have built up the value of our assets either through investments directly in the stock market or through unit trusts, properties, land or, less frequently, jewellery, antiques and painting.

CGT is something to which we must pay attention as soon as we have made an investment. Once an investment shows a profit, it becomes

CAPITAL GAINS TAX

CGT is

- Payable on the balance of gains and losses after allowing for the annual exemption of £6,600 (1987/88).
- Calculated on the net gain after all expenses.
- Losses and gains can be carried forward and are now index-linked.
- Not payable until the gain is actually made and the asset disposed of.
- Payable three months after the end of the tax year in which the gain has been made, or 30 days after the inspector has presented the bill, if that is later.
- Currently charged at 30 per cent.

potentially liable for CGT—but what are called 'chargeable gains' only become so when a 'disposal' of the asset takes place. So, as long as we own them, the question of tax does not arise. But, if you bought a set of shares and then sold them at a profit, you would have to state that profit on your next tax return and would eventually get a CGT bill if the level of profit was above the current level of annual exemption. If you inherited anything which is potentially chargeable, Capital Transfer Tax would have to be paid on the value of the asset on the date you acquired it (any increase in value after that comes into the CGT rules).

CGT does not affect the majority of us, mainly because of the exemptions:

- The most important exemption is any profit made on a principal residence—i.e., the home on which mortgage relief has been available (see pages 70–1)—even if you have paid off your mortgage. The exemption will not include any second home you have bought or inherited.
- Any profit made on the sale of private motor cars is exempt. This would not include profits made by dealers, but they pay not CGT but normal profits tax.
- Any profit made on National Savings Certificates, Index-linked certificates, or any other of the no-longer current Save-As-You-Earn schemes, Defence Bonds or National Development Bonds, or prizes on Premium Bonds, are exempt.
- Gambling wins, including those on the football pools, are exempt.
- Proceeds received on the maturity or surrender of qualifying life-assurance policies are exempt.
- Profits made on the sale of anything which has an expected life of less than 50 years are exempt.
- Profits on the sale of government gilt-edged securities, or marketable securities issued by public corporations and guaranteed by the government, or any fixed-interest stocks issued by public quoted companies are all exempt.
- Compensation monies received for any damages are exempt. These could include a sum of money you were awarded after an accident, or libel damages.
- Any gift you make over to the nation is exempt—this could be paintings, sculpture, or even your house if it has historic value.

202

- Charities are exempt from CGT on any gains they make, as are any contributions they receive.
- Gains from gifts to individuals which are not more than £100 in any one financial year are exempt.
- Awards for gallantry are exempt.
- Anything sold for less than £3,000 is exempt.
- Most important of all, any transfers between husband and wife are exempt.

This list takes in a great deal, and there are even a few further, although less frequent, exemptions to do with debts and the sale of assets for employees' benefits in small companies. For most of us, except the rather well off, only the sale of a second home or an unexpected windfall puts us into the CGT bracket because, after allowing for all these exemptions, we are still allowed to make net profits of £6,600 (tax year 1987–88) without becoming liable for the tax. Husband and wife are treated as one person for CGT, but either can ask the inspector to offset losses against only their own gains, and not those of their husband or wife.

Net profit means not the difference between what we paid for something (or its value when we were given or inherited it) and the price when we sell, but the difference after taking into account any costs involved in purchase and sale. This could include advertising, or commission charged by a stockbroker or an auction house, for example. Then again, even if we have a possibility for CGT, we can mitigate it by looking to see what we ought to sell at the end of a particular financial year, because the new annual exemption begins to apply immediately after 6 April and also because we can offset any gains we make against any losses. So, if we have a gain of say £8,000 on one lot of shares and have sold them in the course of the year, and have a loss on another lot of £2,000, we can avoid CGT by selling the second lot and balancing out the profit and loss at £6,000, which is within the annual exemption. Losses and gains can be carried forward and are now index-linked, so the annual exemption rises each year with inflation. Losses cannot be carried backwards.

A little thought at the end of each financial year—perhaps in consultation with a professional adviser, if you are wealthy—can keep this tax at a minimum if not eliminate it altogether.

Early retirement

Just as many people want to defer their retirement, others wish to retire before the state pension ages of 60 and 65. Where a couple is concerned, this is a matter which should be discussed carefully and its implications fully understood. Normally no one can get a state pension before the official retirement age—although it is permitted in certain professions—so, unless you have a large income from savings and/or access to money from a private pension fund, it is not something that many of us can think about. Women who do not have a pension in their own right also need to be aware that they cannot collect on their husband's contributions until he reaches 65. Where a woman is older than her husband, this means waiting until she, too, is over 65.

Where early retirement on a private pension is being considered, it is probable that the full pension will not be available. In some cases, companies may be prepared to pay in full to an employee who wishes to opt for voluntary redundancy a few years before retirement age as part of a company reorganization plan, but normally there is a sharp drop in pension entitlement for anyone wanting to retire early. The reasons are that (a) contributions cease early, and (b) final pay is also lower than it would have been; moreover (c), the company faces the prospect of having to pay for a longer period.

The employee may be given the option of a lower pension immediately or of having the benefits frozen until he or she is 60 or 65. The latter option will eventually produce more pension, and the individual will benefit as time goes on from any increases announced by the trustees of the scheme. If retirement is only a couple of years or so away and the couple has enough money to survive on until then, there is no doubt that the freezing of benefit is the better choice.

Some schemes do not allow for early retirement at all, and those that do have differing terms on which they calculate the amount of pension per year of early retirement. Some firms do allow full pension for men at any age after 60 and may allow women to go at 55, although the latter does not follow automatically from the former. Others can have very punitive terms indeed. A cut of 5 per cent per year of early retirement is not unusual. For a period, although it cannot be guaranteed indefinitely, state unemployment benefit may make up some of the lost income.

Where early retirement takes place because of ill-health, the employee may well get a full rate of pension, but it will inevitably be lower than it would otherwise have been, because it will be calculated on the final level of pensionable pay you are receiving when you are forced to retire. In such cases, other state benefits may be available to boost income. Some schemes also include disability payments, which can help.

At present, the government is considering proposals to amend the rules on early retirement.

Spotcheck

As your working life draws to a close, have you

- set about minimizing your taxes?
- looked in particular at the questions of Inheritance Tax and Capital Gains Tax, if they are likely to affect you?
- made sure that your savings and investments are the best possible you can get, looking to your retirement years?
- considered the full implications and what you can afford, if you would like to take early retirement?
- recognized your housing needs to see whether a smaller house and more money saved or invested would not be a better plan for you?

THE RETIREMENT YEARS

When we retire, our income tends to fall but, if we have followed a sensible financial plan all our lives, the years we spend in retirement can be just as comfortable financially as any other. There is often a fall in our everyday spending, and the main task now is to ensure that income is not eroded by inflation, because we are no longer earning and cannot expect compensatory wage increases. Unless our level of savings is very low, there is no need to go for maximum income: we can combine some income savings and investments with some form of capital growth. We should make sure that we are getting all the state benefits to which we are entitled as of right. We should reassess our housing needs, if we have not already done so, and look at home income plans if we are a home owner but have limited cash resources. We should ensure that the surviving partner is protected after the first death; and we should start giving away as much of our capital as we can to reduce Inheritance Tax. We may spend many years in retirement, so we should ensure that they are comfortable ones. Finally, we should make a sensible will, which will leave our heirs happy.

20 | Pensions and Benefits

In this last stage of our lives we should, if we have planned carefully, be settling into a comfortable old age with pension and income from savings taking up the slack left when our earnings cease. Alas, this is often not true. Thoughts about pensions are usually far away during the early years when we are setting up our homes. Later, when there are not so many demands on our funds, pensions still remain at the end of the line. Because pension arrangements should be well underway when we are in our 30s, we have dealt with them in Part Five (see pages 158–65). Here we will just look at what financial arrangements we should be making as we reach our retirement years and how to maximize the financial returns from our resources if our pensions are not adequate.

It is important to remember that the day of retirement is not the end of life: women on the whole spend almost 20 years in retirement. Men are less lucky in that they have to work five years longer than women and then have a shorter life expectancy, but even so they average 10 years of retirement today.

Before retirement arrives, it is important to ensure that, as earnings cease, pension payments take over immediately without any break, so the priorities are:

- Apply for your state retirement benefits well in time, and check to see whether you are eligible for any other state benefits.
- Look carefully at your accommodation and decide whether you can afford the running costs and whether you want to: running a home which has become too large for your needs can be a drain on both your physical and financial health.
- Maximize the return on your savings and assets, bearing in mind that there are likely to be changes in your tax position when you retire. Remember that all normal state and private retirement pensions are taxable (the latter should not be confused with the tax-free income which can come from some life-assurance policies, which are only a means of achieving a regular income by using the sum assured due on maturity as income rather than in the form of a tax-free lump sum) and will be added to your income from all sources in assessing the tax you owe.
- Prepare yourself for life alone.

We will now consider each of these areas in turn.

The state retirement pension

The state retirement pension becomes payable to women who have earned a pension in their own right at 60. Men are not eligible until five years later, at 65. A married woman who is not entitled to a state pension in her own right (increasingly fewer in numbers as married women no longer have the option of not paying National Insurance contributions if they work) does get one from the National Insurance contributions her husband has made during his working life. She must then be over 60 and not working, or have reached the age of 65. If she is under 60 when her husband retires, or over it and still working, her husband may still qualify for an adult dependency allowance, which may be reduced or eliminated depending on the level of her earnings.

To qualify for a basic pension, it is best to think of paying National Insurance contributions for the whole of your working life to 60 (women) or 65 (men), although you will get a full pension if you have paid for 90 per cent of it. The rules are that you must have paid: (a) enough contributions in any *one* tax year from April 1975 for that year to be a qualifying year; or (b) 50 flat-rate contributions at any time before 6 April 1975.

The number of qualifying years needed varies depending on how long you have worked. If you have been in employment for between 31 and 40 years, it is the length of your working life, less four years. Five years can be omitted if you have worked for 41 years or over. (People who go abroad to work for an extended period should note this rule: if you are away for more than four or five years, it may be worthwhile to pay the self-employed National Insurance contribution for a time to maintain your right to a full basic pension.) Men normally do not have to pay beyond the age of 60, as they have fulfilled the basic rule by then.

The basic pension for a couple is not worth as much as that of two individuals and, where the wife does have a pension in her own right, the couple do not get the rate for a married man and a non-pension-eligible wife, plus her single pension: they simply get a total of two single pensions. Pension levels are normally adjusted for inflation every year. When one of them dies, the survivor then receives only the single person's pension.

The situation for people retiring today is that they get a flat-rate state pension based on the National Insurance contributions they have made in their working lives, plus (a) an extra earnings-related sum from additional contributions, if they were employees, or (b) further income from a private pension scheme run by their company. A few people do get the earnings-related part as well as a private pension. Some private schemes, however, are not what are called 'recognized' (see page 162). Anyone in an unrecognized fund can top it up with an investment in a private plan with full tax relief to 15 per cent of annual earnings. This situation is about to change under new personal pension rules, but covers the bulk of people retiring now.

Because the earnings-related scheme has been operating only since 1978 and it is only recently that people have been beginning to take full advantage of the allowances for self-employed deferred annuities and Additional Voluntary Contributions, many couples find themselves short of funds at this time in their lives. Even so, a very few people have some reservations about collecting their state pension. It is important to recognize that this has been *paid for by you* through taxes and National Insurance contributions all your working life.

To be eligible for a pension, men and women at the ages of 65 and 60 respectively must satisfy the contribution conditions set out above and be retired from regular work. They must either:

- Not be doing any paid work at all.
- Be continuing to work, but having earnings which are less than the amount allowed under the earnings rule, which operates for men under 70 and women over 65. This level rises each year; for 1987–88 it is £75 a week. The pension is reduced by five pence for every ten pence of the next £4 of earnings and by five pence for every five pence above that figure. Earnings affect only the flat-rate state pension; they do not affect any additional pension from a private fund, any guaranteed pension, any graduated pension (from the scheme introduced in 1961 and dropped in 1975) or any extra amounts paid of the above for putting off your retirement. After the age of 70 (or 65 for a woman), you can earn as much as you want without your pension being affected.
- Be earning more than the weekly amount allowed in the earnings rule, but only occasionally or not for more than 12 hours a week. Retirement is defined as being 'retired from regular employment', a status which is not affected if the person involved works 'only occasionally or to an inconsiderable extent or otherwise in circumstances not inconsistent with retirement'.

Claiming your pension

The local office of the Department of Health and Social Security will send you a form about four months before you are due to retire. Give them a little leeway, but if one has not arrived by three months before your retirement, ask at the office. Fill in the form and send it back without delay. You may of course not know the actual date of your retirement, but give as much detail as you can. Once you have the date, let the DHSS office know.

If you are coming up to the state retirement age but do not intend to retire, inform the DHSS. Once you reach 70 (or 65 if you are a woman and claiming in your own right), you will get your pension whether you have retired or not—but not if you do not claim it. Separate claims have to be made by husbands and wives, and wives must claim themselves if they are applying for a pension based on their husband's contributions, or a pension claimed for a woman taking care of the claimant's children, or for the claimant's children. There will be something for the last two, if you are entitled to child benefit for them.

The form you send to the DHSS must give the date of your retirement. This can be defined in one of three ways:

- the day after you will be giving up your regular job, if you are still working when you reach pension age
- the day that you will reach pension age, if you have already retired
- the date you want to be treated as having retired, if you are carrying on working but will not be earning enough to remove your right to some pension

It is important to make your claim in good time, because you will be told in writing how much you will be getting and how the amount is made up. You may not agree with the figure and the letter will tell you what to do if you don't.

If you find that you do not qualify for the full pension, it will be because

208

you have not fulfilled the pension conditions. These are quite onerous. Just as pensions may be decreased because the pension rules are not met, they can also be increased—by deferring retirement. Anyone who stays in full-time employment is unlikely to be paid any pension at 65 or 60, but when they eventually come to retire, there will be some increment depending on the number of days the pension is deferred for. Additionally, anyone who goes on working after the age of 60 no longer pays National Insurance contributions. This does not affect the rights to a pension when it is eventually claimed, but employers have to have a 'Certificate of Age Exemption' before they can stop making the deductions. Today these should be sent automatically to the person involved, but, if you reach pension age and have not received one, apply to the local DHSS office. Refunds can be made by the employer if by any chance you have continued to pay them, as long as the refund is made in the tax year to which the contributions applied. If that has ended, a refund application form must be applied for at the DHSS office. Those who are self-employed and have been making Class 2 contributions simply hand their contribution card to their local DHSS office when they reach pension age.

How pensions are paid

The long queues of people collecting their pension each week are no longer necessary. As long as a pension comes to more than £1 a week and the pensioner lives in the UK, he or she can choose how to be paid—either weekly, or every four or 13 weeks in arrears. Those who choose to be paid weekly are given a book of orders, covering a year, which can be cashed at a post office. Such orders must be cashed within three months of the date shown on them. If you are paid four or 13 weeks in arrears, the money can be paid directly into a bank or building society. You can change from weekly to the other form of payment at any time.

If you do not live in the UK, your rights to a pension can be affected, depending on where you have chosen to live. The normal rule used to be that, if you went to live abroad, the level of pension that you were getting at the point of departure remained fixed for the rest of your life or until your return to the UK. In other words, you did not benefit from the annual upgradings. Now, however, there are reciprocal arrangements with some countries to the effect that the normal increments are paid; the arrangements may also apply to medical benefits. The countries involved are all the member countries of the EEC plus, alphabetically, Australia, Austria, Bermuda, Canada, Cyprus, Finland, Gibraltar, Iceland, Israel, Jamaica, Jersey and Guernsey, Malta, Mauritius, New Zealand, Norway, Sweden, Switzerland, Turkey, the United States and Yugoslavia. Not all agreements are the same, and not all cover both medical benefits and increases in retirement and widows' pensions.

If you are going to live abroad, it is as well to check just what is covered. Write to the Department of Health and Social Security, Overseas Branch, Newcastle upon Tyne, NE98 1YX. Try to give plenty of notice, because dealing with enquiries takes some time.

Until recently, pensions continued to be paid normally during stays in hospital but now, after someone has been hospitalized for more than eight weeks, the pension goes not to the pensioner (or to the partner who may still be at home) but to the hospital. This can cause hardship for the partner remaining at home and, as always in these situations, help should be sought from the DHSS.

Christmas bonus

Although the £10 Christmas bonus is not a right, it has been given for so many years now that it would be difficult for any government to abandon it. It goes to virtually all British pensioners resident in the UK or in a member state of the European Community or Gibraltar. It is not taxable.

Other state benefits

In addition to the pension, there are a wide range of other state benefits available to the elderly. All except one of these are related to income levels, the exception being National Health prescriptions, which are free to all pensioners as long as they fill in the declaration on the back of the prescription form stating that they are over the state retirement age.

It is recognized by governments today that, if the only income a person has is the retirement pension, this is not enough to live on, and so an additional supplementary pension is granted as soon as either husband or wife reaches 65. The level varies each year; for the period from 6 April 1987 it brought the pension up to £38.65 for a single person and £61.85 for a married couple living in their own homes. An extra 25p is added on the 80th birthday. Changes are planned in this system from April 1988.

In working out the entitlement to supplementary pensions, no account is taken of rent or general rates. When a person becomes entitled to extra benefits of any kind, a certificate is sent to the local authority and the claimant can then apply for full housing benefit.

Claims for supplementary pensions can be made by writing to the local DHSS office. You can pick up a claim form, which is attached to the explanatory leaflet SB1, at any post office or DHSS office. Husbands and wives, or people living together as husband and wife, can make a claim as soon as one of them has reached retirement age, where both are getting a pension from his or her own contributions. In assessing the claim, the DHSS will need to know details of income and other circumstances; all information so given is treated confidentially. If you are uncertain about whether or not you are eligible, call or telephone the DHSS office and discuss your circumstances with them. There is now also a nationwide information and advice service called Freephone DHSS. Supplementary pensions come in a book of orders, and are usually paid from the same book as the basic retirement pension. You must be normally resident in the United Kingdom to qualify for a supplementary pension.

It can happen, of course, that your claim is turned down, so it is worth looking at how your income will be calculated when your claim is assessed. A couple's incomes are assessed together, and the calculation is done on a weekly basis.

- All forms of pension—the basic state pension, the earnings-related part, any graduated pension, or a private pension from a former employer—are taken into account in full.
- Any other National Insurance benefits, like child benefit or family income supplement, are also counted in full.

- Maintenance payments from a former or separated spouse count in full, whether the payment is made through a Court Order or voluntarily.
- A disability or war widow's pension does not have the first £4 a week counted. Nor is the first £4 of most other forms of income, such as regular payments from charities, etc. However, £4 is the *total* amount from these sources which is excluded.
- When it comes to savings and capital, these are ignored if their total value is less than £3,000. If their value is more, there is no entitlement to supplementary pension. The value of the house one is living in is, however, ignored in assessing claims to supplementary pensions— although a second property does count.

If someone is living in your home, it is assumed that they are paying some rent. A notional level is set for this, and it rises with time. It is important to remember that, if one of a married couple is admitted to hospital for a long stay, the amount of supplementary pension will eventually be adjusted because of the saving in household expenses which is reckoned to have taken place during the absence.

In addition to supplementary pension, some people may be eligible for help with heating costs, if they are in poor health, or if their home is difficult and expensive to heat. There is a lower and a higher rate for such benefits, depending on the severity of the medical condition, the nature of the home and the age of the applicant.

As well as regular help with heating costs, single payments for exceptional needs may be made. These could include the costs of purchasing extra blankets and contributions to repairs to heating installations, draught-proofing, etc. Such payments do not come simply on application: any of the claimant's savings over £500 would have to be put towards the cost. There are a variety of lump-sum payments, details of which are set out in leaflet SB16, once again available from DHSS offices or your local Citizens' Advice Bureau. From April 1988 single grants will be replaced by loans from the Social Fund, except in special cases.

Finally, if you are on a special diet and have difficulty in paying for it, there are various weekly levels of allowance which can be as high as £10.85 (from 6 April 1988) for people with renal failure who are being treated by dialysis. From April 1988, weekly payments for heating, special diets and laundry costs will be abolished.

Pensioners who are entitled to supplementary pensions also get free NHS dental treatment; there is no help for private treatment. Similarly, those on supplementary pensions are also entitled to have their fares to and from hospital paid. This is given in the form of a refund, and pensioners should produce their pension order book when they go for treatment. Some pensioners who are not receiving a supplementary pension but who nevertheless are on low incomes may also be eligible for the refund. In this case, form H11 must be obtained from the hospital and sent to the local DHSS office. It will show details of admission or discharge or attendance at an out-patient clinic or day hospital. If you are unable to travel alone and need an escort, the hospital should so state on the form. Some, though not all, health authorities provide chiropody services free to priority groups, which include the elderly. If the authority does not provide it, however, and you have to seek treatment outside the NHS, you will have to pay the cost yourself.

211

Invalidity benefit

The older we get the more likely we are to become invalids. Several forms of invalidity benefit are available. To be eligible for these, you must first of all qualify for the basic invalidity pension, from which the others flow. The total benefit is made up as follows:

- Basic invalidity pension. This is not limited to and is not really designed for the elderly, although they can benefit in certain circumstances. First of all, if you do not retire at 65 (men) or 60 (women), you must be eligible for a pension from your National Insurance contributions or under special arrangements for widows or widowers, or where the incapacity follows from an industrial accident or a prescribed disease. If the retirement pension is paid at the standard rate, so too will be the invalidity pension, if the incapacity has been caused by an industrial accident or a prescribed disease; in the same way, if you qualify only for a pension at the reduced rate, the invalidity pension will be likewise reduced. Those who are widowed or divorced may be able to use their late or former spouse's National Insurance contributions to get an ordinary retirement pension, and can similarly use these for an invalidity pension. Where wives have retirement pensions in their own right, they can sometimes get an invalidity pension at the rate of the two pensions added together up to a certain limit. The basic invalidity pension can continue to be paid after retirement until the age of 70 for men and 65 for women.
- Additional invalidity allowance. This is a payment over and above the basic invalidity pension, and it is based on the earnings-related part of National Insurance contributions. People who were contracted out of the scheme and into private pension plans do not qualify.
- Invalidity allowance. This may be available if the incapacity began before you reached the state retirement age, although anyone with an earnings-related pension or guaranteed minimum pension will have the invalidity allowance reduced or even eliminated. When a man reaches 70 or a woman 65, their retirement pension will be increased permanently by the amount of the invalidity allowance if they were getting it on any day before they reached the state retirement age, if they were at that time entitled to a retirement pension based on their own contributions.
- Increases for wives and dependants. Increases in invalidity pensions apply only to wives who are earning less than £31.45 a week.

    It is rarer for a woman to get an increase in invalidity pension for a husband, but it is possible in certain circumstances when he is a very low earner. It is worth checking the situation. This increase can also be claimed in cases where someone is looking after children, but that is highly unlikely to apply to a woman of pensionable age. Increases are also possible for children where the parent is entitled to child benefit. You must be either the parent of the child or contributing to its maintenance.

Attendance allowance

The attendance allowance is a further state benefit which is not limited to the elderly, although they are more likely to qualify for it than younger people, as their health declines with age. It is paid to anyone over the age of two who is severely physically or mentally disabled and who has needed constant care and attention for at least six months. There are two rates of the allowance (which is not means-tested and which is tax-free). The higher rate is paid to those who require frequent or continual supervision and attention to avoid danger to themselves and others by day and night. The lower rate goes to those who require the same care but only by day or only by night. There are no contribution conditions, but the person needing the care must be resident or present in the United Kingdom.

The attendance allowance is paid on top of National Insurance benefits, industrial injury benefits or war pension, but if a constant attendance allowance is also being paid under the industrial injuries scheme or with a war pension, the attendance allowance may be cut. The formula is that, if the constant attendance allowance is less than the attendance allowance, the difference between the two will be paid. If it is more, the attendance allowance will not be paid at all.

Invalid care allowance

There is a further allowance known as the invalid care allowance. This is paid to people who cannot work because they have to stay at home to look after someone who is severely disabled. A 'severely disabled' person is defined as someone who is receiving either the attendance allowance, at the higher or lower rate, or the constant attendance allowance. The benefit is taxable (to the recipient), but there are no National Insurance contribution conditions and the allowance is not means-tested. Until 1986, married women were not eligible for the invalid care allowance, but became so after a woman took her case to the European Court. She succeeded in her claim that to deny her the benefit was sex discriminatory, and the government immediately capitulated and brought married women into the scheme. This change affects many married women looking after elderly parents, but it is as well to remember that you will not get the allowance unless you claim for it.

Both the attendance allowance and the invalid care allowance are claimed via the Department of Health and Social Security. The claim form for the attendance allowance is incorporated in leaflet NI205 and that for the invalid care allowance in leaflet 212.

Mobility allowance

The mobility allowance is a state cash benefit available to anyone who is unable or virtually unable to walk. Pensioners are eligible as long as they were disabled before their 65th birthday. If they meet that criterion, the benefit can continue up to the age of 75. This allowance is tax-free and is paid in addition to other social-security benefits; moreover, it is the key to eligibility to several others. Recipients can do whatever they like with the money.

If you are blind or have severe mobility problems (again quite frequent with the elderly), you may qualify for the Orange Badge scheme. This gives certain parking concessions either to the disabled person or to someone driving them around. It does not apply in the City of London, the City of Westminster, the Royal Borough of Kensington and Chelsea and part of the London Borough of Camden.

PENSIONS AND BENEFIT RATES (From 6 April 1987)

Retirement Pension (Standard weekly rate)

	Single person	£39.50
	Wife (on husband's contributions)	£23.75
	Married couple	£64.25
Dependency Additions	For spouse or person looking after children	£23.75
Child Dependency Addition		£8.05
Invalidity Benefit	Invalidity Pension	£39.50
Invalidity Allowance	Higher rate	£8.30
	Middle rate	£5.30
	Lower rate	£2.65
Mobility Allowance		£22.10
Severe Disablement Allowance		£23.75
(reduced if other benefits		
are in payment)	Plus for dependent wife or husband	£14.20
	For each child	£8.05
Attendance Allowance	Higher rate	£31.60
	Lower rate	£21.10
Constant Attendance	Normal maximum	£25.80
Allowance	Part-time rate	£12.90
	Intermediate rate	£38.70
	Exceptional rate	£51.60
Invalid Care Allowance		£23.75

Supplementary Benefit (known as Income Support from 1988)

Long Term rates	Single	£30.40
	Couple	£49.35
	Non-householder 18 or over	£24.35
Additions for dependent	16–17	£18.75
children		
	11–15	£15.60
	under 11	£10.40
Help with heating costs	Higher rate	£5.50
	Lower rate	£2.20

NOTE: Other rates and dietary allowances are unchanged

Housing Benefits

Needs allowances	Single person	£48.90
	Single handicapped person	£54.50
	Couple (both handicapped)	£80.45
	Couple/single parent	£72.15
	Couple (1 handicapped or single handicapped parent)	£77.75
	Dependent child addition	£14.75

Income Tax Age Allowance

	Single	£2,960	Married	£4,675
Over-80s	Single	£3,070	Married	£4,845

Age allowance reduced on incomes over £9,800.

Maximizing Income in Retirement

On retirement, the most immediate change is that income from employment ceases and that from pensions takes over. It is unusual for income from pensions and savings to compensate totally for the loss of earnings. This state of affairs is not necessarily a disaster, because on retirement many expenses decrease or cease altogether—e.g., travelling expenses to and from work.

The first thing to do before embarking on a savings and investment strategy is to assess your income realistically. This can be made up of

- basic state pension
- additional pension
- graduated pension (earned from 1961 to 1975 only)
- personal or company pension scheme
- any continuing income from work
- interest or dividends from savings or capital
- social security benefits other than pension.

The total may pleasantly surprise you. Next assess your outgoings, which will certainly change on retirement. If you have planned properly, you may see cuts in your

- mortgage payments
- life-assurance premiums
- regular savings
- travelling expenses
- eating out and other expenses associated with work
- clothing and food

Ideally, you should have timed your mortgage payments to end at your retirement. The same goes for life-assurance premiums; if your mortgage is not repaid, the life-assurance money can often be used to make a lump-sum final payment. Our retirement years are the ones in which we start to use up our savings and reap the benefits of earlier financial planning. Obviously, some expenses may rise in retirement. What we save in travelling expenses to work we may use up in leisure travelling or more expensive holidays. There are many points of balance—we may eat less, but spend more on heating, and so on. Generally, however, many people find that their overall spending budget is smaller.

Think this through in some detail, and then compare your total income with your total outgoings. If you have planned sensibly throughout your life, you should find that you will be comfortably off during your retirement.

Next look at your tax position, which may change sharply on retirement. Recognizing that your income has fallen, the government increases the personal tax allowance to those over retirement age. For 1987–88 it is £2,960 for a single person and £4,675 for a married couple if either is over the age of 65 at any time during the year of assessment. In the 1987 Budget, a new age allowance for the over-80s was introduced at £3,070 for a single person and £4,845 for a married man.

So that the wealthy do not benefit too much from this concession, the age allowance, as it is called, is reduced for those on incomes over £9,800. For every £3 above that level the allowance is reduced by £2, until it falls to the rate available to single persons or to married people who are below retirement age. This means that, by the time a retired single person's income from all sources reaches £10,603 the whole of the age allowance is lost; the figure is £11,120 for a married couple. For the over-80s the figures are £11,375 or £10,768. The single person or couple are then taxed in the same way at the same rates as anyone else.

For many people of pension age, maximizing the income they receive from savings becomes a priority. The path they should follow depends primarily on whether or not they are taxpayers, and marginally on whether or not they are on the borderline between paying taxes. All pensioners need to reassess their savings and make changes if necessary.

One problem can be the timing of savings and investments to ensure that we get a steady flow of money throughout the year. Some savings have interest credited only once or twice a year, and in the case of fixed-interest savings certificates, for example, if we want to get the full benefit of the tax-free growth in the value of the certificates, there is no income at all until they mature after five years. There is no income from index-linked certificates until they have been held for a year. For these reasons, timing can be important.

Bearing all that in mind, plan your savings and investment programme according to your means. First go for savings where the value of your original capital is guaranteed to make sure that you keep your emergency supply of money intact—you may well need it more in your retirement years than ever before—and then move on to savings which provide a combination of growth and income. Finally, if your resources permit, build up a balanced investment portfolio or have a few holdings in different unit trusts.

Non-taxpayers

Non-taxpayers can do little better than put their savings into National Savings. They have three choices, all of which offer high interest, which is paid gross before tax. These are

- The investment account, which is an ordinary savings account. It can have any amount between £1 and £50,000 in it, and can be added to or subtracted from without penalty.
- Income bonds. These are for people with more cash available. The bonds are sold in multiples of £1,000. At present the minimum you can hold is £2,000 and the maximum £50,000.
- Deposit bonds. These are available in multiples of £50, with a minimum purchase of £500 and a maximum of £50,000.

These three forms of National Savings usually offer the highest interest rates available at any particular time. There is usually a slightly higher interest on the two forms of bonds than on the investment account (it varies but will probably be at least 0.5–0.75 per cent), but only one month's notice of withdrawal is demanded on the investment account as opposed to three months for the bonds. Interest is not lost if the full amount of notice of withdrawal is given.

- The National Girobank also has a high-interest deposit account for those with £1,000 or more to save. Anyone who has £10,000 to deposit can get an even higher rate of interest.

Interest on all four is calculated on a day-to-day basis, but income bonds, as their name suggests, pay a regular (monthly) income. This comes after a bond has been held for six weeks and is then paid on the fifth day of each month. The first payment includes all the accrued interest.

In the investment account, interest is added to the account on 31 December. In deposit bonds, it is credited on the first anniversary of the purchase. The Girobank high interest is credited quarterly.

Anyone who becomes a non-taxpayer on retirement should shift their savings from the building society, bank or any other financial institution to National Savings. Otherwise tax will be paid unnecessarily, because in all these institutions the tax on the interest is paid by the institution itself, and cannot be recovered by the non-taxpayer.

Moving into National Savings may put the pensioner close to the tax level, or over it. In such cases, it is then worth considering National Savings Certificates to stay out of the tax net. There are three varieties of these. All are completely free of UK income tax, and details of them do not have to be entered on tax returns. The three varieties are:

- those which offer a fixed, guaranteed initial return on a lump-sum investment
- those which are index-linked and pay no interest, but rise in value in line with the Retail Price Index and so protect the holder from inflation
- those bought on the yearly plan, which guarantees a tax-free income to anyone who agrees first of all to make monthly payments for one year

The tables in Appendix I give details of how all these work in practice.

Aside from National Savings there is one other secure savings medium which pays interest gross, and it will provide you with a cheque book, which is good for non-taxpayers. This is the high-interest cheque account based offshore. This is an account with a bank (or branch of a British bank) based in either the Channel Islands or the Isle of Man. Cheques are subject to a minimum level of withdrawal, and you cannot usually overdraw. Such accounts may allow direct debits and standing orders, and you may even be able to get a cashcard and Eurocheques. The only snags are that the initial deposit must be rather high—£2,000 or £2,500—which would swallow up all the cash of a non-taxpayer, and that there is a charge to pay for cheques drawn after a certain number every quarter. Additions to the account must usually be at least £250. Interest is variable, and changes rather more frequently than that on National Savings. Building societies too run similar offshore accounts.

217

If you pay tax at the standard rate, this is where building societies and banks come into their own. They pay interest net of tax to their savers, but the tax deducted is less than the standard rate, so the saver benefits. For instance, if a taxpayer put money into National Savings, eventually the Inland Revenue would demand 27 per cent (the standard rate of tax) back from the saver. For the private financial institutions, however, the rate paid is only 25 per cent, so there is a 2 per cent direct benefit to the saver. There are many forms of accounts today, with those on longer terms of notice paying rather more than those which allow immediate access to the money. They come in a variety of names, but you will be able to compare one with another by checking the notice terms. (Details are given on pages 237–9.)

The main rule to follow is not to have all your savings in one place. Have something on short withdrawal notice, unless you have an arrangement with your bank that you can overdraw in an emergency—although in that case you must assess whether the overdraft charges will more than wipe out any interest gained by having all your money on long-term withdrawal, rather than some on long-term and some on short-term.

In general, you will be marginally better off in building societies rather than in banks, but the latter are becoming more competitive and so this may change.

If you are a taxpayer, however, you may have enough funds to consider forms of investment other than a simple account. The aim is to increase the value of your capital as well as bring in an income. Depending on the amount of capital you have and what you need to live on, consider in order of priority:

- The Personal Equity Plan. If you hold the plan for the qualifying period, all capital gains and dividends are tax-free. (For details, see pages 51–3.)
- Unit trusts, for a combination of income and growth without too much risk. (For details, see pages 47–50.)
- Gilt-edged securities. Interest here is paid gross. At certain times they can be useful not only for income but for capital growth. (For details, see page 170.)
- Equities. These should be bought only by those with funds which they can risk. (For details, see pages 169–70.)

| Higher-rate taxpayers

The priorities change again for those who are paying tax at higher than standard rates. For the tax year 1987–88, this means anyone (or a married couple) with a taxable income of £17,900 or more. The main concern is to reduce the tax burden, because once you move up from standard rate the tax level jumps immediately to 40 per cent. So the first thing is to get as much into tax-free investments as possible. Basically today this means National Savings Certificates (see page 217). The maximum holding of the normal certificates is £5,000's worth (200 at £25), of the index-linked certificates £10,000 (1,000 at £10), and of the yearly plan (which has a minimum monthly payment of £20 and a maximum of £100 in multiples of £5), £240–£1,200 a year.

After that, the higher-rate taxpayer should seek the highest interest possible from other institutions. Any additional tax owed on any tax-paid interest will have to be settled by the end of the tax year.

Alternatively, the high taxpayer may prefer to look instead to investments in the stock market in order to make a profit on the actual value of the shares held and, by using the exemptions from Capital Gains Tax at the end of each financial year (see pages 201–3), get some of his or her income by taking the profits on some of the shares.

Short or fixed-term saving?

The various forms of saving can be divided broadly into those which allow relatively easy access to their funds for savers and those which are on longer-term withdrawal terms. Anything over six months is usually regarded as longer-term and in such savings interest rates are normally fixed for the full term of the deposit. For the individual the choice should be made:

a) On how long he or she can afford to put the money away. Anyone likely to need money quickly should not put their savings into fixed longer-term accounts. There is usually a penalty for early withdrawal and in some cases it may not be allowed at all, except in the event of death.

b) What you think will happen to interest rates. If you expect them to fall to 6 per cent and you can get, say, 8 per cent guaranteed on your money for a year it makes sense to put your money in a fixed term deposit, if you can rely on not needing the money. If you expect the reverse to happen and that interest rates will rise, it is a mistake to tie your money up for a long period.

Even if you think that a fixed interest deposit is best for you, do not tie your money up for periods of more than 5 years. Choose from Co-operative Society deposits or Local Authority schemes (see page 239).

Annuities

One way of using your capital to increase your income during retirement is to purchase an annuity. These are offered by life-assurance companies, and can be described as a life-assurance policy in reverse. What happens is that the annuitant puts down a lump sum and then gets a monthly, quarterly or half-yearly income. This income is a combined return of capital and interest on the lump sum, which remains in the hands of the life-assurance company, for the rest of the annuitant's life or for a defined period.

Both sides to the deal are taking a chance. The company is hoping to make money—and it will if the annuitant dies before all the capital is used up. The annuitant, on the other hand, hopes to survive past the exhaustion of his or her capital and then start making a profit.

Three things follow from this. First, the older the person taking out the annuity, the more interest (or income) the company will be prepared to offer. Second, no inquiry will be made about the state of the potential annuitant's health. As far as the company is concerned, the best thing that can happen is that the annuitant dies very shortly after taking out the annuity, because it then makes a good profit. Third, annuities differ from life policies in that men get higher interest rates than women, age for age, because they tend to die earlier.

Annuity rates are always good when compared with interest rates generally, and like them they do vary, although they are fixed for the whole of the life of a particular annuity when it is taken out. When rates are very low, annuities are best ignored, and you should never lose sight of the fact that, in an ordinary annuity, the money, once put down, has gone for good, even if you die a week later. Annuities are often suggested to newly widowed women and often, too, when they are at the very youngest ages for annuities. These tend to start at about 50, when they are almost never a good bargain: by the age of 60, the total income will be about 9 per cent more than at 50, by 70/30 per cent better, and by 75 as much as 64 per cent higher. There are many widows around now who 20 years ago supplemented their incomes with an annuity worth £1,000 or £1,500 a year, which seemed a fair sum then, but who have lived to regret the purchase. And, just as annuities are a bad bargain when one is too young, they are not very attractive when one is very old and one's life expectancy may be only a few years. At this stage it is often better simply to begin using up capital, although when interest rates are high a 75-year-old man may get all his capital back from an annuity in little more than two years.

Nevertheless, annuities can be appealing to some people because the rates are often twice the level of interest rates generally. As the savings market has become increasingly sophisticated, however, annuities have lost a lot of their appeal, so the companies offering them have moved beyond the simple annuity, where the annuity ceases on the annuitant's death. Today there is far more variety:

- Basic annuities, which cease on death. These are still liked by the insurance companies because of their simplicity.
- Guaranteed annuities, which offer a lifetime income and some return of capital. These are becoming more popular with customers because they are able to leave some money to their heirs. This can be a sensitive point. It is astonishing how touchy heirs can become at the thought of their parents using their own money for their own benefit during their own lives, rather than maximizing the amount they can pass on!
- Immediate annuities, which are misnamed. The annuitant puts in the capital sum, but does not begin to collect the income immediately, but a short while later. The first payment is generally within six months, with further payments following every six months.
- Deferred annuities, which are a means of getting a higher-than-normal income. These start to be bought many years ahead on an instalment plan—really, in the way one buys a life-assurance policy. Anyone can buy them, but they are especially favoured by the self-employed, who are not in recognized pension plans. As we saw on page 164, they are highly tax-efficient, but only to those not in recognized pension funds, or to those working for themselves. On retirement, the income is paid out like a pension, and is taxable.
- Joint survivorship annuities, which are for husband and wife. They are obviously a sound idea, if an annuity is decided on, because payments continue to be made after the first death, although as a rule the amount then falls by one third.
- Reversionary annuities, which are another form of joint annuity for the

220

benefit of people to whom the purchaser of the annuity is not married. They can be taken out by a person who wishes someone else to have an income in the event of their own death. If the purchaser of the annuity dies before the beneficiary, the income begins to be paid out; if the latter dies first, however, the annuity also dies. Brothers and sisters, unmarried couples, and children of elderly parents all take out these policies. They can be very useful in divorce settlements, in that they guarantee a former wife an income after her ex-husband dies. In law, the reverse also applies today, although the situation is far less frequent.

Minimum or temporary annuities were introduced because of the flagging popularity of the other types, which may not have some final payment on death. Even in guaranteed annuities, the capital sum returned is generally not very generous. Minimum annuities guarantee an income for a number of years, perhaps five or ten. After that there will be an option for the annuitant to take a cash sum or continue with the income. There is some risk in these annuities, because annuity rates are fixed from the moment the annuity starts: rates may have risen during the five- or ten-year period, but equally they may have fallen, so that it might not be possible to achieve as high an income as before for the amount of money involved. Allowing for inflation, this could mean a sharp drop in income when one can least afford it.

Almost all types of annuity can be arranged for either level— unchanged—or increasing payment.

Annuities and tax

The treatment of annuities for tax purposes can be said to be generous, although, as the annuitant is partly just getting back his or her own capital, it is less so than it at first appears or as is sometimes suggested in promotional literature. The Income Tax and Corporation Taxes Act (1970) laid down that, although the interest element of the income is subject to tax in the same way as any other income, no tax is payable on that part which is a return of capital. Further, in calculating the total income of anyone with an annuity, the capital part of the annuity payment is not taken into account. This rule applies only if the annuitant has paid for the annuity him- or herself. This cuts out reversionary annuities bought for someone else (including ex-wives) and also any annuity which comes to an individual by means of a will or a reward for services in employment, or through a pension or superannuation scheme.

Points to watch

If you take out an annuity, always be sure that you know exactly what you are buying. Remember that you are gambling on living and that the life-assurance company in contrast is gambling that you will die earlier than you think. Annuity rates are worked out very carefully by the actuaries who assess risk for all insurance policies; if the companies were to find themselves generally out of pocket, they would change the rates. Remember, too, that once the money is paid the bulk of it is gone for good if you die soon after. Although this may not bother you, many people are concerned about leaving money to their heirs—and the heirs are sometimes concerned about it, too!

Finally, never tie up in an annuity all your money apart from what you may be getting as a pension. We need flexibility in our finances just as much in our later years as we do earlier, and inflation can very quickly eat into our income. As the annuity rate is fixed in most cases, what you get at the beginning is what you will be getting at the end—and that could be 20 or 25 years later.

Home income plans

Not everyone has the floating cash to purchase an annuity which brings a meaningful return, or wants to take a chance on dying soon after purchase. However, people may have an asset which does not normally produce an income: their home. Plans have been devised to unlock some of the capital tied up in this way without the homeowner having to forfeit the house. These are called home income plans.

Home income plans are a means of increasing your post-retirement income—assuming, of course, you own your own home. The chances are that by the time you retire you will have paid off your mortgage, or be very close to it, and in this case, you will have a substantial asset, but one which does not produce an income for you, as it would if the same amount of capital were in savings or investment. Of course, you could sell your home and move to somewhere smaller (see pages 225–6), but you may well not want to do this.

Under a home income plan, the elderly are able to release some or all of the capital tied up in their property. There are two types of scheme, one annuity-based and the other a reversion scheme, whereby the property is sold outright but the former owner then remains in it.

Within the two basic types, however, there are variations, and new versions are constantly coming to the market, so it is worth checking on what is available. It is important to remember that, whatever you choose, you will be unlocking capital while you are alive and therefore reducing the amount which can be left to your heirs. If you feel that it is more important to provide for your heirs than to maintain or increase your own living standards, do not consider a home income plan.

Annuity-based home income plans

In an annuity-based home income plan, a freehold or long leasehold (usually pitched at a minimum somewhere between 60 and 75 years) is mortgaged and the money raised is then used to buy an annuity, which like any annuity provides a single person (or a couple until the surviving one dies) with an income for the rest of life. The mortgage can be repaid at any time; this usually but not invariably happens on the death of the owner. People who move into sheltered housing or into old people's homes, however, will sell their homes and repay any outstanding mortgage at that point. The annuity, of course, once purchased continues to be paid. Naturally, the net value of the home is reduced by the full amount of the mortgage on death or sale, as no repayment of capital is made until death or the sale of the home.

Interest is, however, payable, and it is of course eligible for tax under the MIRAS system (see page 71) for loans of up to £30,000. The net interest payments will be deducted from the gross monthly annuity income before the homeowner gets it.

Where the homeowner is a tax payer, there is also a deduction of tax on the interest element of the annuity. Every scheme is slightly different, although most are available only to men and women over 70 (and it may be 73 for a single woman), or where the combined age of a couple is 150. There may or may not be a minimum property value, but even if there is it is generally very low. There may be a minimum level of loan of about £10,000 and a maximum of about £30,000, but again this is not always the case. Again, there tends to be a maximum percentage loan of 80 per cent of the valuation put on the home, but in some cases it is only 50 or 65 per cent. To simplify things, the mortgage interest rate is usually fixed, and pitched below normal mortgage interest rates.

There are, as almost always in any financial package, charges. Again these vary, but they are rarely very high. First of all there will be, as in any mortgage arrangement, a valuation fee, which depends on the value of the property. There will be a basic fee of perhaps £40 on the first £15,000 and then £1 for every £1,000 above that. There may also be commission on the annuity purchase, or on the property value. Finally, the terms for early redemption vary, and this could be an important deciding factor for some people. If you expect to move into sheltered housing, an old people's home or in with your children, make sure not only that there is no penalty for early repayment before death, but also whether it is permitted at all. Some companies impose no penalties for early repayment; others charge an early redemption fee of three months' interest in lieu of notice.

There is also some choice in the type of annuity, which may give level or increasing payments, and which may or may not—the latter is more likely—have an initial lump-sum payment (seven per cent is typical).

Deciding on which plan to go for demands quite serious consideration, and is best discussed with a professional adviser. If you do not have one, go to your bank and seek help there. Remember, the companies are in it for money—they arrange the mortgage and then offer the annuity through their own companies—so examine at least three schemes before deciding.

It is also worth discussing your plans with your children. In most cases, they are the ultimate inheritors and may prefer to subsidize their parents now so that later they inherit the home free of mortgage.

Reversion schemes

So far home reversion schemes have proved much less popular than annuity-based schemes, probably for the very good reason that the latter leave the property, although mortgaged, in the hands of the homeowner. In reversion schemes, owners sell out their interest entirely. This is rather unappealing to many people, particularly as the price they get is way below the market value. Giving up an asset which may have taken a working lifetime to pay for can be difficult, although the elderly without relatives may find the schemes attractive—because (a) the maximum paid tends to be higher (£50,000 rather than £30,000), (b) there is no mortgage tax relief implication, and (c) monthly payments may come in advance rather than arrears, and may be guaranteed for a period—five years is typical, whether the former homeowner survives or not; if he or she dies, the payments go to the heirs.

Under a typical reversion scheme, the property is not mortgaged but sold to the company operating the plan. The actual sale does not take place until the death of the former homeowner. Until that happens, there is simply a change of property title from the homeowner to the company involved; the company then leases the home back to its former owner for the rest of his or her life for a nominal rate—£12 a year is typical. This sum is simply deducted from the income payments. Note the word 'income': these plans, although they do not involve a mortgage on the property, do sometimes involve the purchase of an annuity. The homeowner will get between 50 and 100 per cent of the value of the home—the level being higher the older you are, because the sooner the company expects to get its hands on the property and realize a profit.

What the former homeowner decides to do with the money is partly up to him or her. Homeowners may decide they want to use it all for the purchase of an annuity; alternatively, they may use only part of it, or, if they happen to be younger when taking out the plan, part now with a top-up later. The balance of the money can be passed on to the heirs at death. Some reversion schemes are available to slightly younger people, and jointly where both are at least 60. And, although there is no contractual obligation for them to do so, the companies running the schemes will consider a variation in the contract so that, if they get the home sooner than expected, they may raise the annuity. Without a contractual commitment to this, however, it is wise not to rely on it.

Taxation

In the mortgage-based schemes, everyone, whether a taxpayer or not, benefits from the deduction of tax under the MIRAS system. It is important to remember, however, that the annuity will bring in extra income, and this may well be enough to push non-taxpayers into the tax bracket. If this is the case with you, remember that the tax will be deducted before you receive the income. Only the interest element of the annuity is liable for tax. Those who still do not pay tax will receive the income gross, but otherwise the annuity holders will receive their payments net of the standard rate of tax, while higher taxpayers will have to inform their tax inspectors so that the correct amount can be deducted. Such taxpayers will have the amount of higher mortgage rate relief included in their tax coding, which should partly make up for the higher amount charged on the interest.

There are Capital Transfer Tax implications in the mortgage. As no capital is repaid during the life of the plan-owner, the mortgage counts as a charge against the estate on death, and the liability for CTT is therefore reduced. In plans normally limited to £30,000, the company will occasionally consider a higher amount as long as the annuity rates are high enough to allow for any loss of tax relief under MIRAS. This usually means that applicants must be older than average, because that is when annuity rates are at their highest.

The annuity income may also affect the right to DHSS payments, although probably to a lesser extent.

In mortgage schemes, the owner keeps title to the house, so that in the event of a sale there is no Capital Gains Tax to pay, under the 'principal residence' rule.

Maintenance and upkeep

In all these schemes, the owner (in a mortgage-based scheme) or the former owner (in a reversion scheme) remains responsible for all the other charges of the home: these include general rates, water rates and all repairs and maintenance. Of course, the annuity itself provides money to pay for repairs, which increasingly require expert help as one gets older.

As in any plan of this kind, there are pros and cons. In order to get the higher income, something must be given up—either title to one's home or a reduction in its value on death, because the mortgage must then be repaid. One of the most difficult problems can be the attitude of the ultimate beneficiaries. Although it should not be a consideration, many people worry about leaving less to their children and the children, just as often if not more often, do not like to see the value of their expected inheritance decrease. They can make this very plain, and it is not all that rare for older people to live at a far lower standard than need be, just so that their children and grandchildren can ultimately inherit the maximum possible. The only sensible advice is: *do not allow this to be a factor when you are considering a home income plan*. It is, however, very difficult to alter attitudes.

Housing in retirement

We have already seen how a home can be used to supplement income during our retirement years, but it is equally important to reassess our housing needs as we get older. The family home will almost certainly be too large for our later years. If the family has lived in the same home for many years, the chances are that selling it and buying a smaller and more convenient one will yield a profit, which can be invested. The amount of this profit will obviously vary from area to area. A smaller home, too, will cost less to run, a consideration which may be important once we start living on a reduced income. A home that was convenient for work may not be exactly what we want to live in when we no longer have this factor to consider.

The decision to move home, however, should not be taken lightly—and it should not be taken on financial considerations alone. You should think about what you really want. For example, many people move to seaside areas and then spend years wondering why they do not see their children and grandchildren as often as they did before.

The first question which must be answered is: do you really *want* to move? If, once you have worked out your financial resources, it is clear that you do not *have* to, then the question can be answered clearly and correctly. If, for example, you enjoy living close to your children, you may want to stay where you are. Many of us harbour romantic thoughts about where we will live in retirement, but the reality may not match our dreams. Living in the country during your later years when you have lived in a town or suburb all your life may prove not to be much fun. If you do make the decision to move, choose your area and then study it before you buy any property. Will you have any social life? Are there good local services, such as meals on wheels and medical services, should you eventually need them? Is there good residential or sheltered accommodation should you eventually want it?

If you get satisfactory answers to all these questions, then look at the financial aspects. Do not rush into anything. However carefully we try, it is difficult totally to ignore the financial side, even when we think we are doing so. It is therefore better to wait until you have actually retired and seen what life is like in your old home before you go ahead and buy somewhere else—or, perhaps, move too soon into sheltered or residential accommodation.

If you decide to stay on in your old home, there may be some mortgage still to be paid off. Now is the time to decide what to do about it. There is nothing to stop you continuing to make mortgage payments from your pension, if you have sufficient funds, but the chances are that you may have a maturing life-assurance policy or some other lump sum to enable you to pay off the loan if you so wish. If it will make you feel more secure to know that your home actually belongs to you and that there are no further mortgage payments to be made on it, then clearly the remaining loan should be paid off. If these considerations do not bother you, then you need to sit down and compare having to pay interest (with tax relief deducted at source) on your mortgage with what you could get from investing the money instead. The interest on this latter may be tax-free, tax-paid or paid to you gross and then liable for tax, depending upon your total income. Whatever the outcome when you do this sum it is still not the total answer, because you must weigh up the benefit of having, in case of emergency, access to money in a bank, building society or National Savings. Once it has been used to pay off a mortgage, the money is no longer available for other uses.

You can look at the equation in two ways. Either you pay off the mortgage and have no savings to fall back on, or you earn an amount of interest which in effect reduces the cost of your mortgage and leaves you with control over your capital. There is clearly a real annual saving when a mortgage is repaid, but this is not simply the amount of the annual payments: it is those less the interest on any amount of capital needed to clear the mortgage. If you work out this sum, and then assess how much interest that amount of money could earn, you will reach a true figure of what you could save by discharging your mortgage. It may be far less than you think. For instance, say you are paying £400 a month in mortgage repayments and your outstanding loan is £40,000. And say savings interest rates are around 7.5 per cent, tax-paid, assuming you are a standard-rate tax payer. The sum you will have to do is 12 monthly payments of £400, which equals £4,800, less £3,000 which could have been earned in interest on your £40,000. So the annual saving is not £4,800, but £1,800. You may of course think that such a saving is well worth while.

New mortgages in retirement

Most people who decide to sell their homes and repurchase smaller properties pay cash for the second home. They reason that it is better not to have new borrowing commitments and pay interest unnecessarily. Among the older generation, too, there is still a feeling that borrowing is somehow wrong, unless one *has* to do it. But the arguments for mortgages in retirement are the same as at any other time in life, except that, because we have fewer years ahead of us, there is less potential for an increase in the value of the home. Mortgages are a cheap way to borrow, and especially so now that tax relief on mortgage interest applies whether or not we are taxpayers, and that inflation is gradually reducing the effective payments we make. Various schemes have been designed by mortgage lenders to suit retired people. Before you commit your cash, look into these to see if it would not be better to have at least a small mortgage so that you have access to a good portion of the profit raised on your former home.

Naturally, married couples have to take this decision jointly, and what they finally do may depend upon the pension arrangements for the survivor of the couple. If he or she is going to be very financially stretched to make the mortgage payments, they may prefer caution and pay cash; if not, a new mortgage is generally to be preferred. After all, the freed capital can always be used at any point to pay off the new loan.

Sheltered housing

Many people—whether they are still a couple or are widowed—decide as they get older that they no longer want to live totally independently, even though they are still fit and able to take care of themselves. The answer here can be sheltered housing. There is a lot to be said for it:

- Purpose-built apartments and houses tend to be compact and efficient to run.
- The share in total services means that things like good central heating and essential services are provided automatically.
- Although residents live independently, there is a warden service immediately available in times of need.
- There is plenty of company, something which should not be overlooked. Old age can be very lonely.
- There is often a choice of whether to buy or rent.

Nevertheless, there can be disadvantages, and these should not be ignored:

- The rent may be relatively high compared with non-sheltered accommodation.
- Where there is an option to purchase, there will be a rule that the property must be sold back to the property company on death, or perhaps when one moves into residential care. It will probably be stipulated in the agreement that the repurchase price is the same as the purchase price, so there is no chance of a profit. Add in a service charge, and one is effectively paying rent for the period in sheltered housing and at the same time sacrificing the interest on capital, if one has paid cash for the home. This may be a price worth paying for the peace of mind sheltered housing can bring, but it is a price which should be recognized.
- Not everyone likes people living closely around them, and it has to be remembered, too, that in a sheltered housing development everyone will be of a minimum age—there will be no young families with children. Although this suits many older people, others prefer a livelier environ-

227

ment. Depression is not uncommon among the old, and living with only other old people can contribute towards it.

- The units are small and, within a single development, not particularly varied. There may be simply two rooms, kitchen and bath for married couples, and single bed-sitters for those living on their own. There may be a rule that, when one member of a couple dies, the survivor has to move to one of the single units. As a couple may have had to sacrifice some much loved furniture to move to the sheltered accommodation in the first place, getting rid of even more on a death may be very distressing.

On balance, however, sheltered housing suits many people, and its use is growing.

Living with our families

If we are lucky, we may in retirement be able to live with one of our children and their family. For those families who can do this, and where it works happily, it can be the best solution to housing in our later years. There has of course to be harmony among the generations, which is by no means automatic; and the children's families may simply not have the space to house an elderly relative adequately. Where these are not factors to be considered, however, there are tremendous advantages for the old person concerned. They have the company of their relatives and friends and the stimulation of young people, and they can contribute to the family income and so help to improve living standards generally. Where they are not too old and infirm, they may be able to make a positive physical contribution to the running of the home, help with the grandchildren, and so on.

A decision to live with relatives should not, however, be taken lightly. It can cause stresses and strains in even the most united families, and there is a real danger that the arrangement might not work out. If this is the case, and the former home has already been sold, making new arrangements may prove financially difficult. So take this step only after you have hammered out any possible difficulties which might arise and assessed carefully whether they are insurmountable. It may seem mercenary, but there is quite a lot to be said for having a written agreement which protects both sides of the family.

If you do go ahead, make sure that you make a proper and regular contribution to the home and its running costs, and raise your contribution periodically to allow for inflation. If you are on a very low income indeed, perhaps with nothing but the single person's basic pension, check to see if your son or daughter can get a tax allowance for contributing to your care (although the allowance is meagre). Also, they may qualify for the invalid care allowance if you are unable to take care of yourself.

Residential care

The time may come when you have to move into residential care.

This may not be a decision that you take yourself; your family or the local health service may do it for you. But you should think about this possibility before the need arises. Residential care is expensive, and good residential care even more so. It is especially costly in London. Many people who have lived at a relatively high standard during their working lives and the early part of their retirement find that they have to share a room with more than one other person, and that even so this is costing them all their resources. If they have a home, it may be sold and the funds transferred to the local authority, which will thereafter pay for the residential care. If you are alone without relatives, you may have no choice about this, but if you have a family, discuss these matters with them while you are in a position to ensure that money is put aside to take care of you properly for the period you have to be in residential care. *Do not assume that it will never happen to you.*

This is not to say that nursing homes are poor and that the care is inadequate, but standards do vary a great deal and 24-hour nursing care does not come cheap. Do not be surprised, if you live in central London and want to stay there, if you have to pay £50 or £60 a day for a single room.

What happens if you are at first able to afford these prices but eventually run out of money? The Department of Health and Social Security may move you to a cheaper home, or, if you are very old and have been in care for a long time, it may supplement what you can afford until you die.

Retiring abroad

More and more Britons are spending at least part of their retirement years abroad. There is much to be said for it: milder climates are kinder to elderly health, and living costs (even if housing and food are at comparable prices to those in the UK) can be lower because heating costs may be sharply lower. With a little care, the tax burden on incomes may also be less.

Nevertheless, anyone contemplating living abroad should think very carefully before doing so, and certainly before selling up property in the UK.

Here are just a few things which should be considered:

- Are medical services adequate in your chosen country? If there is no health service, can you afford to pay for any treatment you may need? Will you need medical insurance? And will the cost be prohibitive?
- Will you be able to cope in a country if you are not fluent in its language?
- Will your family be able to visit you, or can you afford trips back home if you want to see them? Could they accommodate you on visits?
- How would the survivor cope if one of you died?
- Have you carefully checked all living costs, and are you sure you can afford them? Some countries will not allow foreigners to live there unless they have a certain level of income: you may be asked for proof of this.
- Does the country you choose have a 'double tax relief' agreement with Britain? Under these agreements, tax paid in the UK is offset against the liability in the other. If there is no such agreement, you could find yourself paying full tax in the UK as well as in the country in which you are residing. Some countries (although usually only the very wealthy can afford to live in them) levy no income tax at all. You will have to pay tax on any rent you receive from any property in the UK that you let while you are living abroad.
- Will your income be sufficient to cope not only at the beginning but also

later, when there will have been inflation? There can be problems with your state pension. Except in countries with which Britain has reciprocal arrangements, your state pension will be pegged at the level it is when you left the UK; later increases announced by the government will not be added. Such arrangements are with the other EEC countries and with some Commonwealth countries. There should not be any problem with private pensions, and at the moment there is no problem about transferring your assets from the UK to another country, although this could change should exchange control be reintroduced.

- Have you checked the exchange-control regulations where you are going? It is possible that, once you have brought your money into a country, you may have difficulty getting it out again.
- Are there any restrictions on property investment by foreigners? Make sure you have a good agent and, in particular, an honest lawyer. Restrictions may apply not just to buying but also to selling. You may, for instance, be able to buy freely, but may only be able to sell back to locals. This applies in some parts of Switzerland, and it can keep prices of properties bought by foreigners below the normal market level.
- Have you checked the legal costs in buying and selling? These can be very high—stamp duties on purchase are often much higher than in the UK, and Capital Gains Tax may apply on all sales without exemption.
- Are there any local limitations about which you should be aware? In Italy, for example, locals can acquire rights to use land to which they have had free access over some years. You may have to pay to get them to give up this right, even if they have used land without the permission of the previous owner.
- Will you be able to get a residence permit? There is no problem in EEC countries—a citizen of an EEC country has a right to live and work in any other—and many Commonwealth countries allow retired people to join their children, but some countries are not generous with their residence permits. Switzerland, for example, is very choosy about whom it allows to become a permanent resident.
- Are you sure you really want to go? Many people, having had many happy holidays in a place, decide they want to live there permanently. Long-term residence may be quite unlike a temporary summer stay. Would you miss your friends and family too much? It is expensive to make a move, whatever way one looks at it. Moving home again soon after can be costly and, if you have sold your UK property, prices may have moved up too much in the meantime to allow you to buy something which suits you on your return.

If you let out your home while you are abroad you will be liable for some tax on the rental income. Under Section 78 of the Taxes Management Act, your agent is responsible for paying the tax. An agent could be a professional, but might be a neighbour, a friend, or occasionally even a spouse.

Some professional agents insist on keeping the whole of the standard rate of tax back before remitting the rent. Others work out what they think the ultimate liability will be and retain that. Some send all the rental to the property owner, as long as he or she enters a mandate with his or her bank or accountant stating that tax will be paid from the bank account, once an assessment is received.

There comes a point when, almost inevitably, one half of a married couple will have to face life alone. It is usually the wife, both because women live longer than men on average, and because wives tend to be younger than their husbands. It is not unusual for women to face ten years or more of widowhood. There are about six times as many widows as widowers in Britain. As a result, just as social-security payments during our working lives tend to be geared to husbands and their dependants (a notion which is outdated today), social security when it comes to the surviving spouse is geared to women and their needs. Widowers can, as a result, be disadvantaged.

It is important for every married couple to think about what will happen when one of them dies and take what steps they can to mitigate against the survivor's financial loss, if not their grief. There is no point in shirking this issue, but many people do, and both widows and widowers are worse off in consequence. It is too late to start trying to make arrangements once the worst has happened.

Every married couple should take the following steps when they are quite young:

- There should be enough life assurance to carry the surviving partner over the immediate period of the death. If possible, the life assurance should be enough to be able to be invested to make a significant contribution to income, or even provide a regular income, which may be tax-free. (See page 98 ff.).
- Wherever possible, wives should build up pensions in their own right. The income they will get from their husband's pension is quite likely to be only one half or even one third of what they had as a married couple, and expenses may not fall in proportion.
- You should make additional pension arrangements over and above what will be available from the state. The state pension is not generous for a couple, and it is even less so for single people. State pensions tend to be raised only by the amount of inflation every year, and there are signs that relatively speaking they will fall rather than increase in the future. Look at chapter 16 to see what possibilities are open to you.
- Make sure that each of you has made a will. It usually makes sense for husband and wife to leave everything to one another, and so avoid a double dose of inheritance tax. The couple can decide how they want their estate eventually to be distributed, and they should make this decision together while they are both alive. As soon as one partner dies, the other should immediately make a new will, unless a joint will has been made which covers all eventualities. The will has to be proved and, where there is no will, letters of administration, which amount to the same thing as probate, must be applied for (see pages 85–8).
- Make sure that both of you have some basic financial knowledge. There are still many instances where women are left widows and find they know absolutely nothing about money, even such things as where the family income came from, details of savings, or just how much capital is available. It is not all that unusual for women not to know how to write out a cheque! Do not be one of them.

231

These are all items which can be taken care of while both spouses are alive. Failure to make these very simple precautions can add financial disaster to the emotional distress suffered by the survivor.

As widowed men and women are treated differently by the state, we shall look first at what happens to women at the point at which the husband dies and then see how the situation differs for a widower.

A widow's rights

Entitlement to the state widow's pension may come from three sources: (a) the basic pension based on a husband's National Insurance contributions, (b) an additional payment from any contributions he made to the graduated scheme which was in operation from 1961 to 1978, and (c) any payments under SERPS, the State Earnings Related Pension Scheme which was introduced in 1978 (see page 159). Pensions from the graduated scheme are small, although they are increased in line with inflation, and very few people have built up big earnings-related pensions so far. There are also plans to reduce the benefits available under this scheme.

There are differences in a widow's rights depending on whether a woman is under or over 60 at the time of the husband's death.

Women over 60, if they have already been getting a pension based on their husband's lifetime National Insurance contributions (as is still the case for most widows today), must immediately inform the Department of Health and Social Security. The pension will immediately fall to the single person's level. Your pension book will tell you how to go about this and how you can arrange to be paid monthly or quarterly if you wish.

If you are already getting a pension in your own right from your own NI contributions, but your husband was not 65 and therefore not getting a retirement pension, you will be entitled to a widow's pension. If this is more than your pension in your own right, the pension will be adjusted upwards to that of a single person. In addition, there may be an extra over and above the basic level, because of contributions made to the earnings-related part of the state scheme. You have some rights to these from your husband's contributions as well as anything from your own, although the amounts are not large.

If you are between 60 and 65 and still in full-time employment, you will not be able to claim the retirement pension. What constitutes full-time work is not always clear, so it is worth checking. Normally, if you earn less than £75 a week (1987), or work for less than 12 hours, you will not be regarded as fully employed. After the age of 65 there is no limit on how much you can work or earn: you get your pension anyway.

For women under 60 when their husbands die a widow's allowance is sometimes paid during the first 26 weeks of bereavement, and this is the case also if you are between 60 and 65 but your husband was not yet entitled to a retirement pension.

A widowed mother's allowance or a widow's pension go to women with dependent children. They may be paid after the first 26 weeks of bereavement until you reach 60 and become eligible for the single person's pension, or until you retire. To qualify, a woman must be over 40 when her husband dies, or she is not entitled to the widowed mother's allowance. Women who are under 40 get the widowed mother's allowance, but are not entitled to a widow's pension. (There is currently a proposal to raise the qualifying age to 45.) Such widows have no claim as of right to any benefits at all, although they may be able to get supplementary benefit on the usual terms.

The level of the widow's pension varies, again depending on the woman's age when she was first widowed: the younger she is, the less she gets. Women over 50 get the standard rate, while those under 50 get an age-related reduction determined on a sliding scale. It is assumed that, the younger you are, the more likely you are to be able to get a job after your bereavement.

If you remarry or live with another man, you lose all your rights as a widow. If you were separated from your husband when he died, you are treated as a widow, but if you were divorced you are not a widow and have no rights to the widow's allowance and pension. It is important, if you are getting divorced, to try to get some financial rights after your former husband's death written into your financial agreement at the time of the divorce (see pages 191–2).

If you have a dependent child when your former husband dies, you may be entitled to a child's special allowance from the state, via the DHSS.

If you are already getting a widow's pension when you reach the age of 60, you may have a choice until you are 65 between the widow's and the single person's retirement pension. The choice you make will depend on whether you are still working and whether you get a full or an age-related pension.

Widows' benefits

Traditionally in Britain, widows have been treated as a special category when it comes to social security. Widowed mothers have been given allowances, and women who are older when widowed or whose husbands have died when they have passed or are nearing retiring age have been entitled to a widow's pension.

Profound changes are proposed to the system as from April 1988. The main one is that the widow's allowance, which is now paid for six months after the death of the husband, will be replaced by a single lump sum of £1,000. Unlike many social-security payments, the lump sum will not be uprated annually to allow for inflation. Younger childless widows will not qualify for the widow's pension or, naturally, the widowed mother's allowance. They will also lose the current widow's allowance.

From April 1988 the widowed mother's allowance will be paid as soon as the husband dies, rather than 26 weeks later, as has been the case in the past. Women who are not getting child benefit will no longer qualify for the allowance as they do at present.

Another change is that the age of entitlement for a full widow's pension is to be raised from 50 to 55 and, for the reduced rate, from 40 to 45.

All widow's benefits are taxable.

Funerals

The £30 death grant has been abolished. If you cannot afford to pay for a funeral, and if you are on supplementary benefit, family income supplement or housing benefit, you can apply for help from the new social fund.

Making a claim

Do not delay in making your claim. If you wait, you may never get the benefits to which you are entitled as a widow. You must have a very good reason for delaying beyond three months: it is not enough to say that you were too upset to take action. Claims are made on form BW1, which you can get by applying on form BWS (the certificate of Registration of Death) or from the local DHSS office. It will take some time to process your claim, so this is another point in life where planning to have a little reserve of savings becomes vital. Even though you will not immediately receive the pension, your entitlement to it starts the day you make the claim, and any arrears will be made up when you finally get your pension. You can be paid weekly in cash from a post office, or quarterly or monthly in arrears. The widow's pension is not very high and, if it is your only income and you have no savings, you will probably be entitled to extra benefits. Check on this with either the DHSS or your local Citizens' Advice Bureau. Remember that your widow's pension is part of your income and so is liable for tax, should you have other income which takes you into the tax bracket.

Widowers

There is no widower's pension from the state for a man when his wife dies, even though a man may face just as many financial problems as a woman, particularly if he has dependent children. For this reason, it makes sense to have life-assurance cover for women as well as men. If a wife survives her husband, the capital sum from the life assurance when she dies can be used to contribute to any inheritance tax which is then due.

Like widows, however, widowers have only the single person's pension (if they have retired) from the point when their wife dies. This can lead to financial problems unless the widower has another source of income. If he has been in a private pension fund during his working life, there will be no cut in the amount just because he has been widowed, so he will generally be better off than a woman. If his wife was also in a pension fund, however, it is still very unlikely that he will get a widower's pension from her lifetime contributions, in the same way that wives benefit from their husband's schemes. Pension schemes are changing to include widower's pensions, but so far few do.

The needs of widowers are largely ignored by the state, so it is very important for a married couple to consider and cater for the possibility that the husband may be the one to survive.

To see how differently men and women are treated when their spouse dies, let us assume that one or other becomes widowed in his or her 50s. First, the woman will be able to claim the higher married man's personal allowance for the year of her husband's death and for the year after. A man in the same position does not get this allowance in the following year. A woman gets the widow's pension. The man will not qualify for the single person's pension in normal circumstances until he is 65.

If the woman stops working or does not work and has only her basic pension, her children can claim an extra £100 in tax allowances towards any money they may give her: this is not available for any support given to widowers. Then again, the family can buy a house with mortgage tax relief for a dependent female relative to live in, and there is no gains tax liability when the house is eventually sold. This does not apply to male relatives. Finally, under the inheritance-tax rules, money can be passed to bereaved mothers for support without incurring liability to tax. Settlements made to fathers, in contrast, are treated as taxable gifts for inheritance-tax purposes.

The discrimination against men is total, unless and until men are incapacitated by old age or infirmity, at which point they become entitled to all the reliefs on the same terms as women.

Spotcheck

As you retire, have you

- applied for all the state pension to which your National Insurance contributions qualify you?
- looked to see if you are entitled to any other state benefits?
- considered how you can maximize your income in retirement by switching your savings to allow for your new tax position, or taking on a home income plan, or purchasing an annuity (but considering carefully what kind)?
- looked at the whole question of how you want and will need to be housed in retirement?

If you are married, have you

- discussed what will happen to the survivor when one dies?
- made sure that your wills protect each other and that you leave virtually everything to your spouse, if you have not made any provision for inheritance tax on the first death?
- taken advantage of the £3,000 a year exemption on transferring your assets to minimize any inheritance tax which may be due on the survivor's estate?

If you are the survivor, have you

- reported the death to the authorities and claimed your pension and any other benefits to which you are entitled?

Savings Round-up

Savings with the safety of original capital guaranteed

A. NATIONAL SAVINGS

Product	Interest	Tax position	Special features
Fixed interest certificates	Guaranteed for five years; variable extension rates	Free of all income taxes and capital gains tax	Interest accrues until repayment. Not entered on tax return
Index-linked certificates	Guaranteed extra interest after five years	Free of all income taxes and capital gains tax	Extra interest in addition to inflation-proofing. Not entered on tax return
Yearly plan	Guaranteed for five years; variable extension rates	Free of all income taxes and capital gains tax	Monthly payments by standing order by Yearly Plan certificates. Recognized form of saving for Government's Home Purchase Scheme
Income Bonds	Variable	Taxable, but paid in full without deduction of tax	Monthly income paid direct to bank, NSB account, or by post. Recognized form of saving for Government's Home Purchase Scheme
Indexed-Income Bonds	Variable	As income bonds	Monthly income paid direct to bank, NSB account, or by post
Deposit Bonds	Variable	As income bonds	Certificate of value sent on each anniversary of purchase. Recognized form of saving for Government's Home Purchase Scheme
Investment account	Variable	As income bonds	Interest earned every day
Ordinary account	Variable, but two rates generally guaranteed for a calendar year	First £70 of annual interest free of income tax	Free standing orders. Regular Customer Account
Girobank High Interest	Variable	Taxable	Minimum £1,000, rate rises at £4,000 and again at £10,000
Premium Bonds	None. Weekly and monthly money prizes	Prizes free of income tax and capital gains tax	160,000 prizes each month

B. BUILDING SOCIETIES

Product	Interest	Tax position	Special features
Cash card accounts	Variable. Often more for larger amounts	Tax paid	Cash dispenser card. Sometimes standing orders
Cheque book accounts	Variable. Often more for larger amounts	Tax paid	Cheque-book facility
Children's accounts	Variable. Sometimes birthday bonuses	Tax paid. Higher rate taxed parents will have to pay more	Perks such as money boxes, magazines
Gold accounts	Variable, but higher than normal	Tax paid	Higher minimum investment in exchange for higher-than-average interest. Immediate access
Monthly income account	Variable	Tax paid	Interest paid monthly, so worth more rate-for-rate than yearly or half-yearly crediting
Extra interest	Variable, but higher than normal	Tax paid	Loss of interest if money is withdrawn without giving full notice
Regular monthly savings account	Variable, little higher than normal	Tax paid	Savings must be regular, although some flexibility sometimes allowed
Save-as-you-earn	Fixed equal to 8.3 per cent every five years	Tax paid	Must save a fixed amount for 5 years. Interest then paid as a bonus of 14 months' payments
Share/deposit accounts	Variable	Tax paid	Easy access
Term accounts	Variable, but high. May be fixed for six months or a year	Tax paid	High minimum investment

C. BANKS

Product	Interest	Tax position	Special features
Deposit account	Variable	Tax paid	May have a cash card for withdrawals
High interest cheque accounts	Variable	Tax paid	Cheque-book facility. High minimum investment
High interest deposit	Variable but higher than normal deposit	Tax paid	High minimum investment. Easy withdrawal terms
Mortgage Savings account	Variable	Tax paid	Guarantees a mortgage after a period which varies from 1 to 3 years

Product	Interest	Tax position	Special features
Extra interest	Variable, but higher than seven-day account	Tax paid	High minimum investment
Regular monthly savings	Variable, higher than seven-day account	Tax paid	As little as £10 a month can be saved
Fixed rate/ term accounts	Fixed for the term	Tax paid	Minimum varies from £500 to £5,000

D. LOCAL AUTHORITIES

Product	Interest	Tax position	Special features
Lump sum fixed term	Fixed for term	Tax paid	No additions or withdrawals allowed. From 1 to 10 years
Negotiable (yearling) bonds	Fixed for term	Tax paid	One to 5 years. Issued every Tuesday. May be at discount, or bought through stock market, so capital gain possible

E. OFFSHORE

Product	Interest	Tax position	Special features
High interest cheque accounts	Variable	Taxable but paid before deduction of tax	Cheque-book facility. Normally no overdraft

F. CO-OPERATIVE SOCIETIES

Product	Interest	Tax position	Special features
Term account	Fixed for term	Taxable but paid gross	One-year Development bonds, 2-year High Yield Bond. Interest paid either at end or gross

Savings with minimal risk

LICENSED DEPOSIT TAKERS

Product	Interest	Tax position	Special features
Notice accounts	Variable	Tax paid	Half-yearly or quarterly interest
Savings account	Variable	Tax paid	Interest added to account half-yearly
Term accounts	Usually fixed	Tax paid —	Monthly, half-yearly or quarterly interest. Terms under 1 year not worthwhile. Over 5 years not recommended

NOTE: This list is not exhaustive. New schemes are added from time to time. Always check the conditions.

Where to Go for Financial Advice

Many people do not know where to go for advice, and, when they've got it, sometimes cannot be sure that it is the right advice for them. You can get a first-class financial adviser, if you take care and do not rush.

To begin with, you cannot beat personal recommendation, so a safeguard against bad advice is to ask someone you know—a friend, acquaintance, or business colleague—if they can recommend someone from personal experience. However, it is not always possible to find someone this way, so here are a few rules to follow if you need financial advice. They could just as easily be applied when you need a builder, plumber, interior decorator, architect or surveyor.

- Make sure that the person you are going to is a member of his or her professional organization.
- In the case of someone in business on their own account, check to see how long the firm has been in existence. For a first-generation family firm, it's the longer the better; after that, though, the personal touch may be lost.
- If you cannot get a recommendation from a friend, try to get one from your bank manager. A good professional relationship with your bank manager is the first step in long-term financial health. He or she will probably know accountants and solicitors in your area.
- If all else fails, go to the local Citizens' Advice Bureau, or write to the professional body concerned for a list of its members in your local area.

You will find a list of addresses on pages 243–4; this list includes the addresses of the various organizations, etc., referred to over the next few pages.

Your bank manager

A bank manager is the most important financial friend you will ever have. He or she should be able to give general financial advice as well as provide the normal services offered by the bank, and help you out in times of trouble. You, in turn, must play your part in making the relationship successful. Tell the bank manager everything about your financial situation, the good and the bad parts, and, in particular, warn him or her if anything nasty is likely to happen—then he or she will be more ready to help.

Most of us go to a bank branch in our local area, and anyone who is thinking of opening an account should try to see at least two managers in their own area. Talk to people who already have accounts to find out what they think of the service, and then choose the bank you think will suit you best. Remember that it is your money the bank is using and making profits from, so do not be afraid to ask right at the start how they would treat you if you wanted a loan or a mortgage, or what they would do if you were unemployed for a period. The bank may want you to provide references before opening an account, so you are equally entitled to ask them to prove themselves.

Until recently, customers in disagreement with their bank managers had no redress, apart from an appeal to the head office. Now, however, an ombudsman system has been set up to deal with complaints. Although it is supported by the banks, it operates independently of them and can make awards to a justifiably aggrieved customer of up to £50,000.

A solicitor

Finding a good solicitor is more difficult. Different solicitors are good at different things: those who are good at drawing up wills or contracts may not be so good at conveyancing or in divorce cases. This means that it is very important to shop around and check. If you need legal aid, the Citizens' Advice Bureau will give you the names of those solicitors who do this kind of work. There are income and capital limits on who is eligible for legal aid. You can write to the Law Society, who will not recommend a particular solicitor but will send you a list of their members in your area.

Insurance

Bad experiences with life-assurance policies or other insurance are common. There are perhaps more pitfalls in this part of our financial lives than any other. Firstly, many life-assurance policies are not tailored to suit our needs—we may be underinsured on things like contents policies and, all too often, find that our claims are (quite properly) not met by the company. One way to avoid this is to do all this business through an insurance broker who is a member of the British Insurance Brokers Association. People who are not members are not necessarily poor advisers, but if you have any doubts BIBA will send you a list of their members. There is a snag with brokers, too. They often have a connection with a limited number of companies and make their money by commission on the policies they sell, so their advice is not always as independent as you might think.

You can also get insurance advice through your bank or your accountant, but they are not specialists and the value of their advice is limited. Perhaps the best thing to do when you want life assurance is to write to three or four big companies (you'll find them in the Yellow Pages) and ask them what they are offering; read the brochures they send very carefully, choose the one you think suits you best, and then go and talk it over with the company before committing yourself.

If you are convinced you have a genuine claim and all negotiations fail, go to the Insurance Ombudsman (see page 115).

An accountant

The most important thing in choosing an accountant is to know when you need one. Anyone who is self-employed or is just starting a business certainly needs the kind of advice an accountant can give, and so do some people who are involved in very complicated financial covenants or in settlements of divorce cases, and those who have income from trusts. The choice of accountant should be from those who are members of the Institute of Chartered Accountants in England and Wales and the corresponding body in Scotland, or of the Association of Certified Accountants.

Mortgages

You can ask a solicitor, an accountant or a bank manager for help in getting a mortgage. You can of course go directly to a building society, but a lot of the pain can be taken out of getting a mortgage by using an insurance broker, who will also be able to arrange all the life insurance you need to protect your mortgage and your property.

Investing

Stockbrokers can be very choosy about whom they take on as clients. In the stockmarket, the motto is 'my word is my bond', and brokers will buy and sell shares for you on instructions over the telephone. You do not have to send them a written order. This means that they like to be sure that the people they take on will honour their bills. Some do not like private clients—their business is mostly done for the big financial institutions. In the last year or two, however, there has been a big push towards private investors, as brokers have realized that the small customers of today may be the large customers of tomorrow, and will take on people they do not know. You can also deal through a bank or through the high-street share shops which have been springing up around the country (although mainly in the big cities).

Complaining

What happens if you take great care in choosing your adviser and later you feel that you have been badly advised? Firstly, be very sure that you have actually been badly advised. Just because you lose a court case or a divorce suit does not mean that there was anything wrong with the advice: you simply might not have had a leg to stand on. Similarly, you yourself might make a wrong decision about which shares to buy. However, you may be quite right to think that your accountant has got your tax bill wrong, that your solicitor has charged you too much, that you have been misled about the benefits and costs of an insurance policy, that a bank has treated you unfairly, or that a building society has refused you a mortgage simply because you are a woman. In such cases, write first to the professional association of the individual involved, or to the head office, if it is a branch of a nationwide company (e.g., a bank) about which you are concerned.

But be warned: there are thousands of complaints a year and very few of them stand up to scrutiny when investigated by the professional bodies. So make sure your case really is a good one.

Whether you are seeking advice or making a complaint following a bad experience, the organizations to contact are the same.

General
Citizens' Advice Bureau (look in your local telephone book).

Banking
(a) Your bank's head office in London or Edinburgh (easy to find out).

(b) Institute of Bankers 10 Lombard Street London EC4N 1TP

(c) Banking Ombudsman
     Citadel House 5/11 Fetter Lane London EC4A 1BR

Solicitor
Law Society 113 Chancery Lane London WC2A 1PL

Accountant
(a) Institute of Chartered Accountants
     Chartered Accountants Hall Moorgate Place London EC2R 6EQ

(b) Institute of Chartered Accountants of Scotland
     27 Queen Street Edinburgh EH2 1LA

(c) Association of Certified Accountants
     29 Lincoln's Inn Fields London WC2A 3EE

Mortgage
Building Society Association 14 Park Street London W1Y 4AL

Insurance
(a) British Insurance Association
     Aldermany House Queen Street London EC4P 4JD

(b) Life Offices Association
     Aldermany House Queen Street London EC4P 4JD

(c) Associated Scottish Life Offices
     23 St Andrew Square Edinburgh EH2 1AQ

(d) Industrial Life Offices Association
     Aldermany House Queen Street London EC4N 1TL

(e) British Insurance Brokers' Federation
     Fountain Court 130 Fenchurch Street London EC3A 7NT

(f) Insurance Ombudsman Bureau
     31 Southampton Row London WC1B 5HJ

Stockbroker
Stock Exchange London EC2N 1HP

Sex discrimination
The Equal Opportunities Commission
Overseas House Quay Street Manchester M3 3HN

Problems with government services
You may need help and advice in matters of social security, taxes, education or unemployment. You will be able to find the appropriate office or telephone number from your local telephone book, as follows:

Your problem	Who can help	To find the address or number look in a telephone book under
Social security	(a) Social-security office	Health and Social Security, Department of
	(b) Freefone DHSS	A free telephone service: dial 100 and ask to be put through to Freefone DHSS
Unemploy-ment	(a) Job Centre or employment office	Employment Division, Job Centres, and Manpower Services Commission
	(b) Unemployment benefit office	Employment, Department of
	(c) Careers office (for young people)	Careers Service, or name of your local council
Education	Local authority education department	Name of your local authority
Social Services	Social services department (social work department in Scotland) of your local council	Name of your county, district or London borough council (regional council in Scotland)
Welfare rights	Welfare rights officer (usually in the social services department)	As above
Rent and rates	Housing department of your local council	As above
Tax	(a) Tax office	Inland Revenue
	(b) PAYE enquiry office	Inland Revenue
Anything, including the above	Citizens' Advice Bureau	Citizens' Advice Bureau

Index

250